S0-AES-793

A CONCISE HISTORY
OF U.S. FOREIGN POLICY

PRAISE FOR THE FIRST EDITION

"Joyce Kaufman's *A Concise History of U.S. Foreign Policy* is a wonderfully readable guide. It will be a welcome addition to the classroom."
—James Goldgeier, George Washington University

"Sometimes shorter is better. This compact and carefully written text skillfully analyzes the steady growth of American international reach and the irregular patterns of its involvement abroad."
—Barry Hughes, University of Denver

"Written in a lively, student-friendly manner on a subject—the evolution of U.S. foreign policy—with which students are woefully unfamiliar, this slender volume fills a vital role for those instructors who want to acquaint their students with the sweep of the American foreign policy experience without overwhelming the course. I found the discussion of the early Cold War particularly valuable. A recommended supplement."
—Donald M. Snow, University of Alabama

A CONCISE HISTORY OF U.S. FOREIGN POLICY

Second Edition

Joyce P. Kaufman

ROWMAN & LITTLEFIELD PUBLISHERS, INC.

Lanham • Boulder • New York • Toronto • Plymouth, UK

Published by Rowman & Littlefield Publishers, Inc.
A wholly owned subsidiary of The Rowman & Littlefield Publishing Group, Inc.
4501 Forbes Boulevard, Suite 200, Lanham, Maryland 20706
http://www.rowmanlittlefield.com

Estover Road, Plymouth PL6 7PY, United Kingdom

Copyright © 2010 by Rowman & Littlefield Publishers, Inc.

All rights reserved. No part of this book may be reproduced in any form or by any electronic or mechanical means, including information storage and retrieval systems, without written permission from the publisher, except by a reviewer who may quote passages in a review.

British Library Cataloguing in Publication Information Available

Library of Congress Cataloging-in-Publication Data
Kaufman, Joyce P.
   A concise history of U.S. foreign policy / Joyce P. Kaufman. — 2nd ed.
      p. cm.
   Includes bibliographical references and index.
     ISBN 978-0-7425-6709-2 (cloth : alk. paper) — ISBN 978-0-7425-6710-8 (pbk. : alk. paper) — ISBN 978-0-7425-6711-5 (electronic)
   1. United States—Foreign relations. I. Title. II. Title: Concise history of US foreign policy. III. Title: Concise history of United States foreign policy.
E183.7.K36 2010
327.73—dc22

                                                                        2009043131

∞ ™ The paper used in this publication meets the minimum requirements of American National Standard for Information Sciences—Permanence of Paper for Printed Library Materials, ANSI/NISO Z39.48-1992.

Printed in the United States of America

Contents

Preface to the Second Edition

O N JUNE 11, 2009, THE *NEW YORK TIMES* HAD AN ARTICLE on the first page of the Arts Section about the disappearance of traditional courses in American foreign policy and diplomatic history.[1] As someone who both studies and teaches U.S. foreign policy, I found this to be very disturbing. The world we live in changes rapidly. Even though I am a political scientist, I take a historical approach to understanding U.S. foreign policy in this book; one of the lessons of history is that it is as recent as yesterday. And it is often all too easy to miss the important lessons of today—and therefore make the same mistakes—because we did not learn from the past. The cry that the United States "would be welcomed as liberators" that we heard often in the run-up to and early stages of the war in Iraq in 2003 proved to be untrue. However, those same words were used in 1898 to help justify the annexation of the Philippines over the objections of the anti-imperialists, who predicted that such an invasion would "lead to the hell of war."[2] The latter proved to be correct, just as we now know that those who warned of the dangers of invading Iraq more than one hundred years later and the subsequent "hell of war" were also correct. Although not all circumstances will ever be exactly the same, there are still lessons to be learned from looking at and understanding the broad context within which foreign policy decisions were made in the past and analyzing the circumstances within which the outcomes proved to be successful or not.

Since 2006 when this text was originally published, we have a new U.S. president, the first African American to assume this office, who is taking the United States down a far different path both internationally and domestically

than his predecessor did. The decision to go to war in Iraq remains controversial, although by the time of this revision in 2009, it was starting to wind
down with proposed withdrawal dates for U.S. troops and Iraq slated to take
on more of the burden for its own security, albeit with the assistance of remaining U.S. support troops at least through 2010. In contrast, the conflict in
Afghanistan continued with the Obama administration putting greater emphasis on addressing and resolving that conflict, which many feel should have
been at the heart of the military response to 9/11. While NATO nations were
initially willing to assist the United States in Afghanistan, by 2009 the burden
for this war was falling heavily on the United States as the allies, disillusioned
by the lack of progress and responding to the demands and dissatisfaction of
their public, were withdrawing their troops and their support.

If any further proof was needed that we live in a globalized world, an economic recession gripped the globe starting in 2008 and continued well into
2009. Attributed initially to economic failures in the United States that set
off the chain of events, virtually no country has been untouched by it. The
challenge facing all countries now is what to do to respond to the economic
downturn, as countries look to the United States for solutions and not just as
the source of problems.

All these events, both individually and certainly when taken as a whole,
suggest the need for a significant change in the direction of U.S. foreign
policy. Rather than threatening real or perceived enemies, under President
Obama the United States seems to have discovered the art of diplomacy
once again. Rather than seeking to *impose* values such as "democracy" and
"freedom," the United States is encouraging countries to seek out their own
values, especially those that are consistent with America's. Rather than the
"either you are with us or against us" attitude that characterized much of the
Bush administration's foreign policy, at least the early indicators are that the
Obama administration is stressing cooperation and alliances. How successful
these changes will be, whether they actually will result in a more secure country, or whether they will be abandoned in the face of harsh realities once the
honeymoon period ends, remains to be seen.

But the apparently significant changes in direction raise some important
questions about the role that the United States will—or should—take in the
future, especially regarding major international challenges that continue to
perplex, such as how to deal with nonstate actors such as terrorist groups,
or what to do about "rogue states," such as North Korea and Iran, which are
moving toward acquiring nuclear weapons. Some of the policies will continue
to evolve even as this edition goes to press; such is the nature of dealing with a
subject that is dynamic. However, others should be more clearly defined than
they were when the first edition of this book was being drafted. At that time,

we were too close to 9/11 and the policies that were implemented initially to have a sense as to how effective they really were. With the advantage of some time and distance, we should now have a better understanding of the effectiveness of the policies that were applied then and the policies of the Bush administration in general.

The framework for this edition remains much the same as that of the first edition, albeit with factual and typographical corrections. There are some substantive changes, however, beginning with an expanded version of chapter 1, the theoretical framework that sets the stage for what follows. The revised version of the chapter in this edition responds to some of the concerns raised by the faculty and students who have used the book by including some of the specific theoretical approaches to understanding foreign policy, including the feminist perspective.

This edition will also be strengthened by including a short "what would you do if . . ." case at the end of each substantive chapter (2 through 6), which asks the student to think back and put him- or herself into the perspective of the decision-maker of the time who had to make important decisions based only on the information then available. With the advantage of hindsight and knowledge of the consequences of those decisions in each case, what would you have done then if you had the information that you have now? Would the decision be the same or not, and why? Whether and how each case is used is up to the faculty member who teaches the class.

The other major changes in the structure of this edition are in the last few chapters. Chapter 5, "Beyond the Cold War," now begins with Reagan and goes through the Clinton administration. Chapter 6 is now called "September 11 and After" and focuses primarily on the presidency of George W. Bush, beginning with the contested election of 2000 and ending with the changes to foreign policy proposed by the Obama administration. And I have added a new chapter 7, "The Future of U.S. Foreign Policy," that includes materials on the changing nature of the threat, U.S. relations with its allies, and ways in which the United States can address these.

The second edition, like the first, is meant to be a concise guide to understanding U.S. foreign policy, but it is by no means definitive. How it can be augmented by other readings, including the use of primary source documents, is up to each faculty member who chooses to use the book. But, like the first edition, it is meant to be accessible to undergraduates and to anyone else who is interested in learning more about the history and evolution of U.S. foreign policy from the founding of this country to the present. I have learned from conversations with any number of acquaintances that they have read this book as a primer for understanding more about a topic that they otherwise knew little about, a use I did not envision when the book was drafted. That anyone who is not required to read this for a class has chosen to do so out of interest is high praise indeed.

I owe a great deal of thanks to a number of people who have helped me think through the revisions. Especially important have been a number of faculty—John Scott Masker and David Goldberg—both of whom have used this book for a number of years and who have not hesitated to offer their suggestions for improvement. Scott Masker was especially helpful in reading and commenting on various parts of this draft as it was in process. John Morley (Whittier College, class of 2007) also reviewed chapters from the perspective of a student who had taken the class and provided helpful feedback once again. Irene Carlyle, a close friend as well as colleague, also read parts of this draft, as she did the first, and offered her usual incisive comments. Marilyn Chavez, my administrative assistant, was extremely helpful in making sure drafts were printed and formatted correctly, as well as keeping the office running while I was off writing and revising. I also want to thank Leslie C. King (Whittier College, class of 2009), who was in my foreign policy class and who, even after she graduated, was willing to spend part of her summer helping me review all Internet sites. She was a wonderful research assistant during her time at Whittier, and she worked with me on a number of books.

At Rowman & Littlefield, Susan McEachern has been a great source of ideas and has helped me focus on ways to improve this edition. Since we started working together, she has become a good friend as well as editor. Editorial assistant Carrie Broadwell-Tkach answered all my questions quickly and with good humor. I was fortunate to work with Jehanne Schweitzer as the production editor and thank her for all her help once again. The reviews from faculty provided by Rowman & Littlefield also provided insight that helped me think through ways to revise the volume. And, of course, feedback from my students since the book was published provided additional suggestions as to how to improve the book from their perspective.

I owe a great deal to my husband, Robert Marks, who once again lived through the process of thinking, writing, and revising with me. Of all people, he knows full well what that process is like and how important it is to augment the process with diversions such as golf and tennis. I am lucky to have him as my partner in all these endeavors.

Joyce P. Kaufman

1

Setting the Stage for
Understanding U.S. Foreign Policy

W HAT WOULD HAPPEN IF TWO SCHOOLS OF THOUGHT COMPETED to dominate
the making of U.S. foreign policy? One school, led by one of the major
political leaders, stressed the importance of a strong relationship between the
national government and big business and argued that the country needed to
be integrated into the global system, especially the international economy, in
terms that were favorable to it. The other school, led by an opposing political
leader, stressed that the most important thing for the country would be to remain removed from foreign policy and to concentrate instead on safeguarding
the homeland, intervening only when it becomes absolutely necessary. Sound
familiar? These were the arguments between Alexander Hamilton on the one
hand and Thomas Jefferson on the other,[1] put forward when the United States
was created. But it sounds a lot like the arguments that have been made recently. Should the United States be more involved in the world or not? Is it the
responsibility of the United States to help spread democracy? When should
the United States intervene in the affairs of other countries? These are not new
questions, although the answers keep changing as times, circumstances, and
the priorities of the presidents and other political leaders change.

This book on American foreign policy draws on basic political science approaches and theories. However, it is difficult to arrive at a practical understanding of U.S. foreign policy and the decisions that have been made without
grounding them in history. To integrate the approaches, we will use a historical framework to put the major themes and concepts of U.S. foreign policy
into the context of the time at which they were formulated. This requires
looking at the various domestic political priorities as well as the international

context that helped frame the decisions made, for the two go hand in hand in the making of foreign policy. In addition, the text relies heavily on primary documents in order to explore the ideas as fully as possible, using the words of the authors of those policies.

Why is it important to learn about American foreign policy? In other words, who cares? Generally, Americans do not give much thought to foreign policy. They don't make decisions about candidates for office based on the candidates' foreign policy positions unless the country is at war or in a conflict where Americans are dying. In fact, many Americans pay attention to foreign policy only in terms of the value of the dollar against another currency—such as the euro, the yen, or the pound—if they are planning to travel abroad. Some want to know whether a Japanese car is going to cost more or less than it did the last time they bought one or whether there will be a line of cars at the border when they cross into Mexico or Canada. In fact, as the presidential election campaign of 2008 illustrated clearly, the dominant campaign issue had been the war in Iraq until the economic recession started to hit. At that point, Iraq faded quickly as a priority to be replaced by discussion and debates about which candidate had the best solution to fix what was then an emerging problem and one that was seen as more immediate to most Americans than the war.

Most Americans pay little attention to foreign policy unless it appears to affect them directly. But foreign policy *does* affect everyone, not only because of threats of terrorist attacks or the danger of war, but for far more mundane reasons. Look at the label on the last article of clothing that you bought. Where was it manufactured? In China? Bangladesh? What about your computer—where was it made? When you called the technology help line because you had a problem with a product, where was that person sitting? Was it in the United States or in India? All of this is possible because of trade, and trade is foreign policy.

Let's look at it another way. Do you know anyone who is out of work because his or her factory closed and the product is now made overseas? Allowing American companies to be based in another country is a foreign policy decision. Do you know someone who came to this country to get an education and then decided to stay because he or she could get a better job here than would be possible back home? The decision about who can enter the country is a foreign policy decision. In other words, foreign policy is not remote, nor is it important only for diplomats or bureaucrats. Foreign policy can affect everyone.

Most of these foreign policy decisions—what countries to trade with, how many people to allow into the country and from where, whether to allow companies to relocate or outsource—are relatively routine. They become more political, and therefore get more attention, in election years or when something extraordinary happens. The foreign policy decisions that most people know about and follow closely are those that are extraordinary because the stakes appear to be so high. Yet the reality is that many "routine" foreign policy decisions can have a very direct and immediate effect on individual lives.

During the Cuban Missile Crisis in October 1962, Americans were glued to their radios and televisions because of the fear that the world was poised on the brink of nuclear annihilation. (It was only years later we learned how close to truth that was.[2]) The Persian Gulf War of 1991 was a true media event; by the invasion of Iraq in March 2003, reporters were "embedded" with troops in order to quench the public's desire for news about the progress of the war. Furthermore, Americans expected that minute-by-minute account. On the other hand, few people are glued to C-SPAN watching the latest debate on the imposition of steel tariffs. The imposition of the tariff, a decision made by President George W. Bush in March 2002, had important implications for American foreign policy, the relationship of the United States to its allies, and even the price of building or buying a house, something that could affect you or your family. Yet relatively few people followed that discussion or even thought about what it might mean for them.

One could argue that there is little the ordinary citizen can do about foreign policy. Why not simply take the decision-makers' word when they state that U.S. "national interest" is best served by a particular foreign policy decision? As educated citizens, we need to ask what is in *our* national interest. We need to ask *whose* interests are being represented when "national interest" is given as a justification for particular decisions. Before casting a vote on Election Day, everyone should know how to evaluate critically the promises of a politician running for office who claims that she or he will act in the country's "best interest."

Citizens in the world today need to understand that countries are interrelated and that decisions made by one country have implications for decisions made by another, which will, in turn, determine other decisions. You cannot ask meaningful questions or make rational decisions unless you know what foreign policy is and what the related concept of *national interest* means. Not everyone will arrive at the same answers. This is the basis for legitimate intellectual debate. Since the results of foreign policy decisions affect each of us, we all have a right—and a responsibility—to ask these questions.

Make no mistake: this is not an easy process. Understanding foreign policy is an inexact science, often with no clear-cut right or wrong answers. Rather, approaching it requires putting many pieces together, looking at the outputs or the decisions that were made, and then trying to understand the various pieces or factors that went into making the decisions and why.

This book will not provide all the answers to understanding U.S. foreign policy. What it will do is provide insights into the components of foreign policy–making that can inform the questions to ask. It will also help point the reader to ways to determine answers to those questions.

Introduction to U.S. Foreign Policy

In general, Americans are ahistorical. Most have little knowledge of and little concern with the lessons of history.[3] Yet it is impossible to really understand American foreign policy without putting it into a historical context. To do otherwise means that each generation will have to relearn (and often repeat) the lessons of the past. The point here is that little in American foreign policy really is "new." In most cases the formulation of foreign policy is an ongoing process of assessing and evaluating previous or existing policy in light of changing circumstances. An understanding of why and how certain policies were formulated in the past should help you better understand the consequences of those decisions for the United States, for other countries, and even for you personally.

Most students of American foreign policy tend to look at the decisions made as falling into broad categories; for example, should the United States be engaged in the world (*internationalism* or *engagement*), or should it remain aloof from the rest of the world (*isolationism* or *unilateralism*[4])? Should U.S. foreign policy be guided by a single overarching adversary, as it was during the Cold War, or should it be based on a broader and less defined set of goals, such as fighting terrorism, as it is today? Is the "war on terror" really different from the fight against communism, or are they both examples of a conflict against an idea rather than a single country, which is what makes each so difficult to fight? These are not really discrete categories of policies as much as evolutionary (or sometimes revolutionary) changes, where one approach is compared with another, often without regard for the context within which the decisions were made. Foreign policy decisions are not made in a vacuum but are the results of a number of factors, both domestic and international, that are taken into account. Moreover, not all factors weigh equally all the time—to be effective, foreign policy must assign different weights to and reflect changing priorities.

Changes in foreign policy, at least in theory, should reflect the current needs of the country. For example, new foreign policy priorities should reflect the ways in which dealing with actors outside the border—other countries, nonstate actors, international organizations, and others—will help the United States achieve its goals. Specifically, what are the best ways for the United

States to engage with these actors to help the country further its national interest? How have these policies changed to reflect a new or different understanding of how to best achieve that national interest?

This approach to foreign policy is not unique to the United States. In fact, each country's foreign policy decisions should be premised on its own priorities and the ways in which actors outside its national border will help it achieve its goals. In the case of the United States, the student of foreign policy can track and document changes in priorities that will provide important insights into the reasons particular foreign policy decisions were made.

In order to really understand any aspect of American foreign policy from the founding of this country through the twenty-first century and the changing concept of security, the policy must be placed within the framework of both the international situation and domestic priorities. Foreign policy encompasses decisions a country makes that affect actors beyond its own borders. Similarly, the decisions and policies made by other actors (whether nations, corporations, multinational organizations, etc.) have a direct impact on the United States. Both these components, domestic and international, provide the framework that helps define the context for making foreign policy decisions.

Foreign policy decisions cannot ignore domestic factors that can involve a range of issues, including the economic situation of the country, the "mood" of the people, and the cycle of the political process (i.e., whether or not it is an election year). In fact, foreign policy decisions sometimes appear to be made to distract people from the problems within the country. These two components, domestic and international, *both* feed into and affect the foreign policy decisions a country makes. This makes understanding America's foreign policy decisions over time a complex undertaking.

Grasping the general theoretical models and approaches to making policy, along with the assumptions that go with them, are essential to understanding U.S. foreign policy. But those models and assumptions are only the starting points. More important to the understanding of U.S. foreign policy is applying those models and assumptions to the realities of the situation. For example, it is possible to look at and define the concept of "isolationism." However, doing so should also lead to questions about the prevailing view of early U.S. foreign policy, such as whether it really was "isolationist" or whether the United States was engaged in the world but in a limited and clearly defined way, which is closer to a "unilateralist" perspective. That series of questions cannot be answered without first defining the terms and then looking at when—and why—the United States adopted and then deviated from a specific foreign policy type or orientation. This exploration should lead to an understanding of why the United States adopted the policy it did and how that policy, put into the context of the time, was designed to help the United States achieve its goals as defined by its own national interest. Then it will be possible to better understand under what set of circumstances the United States chose to break from that policy and get involved politically and militarily in world affairs. Only by exploring and addressing this range of ideas can you answer the questions posed above and then draw conclusions about the direction of U.S. foreign policy at a particular time in the country's history.

Assessing actual policy against a theoretical model is only one piece of the foreign policy puzzle. When you look at "foreign policy" what you are assessing are *policy outputs*, specifically the *results* of the policy decisions that were made within the government. Here it is important to make a distinction between the *processes* by which these decisions were made and the actual *decisions*. In most cases, foreign policy decisions are the result of a routine process involving bureaucrats in an executive department (such as State, Defense, Treasury, Commerce, etc.) who make decisions based on what has been done before. The president of the United States or the secretary of the agency sets the priorities, and the bureaucrat implements them.

However, this *implementation* process contrasts with the process of *setting the priorities* that will determine what U.S. foreign policy will be. The actual decision-making and the outputs (i.e., decisions) that result are part of the process performed by those in relatively high positions, often under circumstances of crisis or actual conflict, based on their perception of national interest as well as their own priorities and understanding of the political realities.

Here another distinction must be made, that is, the difference between those decisions that are *proactive* versus those that are *reactive*. *Proactive policies* are initiated at a high level (for example, by the president or the secretary of state or defense) and are tied to the creation of a new policy or a dramatic change from an existing one. An example of a proactive policy is the U.S. decision to invade Iraq in March 2003. Here the decision was tied directly to the goals stated in President George W. Bush's "National Security Strategy of the United States," issued in September 2002.[5] This document, which has become known as "the Bush Doctrine," puts forward a new direction for American foreign policy: "defending the United States, the American people and our interests at home and abroad by identifying and destroying the threat *before it reaches our borders*" (emphasis added). In other words, this document states that as part of the foreign policy framework for the Bush administration, the United States will be justified in going to war *preemptively* against any country or group that *potentially* threatens this country or its allies and that it will act alone if necessary. Hence, U.S. foreign policy will be proactive should the country be threatened in any way.

In contrast to a proactive policy, a reactive policy is one where the president and his (or her) advisors are in a position of having to react to circumstances that were thrust upon them, regardless of what established policy might be. The Cuban Missile Crisis provides a prime example of reactive policy, as does the decision to go to war against Afghanistan in response to the attacks on September 11, 2001. In the case of the Cuban Missile Crisis, no matter how carefully President John F. Kennedy and his advisors outlined what their foreign policy priorities should be, such as fighting communism or aiding developing countries, reacting to the information about the missiles in Cuba pushed that emergency to the top of the policy agenda. It also put the United States into a position of responding to circumstances that existed and were initiated by other countries, rather than planning for what the president hoped would happen or would like to see occur.

Similarly, despite warnings about a possible terrorist attack, the government could not expect or plan for the specific events of September 11. Therefore, those events put the Bush administration into the position of deciding what policies to pursue to *respond* to that crisis. These examples stand in contrast to the decision to invade Iraq in March 2003. In that case, the United States initiated the foreign policy decision, choosing when, where, and how to act. In other words, in the case of the invasion of Iraq, the United States did not respond to events thrust upon it (reactive) but took the initiative (proactive) based on alleged evidence of weapons of mass destruction.[6] Knowing the difference between these terms is important to understanding how and why particular foreign policy decisions were and are made. In addition, these cases are examples of how circumstances dictate that decisions be made quickly, with incomplete or even incorrect information. Yet decisions must be made, and those decisions have important ramifications for future policies.

Understanding foreign policy also requires seeing the broader domestic context within which foreign policy decisions are made. For example, an understanding of the Cold War (roughly from 1947 until the collapse of the Soviet Union in 1991) would not be complete without knowledge of the role played by Senator Joseph McCarthy and the Red Scare in the 1950s. The Cold War pitted the United States and its democratic allies against the Soviet Union and other communist countries. McCarthyism, with its desire to ferret out Communists within the United States, fit well within and took advantage of the larger Cold War framework. At the same time, domestically, McCarthy fueled the fear of this ideological enemy. This contributed to public support for foreign policy decisions made during that time.

The role of this short text is not to examine all aspects of U.S. foreign policy decision-making; rather, it is to look at the ideological and political framework of those who made the decisions, to see the ways in which their approach or understanding guided the decisions they made. For example, the change in U.S. foreign policy surrounding the Spanish-American War in 1898 can be attributed in part to the influence of Theodore Roosevelt and his desire to be more aggressive externally, as well as to President William McKinley's reluctance to resist the growing pressure from the media and public to take action. Similarly, the decision to get involved in World War I in 1917 is partly the result of President Woodrow Wilson's deeply held commitment to the ideals of democracy and his belief that the war could be fought as "the war to end all wars" and "the war to make the world safe for democracy." In retrospect, we can look at these idealistic pronouncements and wonder how any leader could ever have believed them to be true. But in the context of the time, they framed the foreign policy decisions that were made, and many of the Wilsonian ideals continue to influence U.S. foreign policy today.[7] Further, at the time, they provided an important rallying cry that garnered the support of the American public.

What does this tell us about what we need to understand U.S. foreign policy? First, it suggests that it is critical to understand the theoretical assumptions (for example, whether to remain unilateralist or to engage internationally) that influenced the decisions made. Second, it tells us that it is important to assess the actual decisions made against the theoretical assumptions or constructs that influenced them. Third, it indicates that it is necessary to look at the context (international and domestic) within which foreign policy decisions were made. Based on this information and a critical assessment of reality versus theory, it will be possible to draw conclusions that allow for a better understanding of U.S. foreign policy.

To start the process, we will begin by delving into the world of theory, that is, what is foreign policy and where does it come from?

What Is Foreign Policy?

"Foreign policy" refers to those decisions made within a country that are affected by and that in turn affect entities outside the country. Initially, foreign policy (and most of international relations in general) pertained to the interaction of nation-states, as those were the primary actors. Hence, foreign policy generally refers to decisions made by one country or nation-state that directly affect another. One of the major changes seen in the recent past is that foreign policy is no longer just about relations between countries. In a broader context, foreign policy now includes a country's relationships with a range of actors, including those that exist outside traditional state borders.

These might include organizations that are made up of nation-states, such as the United Nations, the European Union, or NATO. It could include multinational corporations (MNCs), such as Wal-Mart, that end up influencing the policies of the country within which they are housed.[8] It might include stateless actors, such as the Palestinians, which act as political entities to influence the policies of other countries. It might include nonstate actors, such as Al Qaeda, which exist outside the boundaries of any established country but influence the foreign policy decisions of other countries. Or it might include nongovernmental organizations (NGOs), such as the Sierra Club or Amnesty International, which increasingly have played a role in getting policy issues onto the agenda for international discussion.

The presence of actors that exist outside the traditional nation-state has further complicated the foreign policy process. Generally, countries transmit their policy decisions from one to another through recognized diplomatic channels, whether the head of state, an ambassador, a secretary of state or a foreign minister, or through an established bureaucracy. But the actors mentioned above, especially nonstate actors and stateless peoples, typically do not have such channels or representatives, thereby raising questions about how policy decisions will be transmitted or policy requests made. In some cases, heads of state do not want to meet with representatives of some of these actors because they fear that doing so will grant legitimacy, that is, give the nonstate actors the same status that a country has. However, ignoring these actors or uncertainty about how to deal with them does not mean that they do not have a critical role to play in influencing the foreign policy decisions of a state, even a major power like the United States.

National Interest

Foreign policy decisions are made based on *national interest*. But what does that mean? Exactly what is "national interest"? There are a number of theoretical approaches to guide our understanding of this concept.

Different policy-makers are influenced by different perspectives, which then help frame the policy decisions that they make. If foreign policy involves those decisions that are made within a country that are affected by and in turn affect actors and decisions made outside its borders, it is also important to understand some broad theoretical approaches that decision-makers have used to understand those interactions. These broad theoretical areas of focus have influenced the decisions made by different presidents and other policy-makers. So when we talk about Wilson as an "idealist" or Nixon as a "realist," we need to understand what that really means

The Realist Perspective

In general, relations between countries are the basis of foreign policy. One of the major schools of thought about understanding these relations is the *realist school*, which assumes that nation-states (i.e., countries) are the primary actors in world politics and that each will act in a way that allows it to pursue its key interests or "national interests."

The realist perspective is characterized by the central role that *power* plays, where power is the ability of one actor to influence the behavior of another. According to Joseph Nye, a political scientist as well as policy-maker, power can be defined as "hard" or "soft." *Hard power* includes both economic and military strength that is used to induce others to change their position. In contrast, *soft power* involves persuading others to do what you want through co-option or cooperation, rather than coercion. Soft power relies on values rather than might.[9]

The application of "hard power" is at the core of the realist perspective. In general, since its emergence as an imperial power in the nineteenth century, the United States has relied heavily on its hard power in order to get its way. If the realist perspective assumes that the nation-state is the primary actor in the international system and that it will act in a rational way (to maximize benefits and minimize costs), then states will act to maximize their own power by wielding military or economic might as necessary. At the heart of realist decision-making is the notion that "statesmen think and act in terms of interest defined as power"[10] and that it is in the country's best interest to continue to accrue power using whatever means available.

The United States' decision to provoke a war with Mexico in 1846 and to respond militarily to the explosion of the Maine in the harbor in Havana, Cuba, in 1898 are two early examples of realist foreign policy decision-making. Later, in the twentieth century, President Nixon and Henry Kissinger, who served first as national security advisor and then as secretary of state, are both seen as quintessential realist decision-makers, using the threat of military force when necessary, but also knowing how to play one actor (the Soviet Union) against another (China) to the advantage of the United States. Values and moral principles do not play a major role in realist thinking. Rather, the main goal is getting and using power in the belief that power is equated with security.

In the realist perspective, most critical are what are known as "*core interests*,"[11] those that involve the protection and continuation of the state and its people. These tie directly to a country's security and become the central core of any state's national interest. Only when the country's security can be assured can the government make decisions about other aspects of the country.

For example, concern about global warming, while important, becomes a far lower priority in the face of a direct military threat.

Idealist/Liberal Perspective

Another major approach to relations between countries is the *idealist school*, which looks at countries as part of a collective body where security is best achieved if countries work together rather than in competition. In contrast to realism, the contemporary idealist or liberal perspective is based on values and on the importance of peoples and nations working together cooperatively. *Liberalism* (not to be confused with the political notions of "liberal" or "conservative") grows from the idealist stress on what unites people and countries and leads directly to the creation and growth of international organizations, such as the United Nations, that stress the importance of countries working together in pursuit of common goals for the betterment of all. Advocacy of free trade policies is another example of the application of this theoretical perspective since the assumption is that all countries will benefit from this form of economic cooperation. The use of soft power becomes an important element in this tradition, as it is tied to policies rooted in cooperation. The idealist/liberal perspective gained increasing credibility as a framework for foreign policy with the end of the Cold War and the spread of capitalist economics and democracy through the countries that had been part of the so-called Eastern Bloc.

The foreign policies advocated by Woodrow Wilson are perhaps the clearest application of this approach in American foreign policy. From Wilson's decision to enter the First World War, justified in part on the need to make the world safe for democracy, to his advocacy for an organization that would bring all countries together to thwart expansionist tendencies of other countries, his foreign policy was steeped in idealism. George W. Bush, with his emphasis on the belief of the importance of spreading the values of freedom and democracy, is a recent example of this way of thinking.

Underlying the goals of the idealist/liberal approach to foreign policy is the idea that the country's security and national interests are better served by working *with* other countries than by trying to compete with or overpower them.

Feminist Perspectives

Another approach to foreign policy and international relations grew out of the *feminist critique*, which advocates the need to look not only at who made policy and why (generally men who followed the realist approach), but also at the impact of those decisions on the people who were most affected and often had the least access to the decision-makers: women and children. And, as feminist writers point out, women have been an important—if unacknowledged—part of U.S. foreign policy.[12]

The *feminist perspective* argues that those who make foreign policy decisions are largely men who have different interests from the groups affected by U.S. policy, especially when the policy decision is to do nothing. (It is important to remember that doing nothing is a policy decision in and of itself.) It focuses more on understanding who has the power and how that power is used than on the processes by which decisions are made. The feminist perspective would remind us of the importance of understanding the impact of decisions on all people and of the ways in which gender might influence our understanding of foreign policy decisions.[13]

When we look at the characteristics generally associated with foreign policy, especially hard power, they are the traits that we tend to think of as masculine: power, military might, strength, and coercion, to name but a few. In contrast, the notions of cooperation and peace, which are typically associated with women and are seen as feminine, are perceived as less important in ensuring a country's security. However, in order to get a more complete understanding of U.S. foreign policy, we need to look at the world through "gender-sensitive lenses." In doing so, we can see that women are an important part of the foreign policy picture, even though they are often obscured by the prominence of men, and that foreign policy is neither necessarily masculine nor feminine. Rather, it is about making decisions perceived to be in the best interest of the country.

The emergence of women as prominent foreign policy decision-makers both in the United States and in other countries has made it clear that women are as capable of making tough decisions as men. In the United States, Hillary Clinton, Madeleine Albright, and Condoleezza Rice are all examples of women who rose to hold the critical position of Secretary of State. Before them, women like Margaret Thatcher in England, Indira Gandhi in India, and Golda Meir in Israel all became prime ministers in their respective countries. But it is important to bear in mind that many of the qualities ascribed to these women were masculine in character (ambitious, ruthless, hard-headed), and not necessarily seen as positive qualities for women to have.

Security and the Concept of Threat

Regardless of which theoretical approach you take—realist, idealist/liberal, feminist—achieving the country's security is paramount. Inherent in the concept of security is also the notion of threat, that is, anything that endangers a country's core interests, people, or territory. Although this generally refers to physical danger, the concept of threat is far broader than that and can apply to anything that can harm or interfere with the way of life, ideals, philosophy, ideology, or economy of the country. During the Cold War the primary threat coming from communism was far more than the fear of military attack; communism was also seen as a danger to the democratic ideals and capitalist market economy on which the United States was founded. More recently, the concept of threat was broadened still further to refer to the dangers posed by environmental degradation, the spread of disease, and human rights abuses— all of which run counter to the ideals that are considered important to the United States.

One test of national interest and core values is whether the threat is important enough to go to war about. Would the American public support the decision to deploy U.S. troops against the perceived threat? Clearly, in the face of armed attack on the country, such as the Japanese attack on Pearl Harbor on December 7, 1941, or the terrorist attacks on September 11, 2001, there was little debate about whether a military response was appropriate. But what about the case of human rights abuses abroad, such as those that have taken place in Rwanda or Bosnia or Sudan? Because protecting basic human rights is a central value dear to the United States, should the United States use its military might to help those whose rights are being abused? This is a much harder question to answer, and the response can be debated. Some people believe that the United States has a moral responsibility to intervene in those cases. Others believe that fighting against human rights abuses in foreign countries is not in our national interest because it does not affect this country directly. Therefore, they conclude, the United States should not get involved. Because of the need for public support for military intervention, the resulting foreign policy decision as to whether or when to intervene in such cases is an example of the ways in which international and domestic factors coincide.

As the one who sets the foreign policy priorities, it is up to the president to make the case that (military) intervention is in the national interest, and it is the president who is held accountable by the public. Former assistant secretary of state for democracy, human rights, and labor, John Shattuck, notes that in these cases, "strong public support is unlikely until the president has stimulated it by cogently explaining that the redefinition of U.S. national interests include the prevention of human rights and humanitarian disasters that might destabilize the world."[14] In other words, while it is easy to make the case for war in the event of direct attack on the country or on U.S. citizens, it is far more difficult to explain why it is necessary or in the national interest to get involved in a country on the other side of the world to prevent human rights abuses or humanitarian catastrophe there. If the president believes that such intervention is necessary, it will fall on him or her, as the leader of the country, to clearly explain why.

A corollary is that once the president makes the decision to intervene militarily, the public must see results, or support for that effort will wane over time. This was the case with Vietnam. In 2003 President Bush took his case to the Congress and the public and received the support necessary to go to war against Iraq. However, by June 2005, two years after the war was declared "over," with combat troops still fighting and no known exit strategy, public support started to decline.[15] By April 2008, as the presidential campaign was heating up, according to a Pew poll, 52 percent of Americans believed that the war was going not too well or not at all well, and 57 percent believed that the war was the wrong decision.[16] Regardless of initial support for the war effort, over time and with little end in sight at that time, support was waning.

Another component of the concept of threat is tied directly to the ways in which the nation perceives its own power and capabilities as well as its perception of the power and capabilities of an adversary. A nation will pursue a foreign policy that it believes will increase its own security and diminish the threat. This suggests that many foreign policy decisions are tied to intangibles, such as perceptions. For example, it is possible to measure quantitatively one country's military might, such as the number of fighter aircraft, aircraft carriers, tanks, and troops. But what should also go into this equation (and is much harder to measure) is the nation's willingness to use those capabilities, that is, its *credibility*. This is an intangible but very real factor when one country is trying to determine whether other countries represent a threat or, conversely, how it can protect itself from a threat. Most will agree that a country with no military force or with a military that could easily be overpowered poses little direct threat to the United States. But what about a country such as North Korea or Iran, both of which are believed to be developing nuclear weapons? Each of those countries is as a threat because of the fear that it might use those weapons. Thus, a country's credibility enters into the foreign policy equation, and perceptions directly affect the making of foreign policy, where credibility is based on the belief that a country has weapons and is willing to use them to achieve its foreign policy goals.

Foreign Policy Orientations

How does a country pursue its national interest? Countries have various foreign policy options or orientations available to them. The particular option that the decision-makers choose to pursue assumes a number of things: that they know or have formulated what is in the national interest; that the decision-makers will then make decisions that are tied to or that will further the national interest; and that the first priority will be to ensure the country's security and that of its people.

We will look at a number of foreign policy orientations in this book: *unilateralism, isolationism, neutrality,* and *engagement.* The United States has predominantly pursued two of these in its history—unilateralism and engagement—although it was isolationist in the period between the two world wars. The United States initially declared neutrality to try to avoid involvement in World Wars I and II, but this was very limited in scope. In reviewing these foreign policy orientations, it is important to remember that they are generalizations or theoretical types and that few countries pursue one or another in its purest theoretical form. Rather, the application of the particular policy will be a function of the country and its goals at a given time.

Of these orientations, *neutrality* is the only one that has a very specific meaning within the international system. When a nation pursues a policy of neutrality, it chooses *not* to engage in any military, political, or security alliances. In other words, it remains apart from any aspect of the international system that would require it to take sides or get involved militarily. Because of its unique status, a country that is neutral generally is willing to accept specific roles and responsibilities within the international system. Often such a country—Switzerland is a classic example of this—is used as the site for various international negotiations so that no one country in the negotiation has the "home team advantage." Switzerland, moreover, is an international banking center because it is considered "safe." A declaration of neutrality also means that other countries will (or should) respect that position and not invade or attack a neutral nation.

The declaration of neutrality became especially important during the Cold War, when states did not want to be put into a position of having to take sides between the United States and its allies and the Soviet Union and its allies. In fact, a group of countries, primarily smaller developing ones, further assured this special relationship by creating their own bloc called the "neutral nonaligned" (NNA) countries. Led by Egypt under Nasser, Yugoslavia under Tito, and Indonesia under Sukarno, this group of countries met in 1961 to create an organization that would combat colonialism and also assure political and military/security independence for their states at the height of the Cold War. In addition to protecting their countries' national interest by allowing them to remain outside the U.S. and Soviet orbits, these countries also worked together to further a common agenda that would benefit them, including economic cooperation and growth. Many of these countries were very successful at playing the two sides off against each other in order to get economic aid and assistance; both Tito and Nasser were masters of this political maneuvering, for example.

As noted above, the United States tried to pursue neutrality at various points, primarily to stay out of the two world wars, at least initially. But, as will become clear later in this text, generally the United States chose not to pursue this foreign policy option.

Unilateralism and Isolationism

In the early years of the United States, the prevailing foreign policy was one of unilateralism,[17] which allowed the country to have a certain amount of freedom. The policy gave the United States freedom to engage with other countries economically while also protecting it by keeping it out of any formal alliances or agreements. This "policy of aloofness" or political detachment from international affairs was advocated by Thomas Jefferson, George Washington's secretary of state, who saw this as "the best way to preserve and develop the nation as a free people."[18] This approach was consistent with that advocated by other founders of the country. John Adams, the second president, advocated that "we should separate ourselves, as far as possible and as long as possible, from all European politics and wars." And in his often-quoted farewell address as president, George Washington warned the leaders of the new country to "steer clear of permanent alliances with any portion of the foreign world." He asked the country why we should "entangle our peace and prosperity in the toils of European ambition, rivalship, interest, humor, or caprice."[19]

What did the policy of unilateralism really mean for the United States? Here, again, it is important to think about national interests *within the context of the United States at that time*. When the United States was founded, the highest priority was to grow from within. As a new country, the greatest need was to pay attention to internal priorities, including political stability and economic independence, and the best way to do that, according to the founders of the country, was to remain outside the framework of European wars. Instead, the emphasis would be on economic strength through trade and commerce. This emphasis was essential to the growth and expansion of the country.

Europe in the eighteenth century was in a constant struggle for power, with France and England especially vying for prominence. America's founders warned the future leaders of the United States that it would not be in the national interest to get involved with those struggles, but rather it would be in the country's interest to stay clear of them. Yet "the evidence suggests that the U.S. economy was at least as dependent on foreign trade in 1790 as it was two hundred years later,"[20] and much of that trade, and in fact the United States economic system, "was inextricably bound up in the British economic system."[21] Hence, while the United States in its early years remained removed from the politics and wars of Europe, it was linked directly to Europe economically.

Pursuing a foreign policy of unilateralism allowed the United States to pick and choose when, where, and how to be involved with other countries, which was what allowed it to grow. Unilateralism provided the framework for geographic expansion through what would become known as America's "manifest destiny," and it allowed the country to strengthen economically through trade and, eventually, industrialization. And as U.S. trade and commerce grew, a military (especially a navy) was needed to protect U.S. interests. In short, unilateralism allowed the United States to become a "great power" by the end of the nineteenth century.[22]

The other major policy orientation that the United States pursued was one of *engagement,* or *internationalism,* which has characterized U.S. foreign policy from 1945 to the present. Internationalism deals with the decision to become actively engaged in all aspects of international relations, including the military and political alliances that the United States shunned prior to World War II. Again, the critical question is why the U.S. decision-makers chose to pursue that course of action. How and why was it in the best interest or national interest of the United States to become involved militarily and politically as well as economically?

An important point is that involvement internationally has both a cooperative and a conflictual component, with a country sometimes pursuing both at the same time. For example, during the Cold War, although the United States and the Soviet Union were major adversaries, they were also trading partners, at least since 1972, because this served the best interests of both countries economically.[23] And while the Bush administration labeled North Korea an "axis of evil" country, under the terms of an agreement signed between the United States and North Korea in 1994, the United States sent fuel to that country.[24]

Theory and Context

Over the course of its history, the United States has pursued two major foreign policy orientations at different points, first unilateralism and then a policy of internationalism or active engagement in the international system, although at different periods it also was either neutral or isolationist, albeit briefly. Deciding which one to pursue and why, and when and why to break from that particular pattern, was tied to what was perceived to be in the national interest of the United States at various points. It is important to note that each of these approaches represents an ideal type and, as we will see, the actual application of each policy was not nearly as pure.

In order to understand which approach the United States opted for and why, it is necessary to place the particular policy into the context of the period during which it was made. American foreign policy is the result of a number of often-competing priorities and issues, as well as the result of the perspectives of the people who make policy. All of these factors change over time. Therefore, it is important to explore when and why the United States broke from its policy of unilateralism, temporarily as well as permanently. We must also examine why U.S. policies since the end of the Cold War have been different from those pursued during the Cold War, although all could be termed "internationalist," though for different reasons. In other words, understanding U.S. foreign policy is tied to an understanding of history and the context within which decisions were made—both domestic and international.

Fully understanding and appreciating American foreign policy (or that of any country) requires looking within the nation to see who makes policy and speaks for the nation. Generally, the more developed and democratic the country, the more complex the foreign policy decision-making apparatus. In the United States, policy is generally formulated by the executive branch, specifically, the president, his advisors such as the assistant to the president for national security (the national security advisor), and the secretaries of state and defense, although other components of the executive branch (the bureaucracy) weigh in as well. Other actors, such as Congress, play a role, although a less direct one. The media play both a direct role, through the stories they cover and how they cover them, and an indirect one, as a vehicle through which the public gets its information. But the power of these other groups to influence policy outcomes diminishes the farther they get from the president and the members of the executive branch.[25] Knowing who makes policy and the relationships these various actors have to one another is a critical part of understanding the process of making foreign policy.

Identifying Themes

Thus far, we have identified a number of themes that characterize and explain U.S. foreign policy. We can look at the policies based on how involved the United States was with other countries and the extent of that involvement (unilateralism or isolationism versus internationalism or engagement). We can look at who made the policies and the competing role of the president versus the Congress. We can ask who influenced the policies and who are affected by them, both domestic actors and international. And we can ask how U.S. foreign policy at different points in time reflects changes from previous policies and, if there are changes, why these occurred.

One of the points raised in reviewing the history and evolution of U.S. foreign policy is that while the broad shifts might be startling (e.g., unilateralism to engagement), on closer examination hints of those changes actually existed before they were implemented. This, too, is important to note. For example, the ideological battles between democracy and communism following World War II in many ways were extensions of the fight for the spread of democracy advocated by Woodrow Wilson. Hence, as the United States moved into the Cold War, it was possible to hear echoes of earlier ideas about the primacy of democracy and about the need to "make the world safe for democracy." What was different during the Cold War was the fact that military and political engagement in support of those ideals became the norm rather than an exception.

As we explore the evolution of U.S. foreign policy, we will keep returning to these themes in order to place the foreign policy decisions into a broader context for understanding.

Who Makes Foreign Policy and Why Are Particular Decisions Made?

The Constitution set out a framework for making U.S. foreign policy. Like many other decisions made in the early years of this country, the particular approach built into this document was designed to limit the power of any one branch and to ensure that the system of checks and balances would be applied.

The Actors

The executive branch, headed by the president, and the legislative branch, the Congress, are the two parts of the government that have been given most of the responsibility for making—and for implementing—foreign policy. Although the judicial branch is usually not considered part of the foreign policy process, it does get involved when a particular law is in dispute, and it has been used to interpret the Constitution in order to clarify the relationship between the other two branches on a range of issues.[26] However, that does not happen very often.

In the early years of the country especially, with a relatively weak and part-time Congress, it is not surprising that the executive branch, primarily the president, set the foreign policy priorities. It was assumed at the time that only the president could look at what was in the national interest and then give the orders necessary for that policy to be implemented. More important, it was also assumed that only the president represented the country as a whole. In an era before cell phones, faxes, and Internet, the primary means of communication was through letters and direct conversation. Hence, the president had to rely on information supplied by U.S. diplomats and emissaries who traveled and lived abroad, representing the United States, as well as information from other countries' diplomats who served as the representatives of their countries here. It was the job of these officials to relay information back through the State Department, where the secretary of state could inform and advise the president, who could then make decisions.

Just as the means of communication were slow, so decisions could be made more deliberately. Crises did not escalate overnight, nor did circumstances change by the minute. Rather, there was an established international order, and the primary shifting that took place was over the relative power that different countries had within that order.

In the late eighteenth century, the United States was a relatively new country compared with the European nations such as Britain or France, or with the Asian nations of Japan and China. Fearing what would happen if the country got involved with those countries, the founders decided that the highest priority for the United States was to establish itself as a nation and to stay removed from those others politically and militarily.

Over time, circumstances changed. Among the most significant in the making of U.S. foreign policy was the growth of the executive branch following World War II, and subsequently the assertion of congressional power into foreign policy decision-making. Later chapters will explore the various changes and the reasons for them; however, a brief overview will help set the stage for what will follow.

Shifting Balance of Power

As the United States grew as a nation, so did U.S. relations with different parts of the world. With more involvement internationally came questions about the wisdom of the decisions that were made and whether the president really did speak in the best interest of the country or whether he represented the interests of a group, such as big business. As a result of such questions and the political pressure that came with them, Congress became more assertive at accepting the role it was given in the Constitution to balance the power of the president. Perhaps one of the first assertions of congressional prerogative came after World War I, when the Republican majority in the Senate opposed the creation of the League of Nations advocated by President Wilson. Where Wilson saw this organization as one way to avoid war in the future, the Senate feared the opposite—that being a member of the League would guarantee U.S. involvement in future wars outside the country.

This example illustrates different interpretations of national interest that resulted in a clash between the two branches and shows the tension that the Constitution created when it assigned foreign policy powers to two branches, albeit different powers, but in the same arena. For example, Article II, Section 2 of the Constitution grants to the president the power to make treaties, but "with the Advice and Consent of the Senate . . . provided two thirds of the Senators present concur."[27] In the case of the League of Nations, because the Senate did not concur, the legislative branch prevailed.

There are other areas where the power of the two branches at best overlap or at worst conflict. One of the most dramatic has to do with the decision to go to war. Here, too, the Constitution builds in ambiguities. Article II, Section 2 states, "The President shall be Commander in Chief of the Army and Navy of the United States."[28] But Article I, Section 8 states very clearly, "The Congress shall have Power . . . To declare War."[29]

When Pearl Harbor was bombed, President Franklin D. Roosevelt went to Congress to ask that body to declare war, and Congress complied. Subsequently, the authority of the president to take the United States to war (or even what "war" meant) grew increasingly murky. President Harry Truman did not ask for a declaration of war when the United States went into Korea in 1950. Instead, he issued a statement noting that he had ordered "United States air and sea forces to give the Korean Government troops and cover," under the auspices of and in response to a request by the United Nations.[30] When President Lyndon Johnson wanted to escalate military operations in Vietnam—which was termed a "limited war" rather than a formal "war"— he did not seek a declaration of war. Instead, he asked that Congress pass a resolution allowing him "to take all necessary measures," thereby giving him a blank check to do whatever *he* deemed necessary to prosecute that war. It can be argued that when Congress did so, it abrogated its responsibilities under the Constitution. Subsequently, Congress sought to return the balance by reversing the Tonkin Gulf Resolution in 1971 and then by passing the War Powers Resolution two years later.

The passage of the War Powers Resolution in 1973 was a clear assertion of congressional authority. Congress also designed this act to ensure that the power of the president to take the country into an undeclared war was balanced by the congressional oversight guaranteed in the Constitution. However, since that resolution was passed, its constitutionality has been questioned, and presidents have found ways either to work outside its strictures or to skirt them. Both Presidents George H. W. Bush and George W. Bush asked

Congress to support their decisions to send U.S. troops to fight in the Middle East, in the first case, the Persian Gulf War of 1991, and in the second case, the "war on terror" (against Afghanistan and also Iraq). In both cases, they used the Tonkin Gulf Resolution of 1964 as a model to secure open-ended support for the action rather than requesting a formal declaration of war.[31] Given the brevity of the 1991 Persian Gulf War, the wisdom of congressional approval was not debated subsequently, although it passed initially only by a narrow margin.

That stands in contrast to the case of George W. Bush and the war with Iraq that started in 2003. The longer the conflict continues and as more information becomes available that makes it clear there were no weapons of mass destruction (the original rationale for that war), the more public support dwindles. Waning public support for the war means that members of Congress undoubtedly will raise questions about the wisdom of voting for open-ended support as they are pressured by their constituents and respond to public opinion.[32]

President Bill Clinton did not go to the Congress to request approval to send troops to Haiti in 1993, nor for U.S. involvement in Bosnia in 1994 and in Kosovo in 1999. In the case of Haiti, Clinton argued that as commander in chief he possessed the authority to send U.S. forces as needed; in the case of the Balkans, he claimed that these were NATO missions (as opposed to U.S. military actions) and that therefore the United States was obliged to participate under the terms of the NATO treaty.

The point here is that tensions do exist between the two branches regarding the conduct of U.S. foreign policy and especially the commitment of troops. Those tensions are exacerbated by domestic political issues, including public (and therefore congressional) support for the mission.

Role of Economics

Despite the claims of pursuing a unilateralist or isolationist foreign policy in the early years of U.S. history, successive presidents made decisions to get involved with various parts of the world. This happened incrementally, first by establishing a "sphere of influence" in the Western Hemisphere (i.e., the Monroe Doctrine and the Roosevelt Corollary), and then by expanding that sphere to encompass more countries, such as Japan and China, in which the United States had economic and business interests.

An important point here, and it is one that can be seen throughout this brief exploration of American foreign policy, is that very often the decision to expand U.S. involvement with different parts of the world was made for economic reasons. In some cases it was to protect business interests, such as the case of U.S. investments in Cuba before the Spanish-American War; in some cases to expand trading opportunities, as was the case with U.S. expansion into Japan in 1853 and China at the end of the nineteenth century. In other cases it was with a desire to increase access to foreign capital and investment, which drove much of America's relations with Britain. But the bottom line is that economic motives and the need to protect U.S. businesses often drive foreign policy decisions. These decisions were (and are) made by the president based on his perception of national interest.

Another constant in reviewing the history of U.S. foreign policy is that once the United States started to get involved with a particular part of the world, it did not retreat from that area as it became more involved with other parts. U.S. involvement in different parts of the world can be seen as an inverse pyramid, starting with a narrow base, where involvement was limited to a small number of countries in the early years, growing to a very broad platform at the top by the 1960s, as the United States was involved directly on every continent in some way.

Role of Domestic Politics and Factors

That brings us to the next important generalization about making and understanding American foreign policy—the role that domestic politics and other domestic factors (economic, social, etc.) play. An examination of the history of U.S. foreign policy illustrates clearly the role of domestic politics. Support at home for Cold War foreign policy was increased by Senator Joseph McCarthy and his "Red Scare." Conversely, the decision to pull out of Vietnam was accelerated by an American public that was withdrawing its support for the war and was also losing its faith in the government because of the then-breaking Watergate scandal.

Many African Americans in this country are concerned about and question why the United States has not been more involved with Africa, especially given the genocide that took place in Rwanda in the 1990s and in Darfur in Sudan starting in 2004. Here, too, the easy answer lies, at least in part, with domestic politics. The United States claims that it has (or had) no vital national interest in these regions. More important, despite pressure from the Congressional Black Caucus and the commitment of secretaries of state Colin Powell and Condoleezza Rice to pay more attention to Africa, the reality is that there has not been a critical voting bloc or a powerful domestic political voice for that position, at least when weighed against the voices of those who oppose deploying U.S. forces in distant lands for humanitarian reasons that are not clearly linked to U.S. national interests.

As noted above, economic factors play a major role in influencing the direction of foreign policy decisions spurred by business interests that are important to the political process as well as the economic well-being of the country. Big business especially tends to have ties to the political system, through lobbies, campaign contributions, and the interrelationship of business and foreign policy/security through what President Dwight Eisenhower called the "military-industrial complex."[33] Hence, U.S. involvement in many parts of the world has often been tied directly to the need to protect economic and U.S. business interests abroad as well as resources such as oil.

Who Is Affected by U.S. Foreign Policy Decisions?

This brings us to the next logical question: who is affected by U.S. foreign policy decisions? The most obvious answer to this question is those countries with which the United States is involved. But people at home are affected as well. Another category to consider is the least powerful, or the powerless. Each of these is explored briefly below.

Impact of U.S. Foreign Policy Decisions on Other Countries

Since foreign policy is a continuous process where a decision made by one country directly affects the decisions made by another, any change in existing policy will have an important and perhaps long-standing impact on other countries. A good example of this is the U.S. relationship to its European allies. Joined together through NATO, the United States and the countries of Europe have remained allies because it was in all their interests to do so. Despite rocky periods, such as French President DeGaulle's decision to remove France from the military structure of NATO in 1966 or many of the European countries' responses to the war in Iraq, the alliance has been able to function as a whole. In fact, after September 11, it was the Europeans, not the United States, who requested invoking Article 5, the collective defense clause, of the NATO treaty in order to allow for a unified NATO response.[34]

The Bush administration's decision to go to war against Iraq in March 2003 without UN Security Council approval put it at odds with some of its NATO allies. While some NATO members, such as Great Britain and Poland, supported the United States, others, most notably France and Germany, were outspoken in their objections to this decision. Nonetheless, they all remained allies, bound together by common interest.

Another example is the Cold War, which was premised on competition between the United States and the Soviet Union. The United States based its early Cold War policies on assumptions about Soviet military capabilities and, specifically, the ways in which they lagged behind those of the United

States. When the USSR tested an atomic weapon in 1949 and then launched Sputnik in 1957, the United States had to rethink its own policies, including the need to accelerate some of its weapons programs. This led to an arms race that ultimately contributed to the economic bankruptcy and collapse of the Soviet Union.

This leads to another important conclusion: foreign policy decisions often have unintended consequences. No matter how carefully foreign policy decisions are analyzed and assessed, not all results can be anticipated. It also means that decisions are made based on assumptions and information available at the time. It is only later, as more information becomes available, that the full range of options (and dangers) becomes clear. This often puts the United States into a position of making policies that are reactive rather than proactive.

Domestic Constituencies

The American public is directly affected by foreign policy decisions, although different groups are affected in different ways. Foreign policy decisions can affect each of us, whether we are aware of it or not. The *Wall Street Journal* published an article on August 11, 2004, entitled "Sticker Shock at the Lumberyard." The article, which is subheaded "Remodeling Gets Costlier as Price of Wood Surges; Impact of China and Iraq," is a good example of the ways in which foreign policy decisions have an impact on "ordinary" Americans.[35]

An increase in the price of lumber can be attributed to a number of domestic factors, such as a housing boom in the United States that has increased the demand for lumber. Foreign policy comes into this as well: a building boom in China that has increased demand, a 27 percent tariff on lumber imported from Canada (which supplies 30 percent of all U.S. lumber), and a weak dollar that makes imports more costly all mean that Americans are feeling the impact on their pocketbooks. Those who are remodeling or renovating a house, doing any home improvement, or buying a new house will be paying more for lumber than they would have one year earlier.

Almost every group in this country has some representative who is looking out for and advocating for its interests. Virtually every type of business and labor organization has a lobbying group that represents it in Washington, as do special interest groups that have been formed to advocate for policy areas they care about, such as the environment. Even foreign governments have interest groups to represent their point of view. The goal of these various groups is to make sure that policies enacted by the president and Congress will not harm and ideally will help the constituencies they represent.

However, the success of these groups to influence policy decisions will vary, depending on who is in office, how broad their constituency is, and the amount of access that they actually have. For example, under the Clinton administration, environmental groups were extremely successful in advocating for protection of natural wilderness areas and for policies and agreements to protect the environment, such as the Kyoto Protocol. Part of the reason for their success was a president who was sympathetic to their cause and a vice president who was actively committed to improving the environment. In contrast, the administration of George W. Bush, which was tied more closely to business interests, reversed many of the Clinton administration policies to allow logging and road building in national forests, a position the Bush administration justified on domestic economic priorities. Shortly after taking office, the Obama administration again reversed many of the Bush administration decisions on the environment.

Clearly, each administration responded to a different set of needs, priorities, perception of national interest, and interest groups, and the policies enacted had a direct impact on different groups of Americans. But in addition to politicizing the issue domestically, changes in policy send confusing and ambiguous signals to other countries, which are trying to make their own policies based, in part, on what the United States is doing. Hence, under a Bush presidency, the countries that worked with the United States to reach agreement in Kyoto had to form a new coalition, recognizing the fact that they likely would have to move forward without U.S. help or support. This is likely to change again under Obama.

The "Powerless": The Feminist Perspective

As noted above, in asking "who is affected by policies," the feminist critique becomes especially important. The feminist critique argues that often those who are most affected by decisions are the ones who are the least powerful and, therefore, with little direct access to those who make the decisions. Who represents the interests of these groups? And is protecting these groups, whose interests fall under the broad category of "human rights" and "humanitarian interests," for example, a valid basis for making foreign policy? Are they tied to U.S. "national interest"?

The case of the Vietnam War is instructive when we look at the groups that are both affected by policy decisions and also most powerless to do anything about them. The "peace movement" grew from a small fringe group in the early days of the war to become all-encompassing. While many in this country still supported the war, the violent actions at Kent State University in May 1970, in response to what was seen as the illegal bombing of Cambodia, which was neutral in the conflict, galvanized members of the "silent majority," some of whom later joined with students to protest the war. Clearly, male students had the greatest stake in the outcome, as they were the ones being drafted to fight and die in Vietnam, but they were also generally removed from the formal political process. By 1968 the voices of public opinion were loud enough to keep Lyndon Johnson from running for reelection and were strong enough to persuade Nixon that he needed to find a way out of the war.

Setting the Stage

This chapter introduced some important concepts about American foreign policy that will help frame the approach taken throughout this book. It also laid out some basic questions about the foreign policy process, including asking who makes these decisions and why. But this introduction to the theories and concepts is just the starting point—now we have to apply them.

The next five chapters use a historical approach to U.S. foreign policy and break the more than two centuries of American history into five basic parts. Chapter 2 looks at a rather long period, from the founding of the country until just after World War I, years in which U.S. foreign policy was largely tied to the concept of unilateralism. We start with a review of why that particular approach was chosen in the context of international politics in the eighteenth and nineteenth centuries, as well as within the context of domestic priorities. But in order to really understand this concept, it is important to explore the circumstances under which the United States broke from that orientation and chose to get involved in international affairs, and why those decisions were made, as well as who made them. In many ways, exploring those exceptional cases, such as the Spanish-American War, provides insights into the foreign policy process.

Chapter 3 looks at the period from the end of World War I through World War II. This was a difficult period for the United States, which had to deal with economic depression as well as expansionist countries such as Japan and Germany. As both of these countries started to conquer others, calling into question the viability of the League of Nations and the concept of "collective security," the United States had to make some tough decisions about whether to intervene in world affairs, and when.

Chapter 4 explores the period in which the Cold War dominated U.S. foreign policy, from the end of World War II until the election of Ronald Reagan in 1980. This was a period characterized by active engagement with the international system and the creation of a foreign policy and defense bureaucracy that could support the changing role for the United States. All of U.S. foreign policy during this period was designed with an eye toward containing communism, which influenced not only U.S. policies, but relationships with other countries as the United States built its system of alliances. As we will see, the United States became involved with different parts of the world—from Europe and parts of Asia to the Middle East and Africa—but did not retreat from any. Therefore, within a few decades after World War II, the United States was involved on virtually every continent. And along with the expansion of political and military ties came broadened economic ones.

Chapter 5 looks at the period beyond the Cold War, starting with the administration of Ronald Reagan (1981–1989), which marked the beginning of the end of the Cold War, and going through the administrations of George H. W. Bush (1989–1993) and Bill Clinton (1993–2001). During this period the Soviet Union collapsed, and democratic movements swept the countries of Eastern Europe. While these changes brought with them a sense of euphoria, as the United States and forces of democracy triumphed over communism, they also brought new challenges that were largely unforeseen, such as increased civil wars and ethnic strife, and the growth of terrorism. What made these events especially difficult for the United States was that the entire foreign policy apparatus to that point was tied to the old Cold War structure and so was not appropriate to or adequate for meeting these new threats. Not only was a rethinking of foreign policy necessary on the part of the decision-makers, but it also required an articulation of the new or revised concepts to the American public at a time when their attention was focused inward ("it's the economy, stupid"). To many students of American foreign policy, the result has been a muddled and unfocused policy that puts the United States in the position of responding to the latest challenge rather than proactively pursuing policies deemed to be in the national interest.

Chapter 6 focuses on the presidency of George W. Bush, beginning with the contested election of 2000 and ending with the changes proposed by the Obama administration, which took office in January 2009. Despite the course that the Bush administration appeared to be on when coming into office, everything changed with the events of September 11, 2001. How that administration responded to the attacks that day and the changes in direction in U.S. foreign policy as a result are the focus of this chapter, as are the responses of the Obama administration to the policies that it inherited.

Chapter 7 will return to the basic questions raised in this chapter, with an eye toward answering them in light of what you have learned in this book. It will focus on the changing nature of the threat, U.S. relations with its allies, the wars in Iraq and Afghanistan, and how the United States can address all these in a way that will allow it to regain its role as global leader—if that is the intention. All of these will be framed within the context of a changing economic situation.

The goal in this book is not to pass judgments about the wisdom or "rightness" or "wrongness" of any single foreign policy decision as much as it is to provide the tool for understanding those decisions.

2

Unilateralism to Engagement

The Founding to the End of World War I

WORKING DEMOCRACIES ALWAYS NEED TIME TO DEVELOP, as did our own. We've taken a 200-year journey toward inclusion and justice, and this makes us patient and understanding as other nations are at different stages of this journey."[1] So said President George W. Bush in November 2003 about the need for governments in the Middle East to make democratic reforms. Yet, as the president noted, a two-hundred-year journey has taken the United States along a range of different paths, from unilateralism/isolationism to active engagement in the international system.

The early years of U.S. foreign policy were defined by those men (and they were all men) who believed that the highest priority of the country should be to look inward and build a stable and prosperous country removed from the affairs (and wars) of Europe. This did not mean that the United States would not be involved with other countries. Rather, it meant that foreign policy decisions would involve choosing when, where, and how to get involved with other countries while at the same time building our own.

The first chapter of this book outlined a number of foreign policy orientations, including unilateralism. This policy presumed that the United States would remain removed from the political and military affairs of the rest of the world but would be engaged in limited ways and in areas of its choosing. Many political science texts refer to the early years as a period of isolationism, meaning that the United States remained removed from the political affairs of the rest of the world, limiting its international engagement to economics and trade. This chapter will explore the policy of unilateralism (as opposed to isolationism) to describe how the leaders of the United States chose when,

where, and how to be involved internationally and how those decisions allowed the country to grow into a great power by the end of the nineteenth
century.

We will begin by looking at the perception of national interest at the time that
this country was created, and why the founders believed that being removed
politically and militarily (i.e., "aloof") from other countries was in the national
interest. Nonetheless, as we will see, the country broke from this policy at various points in its early history. Understanding when and why the country deviated from this policy will give you a better understanding of the foreign policy
process as well as the ways in which domestic priorities affected the definition of
"national interest" when applied to U.S. foreign policy. It will also give you an
understanding of why knowledge of the past can provide insight into the direction that U.S. foreign policy ended up taking at various points in time.

The Beginning

The newly independent United States had to develop policies and processes
for governing domestically and for setting priorities internationally (foreign
policy). Much of what the founders of the country did was simply react to
(and against) what they had seen in England, especially the tyranny of the
monarch. However, they were not in agreement on how to create a new governmental structure that would replace the monarchy they had known and
that was the norm at the time.

Creating a Foreign Policy Framework

The Articles of Confederation, drafted in 1777 and ratified in 1781, created
a loose union of sovereign states and was the first attempt to frame a new form
of government. Given the priorities in the 1770s, the Articles "were designed
primarily to facilitate a unified approach to foreign policy and national defense,"[2] with the Congress given primary responsibility for speaking on behalf
of the whole. In contrast, domestic priorities rested with each of the states.
Although the Articles of Confederation failed for a number of reasons, the
idea of the country speaking with a single voice on foreign policy remained an
important concept that would continue through the evolution of the government to its present form. However, the voice would shift from the Congress to
the president, although the power for making foreign policy would be divided
between the executive (the president) and the legislative branches.

A Continental Congress convened in Philadelphia in 1787 specifically to
revise the Articles of Confederation. The goal was to create a strong central

government that would have responsibility for the domestic affairs of the nation (as opposed to the states) and would speak on behalf of the country on foreign affairs. As embodied in the new Constitution, power in foreign policy would be vested in both a president and Congress, with each given certain tasks to ensure that there would be checks and balances. For example, while the president would be the commander in chief of the armed forces, it would be up to the Congress to declare war. While the president, as head of state, could negotiate treaties with foreign governments, two-thirds of the Senate must concur through its "advice and consent" function.[3] In this way the founders believed the national interest of the country would be served because no one person or organization within the government could become too strong. The design of this structure also assured that various constituencies would be heard and represented.

The Constitution also specified the powers that would be given to the states as well as to each branch of the federal government, and it reflected many of the divisions that existed within the young country. As is the case today, there were divisions between the rural areas and the cities, between those Americans who were educated and well traveled and those who were not, between the farmers and the merchants, and between those who lived on the coast and those who were inland. Those divisions also reflected the differences in how each of the groups viewed the world beyond the borders of the United States. Ultimately, Gouverneur Morris of Pennsylvania reflected the view of the founders of the country when he stated that the president was "the general Guardian of the National interests."[4] This has not changed over time. What has ebbed and flowed is the relationship and relative power of the president versus the Congress to make foreign policy. The "push-pull" has often led to tensions between the two branches. The sometimes difficult relationship between the branches, as well as the reasons for the tensions, became more apparent during the Cold War and will be explored in more detail in later chapters.

Beware of Entangling Alliances

The first three presidents of the United States—George Washington, John Adams, and Thomas Jefferson—were wary of foreign involvement that could wreck the young country. Yet each also brought to his position an understanding of the world beyond the United States, as well as the dangers of involvement in foreign wars. Washington was the first commander in chief and, as a general, saw firsthand the havoc wrought by war. Adams came to the office with a diplomatic background, as did Jefferson. Each of them feared what would happen if the United States got too involved in the wars of Europe at the expense of "domestic tranquility."[5]

In many ways the primary dispute over U.S. foreign policy and the definition of national interest was between Alexander Hamilton, the first secretary of the treasury, and Thomas Jefferson, the first secretary of state. Hamilton laid out many of his ideas on foreign policy in *The Federalist Papers*, written with James Madison and John Jay between October 1787 and July 1788. Hamilton believed that the United States needed the capabilities to develop into an important power, with a critical role to be played by an alliance of the government and commerce (business). Because of his emphasis on commerce, he advocated for a navy that could protect America's interests on the high seas, and he wrote of the importance of an army to make sure the United States could withstand the dangers surrounding it, from "British settlements" to "the savage tribes on our Western frontier."[6]

Jefferson saw the world differently. Rather than using limited U.S. resources to create a military, he emphasized trading with other countries and negotiating commercial treaties that would be in U.S. interests. While he allowed that the United States might need a small navy to protect its commercial interests, his priority was in securing the country's place in North America. The Louisiana Purchase of 1803 and the acquisition of the port of New Orleans resulted from Jefferson's desire to promote commerce. The decision to acquire this territory began a pattern of growth and expansion of the United States that would continue for the next fifty years and, ironically, would be aided directly by the decision to build a navy, as advocated by Hamilton.

The primary rivalry for "great power" status in Europe at that time was between France and Britain, each of which was building its empire, sometimes at the expense of the other country. Although Spain, the Netherlands, and Portugal had also established themselves as colonial powers in the "new world" by that time, each of the first three U.S. presidents saw France and Britain as the primary danger. However, the early American leaders did not agree which country posed the greater threat. What was clear was that the dangers of getting involved in foreign wars or in any rivalry among the major European powers had the possibility of creating a real threat to the homeland.

Despite these dangers, in 1778 the United States entered into an alliance with France, Britain's primary rival. Using realist political thinking, the early founders saw this alliance as a critical balance to the power of Britain, against which the United States was fighting for its independence. Ultimately, relations between the United States and France soured, with some of the early Federalists calling for war against France. From 1796 until 1800 the French claimed the right to seize any ships potentially bound for their enemy (Britain) and seized more than three hundred U.S. vessels. In 1800 the United States and France negotiated a treaty to end this "quasi-war." The United States agreed to drop all claims against France "in exchange for abrogation of the Franco-American Alliance of 1778."[7] This early alliance made clear to the United States the risks of involvement with the major European powers.

On September 17, 1796, George Washington delivered his Farewell Address to the nation upon his retirement after serving two terms as president. This address laid out his perspective on U.S. foreign policy based on his reading of the priorities at the time and the dangers that seemed to threaten the young country. While he advised the country to "steer clear of permanent alliances," the address contains much more regarding Washington's understanding of the world at the time and what it meant for the United States. For example, he advised the United States to "observe good faith and justice toward all nations. Cultivate peace and harmony with all." He told the country that "nothing is more essential than that permanent, inveterate antipathies against particular nations and passionate attachments for others should be excluded, and that in place of them just and amicable feelings toward all should be cultivated." In other words, it would be in the best interest of the United States to deal with all countries equally and fairly and in a positive way.

Washington also said "The great rule of conduct for us in regard to foreign nations is, in extending our commercial relations to have with them *as little political connection as possible*" (emphasis added). Thus, he warned that while it is important to trade with other countries, the United States could do so while also remaining politically removed from them. And he warned that "Europe has a set of primary interests which to us have none or a very remote relation. Hence, she [Europe] must be engaged in frequent controversies, the causes of which are essentially foreign to our concerns. Hence, therefore, it must be unwise in us to implicate ourselves by artificial ties in the ordinary vicissitudes of her politics or the ordinary combinations and collisions of her friendships or enmities."

Given the dangers and warnings that Washington laid out, it is logical he would then advocate "our policy to steer clear of permanent alliances."[8] And John Adams, the second president, agreed with Washington about the need to "separate ourselves, as far as possible and as long as possible from all European politics and wars."[9] Consistent with the belief that a strong executive should set foreign policy priorities and speak for the country, these men defined the path the United States would take in foreign policy for more than the next century. Initially, at least, the United States remained removed from European politics and did not enter into formal alliances; instead, the goal was to strengthen the country economically by *trading* with those countries. This policy of limited involvement, and the decision to become involved with other countries when and where the United States chose to, became the basis for the U.S. policy of *unilateralism*.

Manifest Destiny, the Monroe Doctrine,
and Westward Expansion

The death of Alexander Hamilton in 1804 meant his voice regarding the direction of U.S. foreign policy was stilled, although his influence and ideas remained important. What guided U.S. foreign policy in the 1800s was the notion of "manifest destiny," or "the belief that it was the destiny of the United States to spread across the continent." Further, "Manifest destiny embodied the conviction that Americans had a higher purpose to serve in the world than others. Theirs was not only a special privilege, but also a special charge: to protect liberty and to promote freedom."[10] Examining manifest destiny from that perspective—that higher ideals were central to the founding of the country and it was the role of the United States to serve and promote them—makes it possible to identify a pattern of idealism and also expansionism that provided the framework for foreign policy, including the justification for the breaks from the policies of unilateralism and sometimes isolationism that predominated from the founding until World War II.[11]

It is important to remember that most of North America had been colonized by European countries by the end of the eighteenth century. Consequently, if the United States was to expand further, it had two options: it could deal with those countries in a way that could be cooperative (e.g., negotiating treaties) or in a way that could lead to conflict. There seems to be an inherent contradiction between the policies of manifest destiny and expansion versus unilateralism. On the one hand, the United States had no desire to get involved politically with Europe. On the other hand, if it was to grow and expand, the United States had to engage in various ways with the same European powers that had already colonized parts of the continent and that could, potentially, threaten the United States. Didn't that mean breaking from a policy that was unilateralist or even isolationist?

What made the desire for expansion compatible with the overall doctrine of unilateralism was the belief that the United States was not engaging in political alliances nor in European politics or wars but was simply protecting itself and fulfilling its mission—its "destiny." Hence, the U.S. conquest of North America did not seem to contradict what Washington had warned of or the course that he and Adams had set.

Domestically, by the early 1800s the young nation became more stable as a democracy with the assurance that the processes and structures of government that had been embodied in the Constitution worked. Events in Europe further helped the United States pursue its manifest destiny. As the United States began its march westward while building an economy based on trade and commerce, Europe was fighting the Napoleonic Wars. The end of those wars in 1815 marked a change in the politics of Europe as alliances and the power balance shifted. What had been the Spanish empire in the new world started to disintegrate as Argentina, Bolivia, and Chile gained their independence from Spain. Meanwhile the United States negotiated with Spain to purchase Florida, which was ceded to the United States in 1819. In 1822 the Monroe administration extended diplomatic recognition to the newly independent Latin American republics of Argentina, Chile, Colombia, Mexico, and Peru.

In Europe, the usual intrigues were ongoing, with suggestions that France and Spain were aligning with Russia, Prussia, and Austria to wage war on the new republics in Latin America in order to help Spain regain its territory. In response, Britain proposed that the United States join Britain to ward off French and Spanish aggression in the new world. However, Washington's early warnings were not lost on President James Monroe or on John Quincy Adams, his secretary of state. On December 2, 1823, in response to Britain's overtures, Monroe delivered an address to Congress that defined the U.S. position: the United States would continue to stay removed from European affairs but, in turn, the European powers were expected to stay out of the new world, which the United States declared was within its own sphere of influence (i.e., tied to its national interest).

"Our policy in regard to Europe, which was adopted at an early stage of the wars which have so long agitated that corner of the globe, nevertheless remains the same, which is, not to interfere in the internal concerns of any of its powers," Monroe said. "It is impossible that the allied powers should extend their political system to any portion of either continent without endangering our peace and happiness; nor can anyone believe that our southern brethren, if left to themselves, would adopt it of their own accord. It is equally impossible, therefore, that we should behold such interposition in any form of indifference."[12]

With the Monroe Doctrine the United States reiterated its promise not to interfere in European politics. In turn, the Americas were no longer open to European colonization. The only country that now had claim on the region was the United States.

Continued Expansion

The Monroe Doctrine made clear the intentions of the United States to continue to expand on its own continent. Over the subsequent decades, the country did so by annexing Texas (which had won independence from Mexico) in 1845, acquiring the Oregon territories from the United Kingdom in 1846, and expanding into the western part of the country (that is now

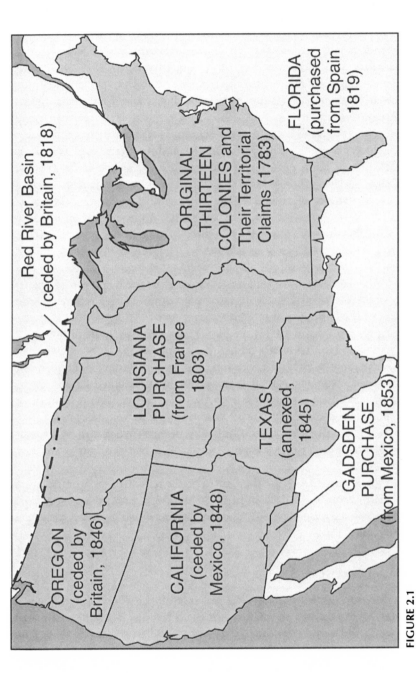

FIGURE 2.1
U.S. Westward Expansion.

California, Nevada, Arizona, and parts of Utah and Colorado) in 1848 (see figure 2.1). Not all of this was done peacefully. The United States gained some of that territory as a direct result of war. It is clear that U.S. national interest and priorities at the time were best served by ensuring that the United States was no longer surrounded by foreign powers and by asserting primacy over its own lands, even if that meant war. This framework was to guide U.S. foreign policy throughout the nineteenth century and well into the twentieth.

Consistent with the notion that the president defined the national interest, when James K. Polk became president in 1844, he made it clear that he would accelerate the policy of territorial expansion toward the west. One of the prizes was the Mexican territory of California, with its known port of San Francisco. The other area Polk wanted was the Oregon territory, held by Britain. In the latter case, Polk was willing to negotiate with Britain, building on negotiations started earlier by John Quincy Adams. In June 1846, the British proposed a treaty that Polk accepted and sent to the Senate, which ratified it by a vote of 41 to 14. Despite Polk's claim of "Fifty-four forty or fight," suggesting the territorial lines that would be ideal, he was willing to compromise with a border at the forty-ninth parallel rather than risk the domestic political battles and costs of war with Britain.

Unlike parts of the Oregon territory, which were described as "wholly unfit for agriculture & incapable of sustaining any considerable population"[13] (and thereby worth giving up), California was seen as worth fighting for. Initially Polk tried negotiating with Mexico to persuade the country to sell California to the United States. When that failed, Polk resorted to the use of hard power and ordered troops to the Rio Grande, the border area, where they quickly engaged with Mexican forces. Congress responded to the clash between U.S. and Mexican forces by endorsing Polk's request for a declaration of war.

Military historian T. Harry Williams describes the Mexican-American War this way: "The Mexican War has always occupied an ambiguous position in the national historical consciousness. Depending on the prevailing mood of intellectuals and historians, it has been denounced as a wicked war of aggression against a weaker neighbor or justified as an inevitable phase in the expansion [of the United States]." He also describes this war as "significant because of the number of 'firsts' associated with it. It was the first overseas war. . . . It was also America's first successful offensive war, the first in which the strategic objectives were laid out with some clarity before hostilities were joined, and the first to be conducted with a large measure of technical proficiency and with relative efficiency. Finally, it was the first war in which the president really acted as commander in chief."[14]

Though it was controversial, the Mexican-American War (1846–1848) was important to the growth of the United States, a priority at that time, and was seen by the leaders of the country as necessary to secure parts of the hemisphere that the United States claimed as its own. Despite its large cost to the United States (more than five thousand eight hundred Americans killed or wounded in battle, eleven thousand soldiers dead from disease, and a financial cost estimated at more than seventy-five million dollars), the United States acquired approximately five hundred thousand miles of territory.[15] At the end of the war, U.S. territory extended from the Atlantic Ocean to the Pacific and included the areas now known as Nevada and California, both of which had gold and silver deposits. The promise of wealth from gold and silver helped fuel the westward movement of the population that was necessary to the growth of the country. The acquisition of California also meant that the United States had ports on both coasts, which helped further the goals of increasing trade and commerce.

During the period from December 1845 through the end of the Mexican-American War in 1848, "the United States had grown by about 1.2 million square miles, or about 64 percent."[16] How was this expansion possible? Who paid for the purchase of these new lands or to finance these wars? How could the United States assure the security of this ever-expanding country?

In many ways, the answers to these questions can be found in the concept of what we now call *globalization*, which linked the United States to other countries economically, even as it stayed removed politically. As Walter Russell Mead has argued, "Economically the United States was more dependent on the rest of the world in the nineteenth century than it was during much of the Cold War." In fact, the United States took seriously the need for commerce and trade and depended on foreign investment to provide the funding to sustain much of this growth westward that was seen as critical to the national interest.[17] The only alternative would have been to raise taxes, and that was unpalatable politically. To some Americans this foreign investment was a cause of controversy or resentment, and they were concerned about the influence these investors might have on U.S. policy. But there was little that they could do about it.

The decision to trade with and secure investments from other countries, especially Europe, while positioning itself in the Western Hemisphere is the essence of the early U.S. policy of unilateralism. Pursuing this policy allowed the United States to achieve what it had defined as its national interest, its "manifest destiny," while simultaneously protecting it from the intrigues of Europe.

As the United States expanded westward in the mid-nineteenth century, it also was starting to make a mark internationally. With the Atlantic and Caribbean claimed by Europe and the Atlantic waters nearly exhausted by European whalers, the American whaling trade needed other waters to explore. After 1848, when U.S. territory extended to the Pacific, it was only natural that the United States look in that direction for trade and commerce that would allow it to compete with Europe economically. In 1853, U.S. Commodore Matthew Perry arrived in Japan, a country then untouched by the West. He offered Japan a choice: trade with the United States peacefully, or run the risk of war. When he returned early in 1854 with a fleet of ships, Japan granted the United States the right to use the Japanese ports of Shimoda and Hakodate, and by 1856 the United States negotiated a trade treaty with Japan. Japan soon extended similar terms to the European countries of France, Britain, the Netherlands, and Russia, but it was U.S. ambition that opened the country to the West.

The U.S. venture into Japan was an example of the growing power of the U.S. navy, initially created to protect U.S. commercial interests but also to be used as an instrument of policy. Here, too, we see one of the apparent contradictions of the policy of unilateralism, that is, growing U.S. presence globally: "During the period of American innocence and isolation, the United States had forces stationed on or near every major continent in the world; its navy was active in virtually every ocean, its troops saw combat on virtually every continent, and its foreign relations were in a constant state of crisis and turmoil."[18]

Clearly, a unilateralist foreign policy did not mean being removed from the world. Rather, it meant that the United States would chart its own course and become engaged internationally at times and places that it chose, when it was perceived to be in the national interest to do so.

The Civil War

By the time the American Civil War broke out in 1861, the United States was well on its way to becoming a major economic power. While the countries of Europe had been diverting economic resources toward their militaries, the United States had focused instead on internal needs. The thriving trade between the United States and England (the United States exported raw materials, especially cotton, to England in exchange for British manufactured goods) tied the two countries closely together and further fueled U.S. economic growth. Pragmatically, one of America's former adversaries became one of its major trading partners.

The Civil War required the U.S. government to divert resources for military purposes. According to Paul Kennedy, the Civil War was "the first real industrialized 'total war' on proto-twentieth-century lines."[19] By the end of the war, the industrial output of the United States had increased, and along with that came modernization of military technology. Coupled with the relative stability of the international system in the later part of the nineteenth century, the United States could grow economically and industrialize even further, thereby preparing it to take its place in the "modern" world.

The Spanish-American War

The Spanish-American War of 1898 represents one of the clearest cases where the United States broke from its unilateralist policy (as defined by political and military aloofness from other parts of the world) to become actively engaged internationally, both militarily and politically. The United States earlier had acted aggressively against Mexico to acquire contiguous territory seen as essential to the country's manifest destiny. But the Spanish-American War represents a different case. The question to ask here is why the United States chose to declare war against Spain, a European country. How did this serve the national interest? Here we see the confluence of international and domestic politics, both of which must be considered in order to answer these questions.

The United States had had a troubled relationship with Spain for decades. Spain claimed some of the land that the United States wanted for its own. For example, the Florida cession in 1819 was the result of a long diplomatic campaign that was characterized by threats, bribes, and intimidation. At that time the United States also made it clear to Spain that any attempt by that country to reestablish its control over the colonies in the Western Hemisphere that had gained their independence (e.g., Argentina, Bolivia, and Chile) would result in war between the two countries. This history between the two countries helps frame the issues surrounding the Spanish-American War.

The U.S. decision to go to war against Spain in 1898 resulted from many factors, all of which reflected what was then understood as the "national interest." The result was a more aggressive foreign policy and an expansive interpretation of U.S. territory to include the Pacific Ocean. Spain's possession of the Philippines and Guam interfered with the U.S. desire to strengthen its role in the Pacific, especially after the opening of Japan in 1856, which was followed by a treaty with Korea in 1882.[20] And the United States saw Spain's control of the island of Cuba, ninety miles off the coast of the United States, as an infringement on its hemisphere. In addition, American businesses, which had invested millions of dollars in Cuban sugar, were pushing the government to do something about the political instability on the island.

McKinley was elected president in 1896 on the twin promises to protect American business and to free the Cuban people. The press exacerbated U.S.

claims on Cuba and pressure to go to war against Spain to "protect" the island. One newspaper, William Randolph Hearst's *New York Journal*, printed a letter written by the Spanish ambassador, Enrique Dupuy DeLome, that had been stolen by Cuban rebels. The DeLome letter described President McKinley as "weak and a bidder for the admiration of the crowd, besides being a would-be politician who tries to leave a door open behind himself while keeping on good terms with the jingoes of his party."[21] Although the ambassador subsequently resigned, the letter had the desired effect of further inciting "war fever" within the United States when it was published on February 9, 1898.

A few days later, on February 15, 1898, the U.S. battleship *Maine* blew up in Havana harbor, allegedly by an underwater mine, although a later investigation indicated that the explosion was caused internally.[22] Again, the press snapped into action and called for war against Spain, using the slogan "Remember the *Maine*" to rally public support. On April 11, McKinley went to Congress and asked for authority to "intervene" in Cuba, despite the fact that Spain had agreed to give Cuba its independence. Although this was not a formal declaration of war, Spain perceived it as such. In response, Spain declared war on the United States on April 23. By late July, the United States had overwhelmed Spain militarily in the Atlantic (Cuba and Puerto Rico) as well as in the Pacific (the Philippines), and peace negotiations started between the two countries. They signed the Treaty of Paris on December 10, 1898. As a result of the peace negotiations, Cuba was given its independence from Spain, Spain agreed to give Puerto Rico and Guam to the United States, and the United States purchased the Philippines for twenty million dollars. The U.S. position in the Western Hemisphere, from the Atlantic into the Pacific, was secure.

Implications of the Spanish-American War

The United States justified the decision to go to war against Spain in part by the principles put forward in the Monroe Doctrine and the need to solidify its sphere of influence in the Western Hemisphere. Tied to this were humanitarian goals, as some U.S. political leaders believed Cuba needed to be "saved" from Spanish exploitation. But the decision was primarily the result of a combination of commercial, political, and growing expansionist sentiments perpetrated in part by political leaders and members of the media.

To be understood fully, this decision must be put into a global context. For the countries of Europe, this was a time of imperialism, as each of the major powers scrambled to claim colonies in Asia and Africa. By confining itself to North America, the United States was being left out of this global power grab that threatened to undermine the place that the country was slowly securing for itself internationally. The Spanish-American War unambiguously made the United States an imperial power, rivaling the major powers of Europe. No longer seen as a new, young country, the United States now had its own colonies, which brought with them responsibilities. The United States could no longer be removed from the rest of the world, nor could it only look inward. Rather, its national interest now required that it protect its colonial interests as well as be more involved in world affairs. The foreign policy of the United States was changing.

It also is important to look at the role that domestic politics played in pushing the United States to war against Spain and toward expansionism. First, Americans were united against a common enemy, Spain, for the first time since the Civil War had divided the country. Northerners and southerners fought side by side, thus helping to heal the bitter divisions, at least temporarily. Second, foreign policy, especially the role of the United States in the world, became an important issue in the presidential election of 1900. Theodore Roosevelt, leader of the Rough Riders, which had gained fame during the war, was on the ticket as McKinley's vice president, and he espoused an imperialist/expansionist agenda that he was able to enact once he became president upon McKinley's death in 1901. Finally, we see the power of the press, lead by William Randolph Hearst, who used newspapers to foment public sentiment in favor of war. This fact alone marks an important transition in the role of the media in influencing policy.

The Spanish-American War and the defeat of Spain ended more than four hundred years of Spanish power and influence in the Western Hemisphere and Pacific and solidified the role of the United States as the major power in the region. This meant that the United States faced the new century in a different position internationally, and its foreign policy reflected that shift. But it also had unintended consequences for the United States. (See the case study of the Spanish-American War at the end of this chapter.)

The Scramble for Concessions

As a result of the Spanish American War, the United States had a firm claim to the Pacific. But by 1899, the "scramble for concessions" in China threatened to leave the United States out of this market. To ensure its place and to protect its commercial interests in China, Secretary of State John Hay sent his Open Door note to the governments of Germany, Russia, and England; similar notes were subsequently sent to Japan, Italy, and France.[23] This document called on the other imperialist countries to open their Chinese concessions (areas of interest) to trade and investment equally to all. The Open Door note was another assertion that the United States was a player in the international system.

The Roosevelt Corollary to the Monroe Doctrine

In 1902, Venezuela defaulted on debts to many of its European investors. In response, Britain, Germany, and Italy sent gunboats to blockade Venezuela's ports. In the United States these actions raised old fears that European powers would try to undermine U.S. dominance in the region. President Theodore Roosevelt used the opportunity of an address to Congress to state clearly the U.S. position regarding the Western Hemisphere:

> It is not true that the United States feels any land hunger or entertains any projects as regards the other nations of the Western Hemisphere save such as are for their welfare. All that this country desires is to see neighboring countries stable, orderly and prosperous. . . . Our interests and those of our southern neighbors are in reality identical. They have great natural riches, and if within their borders the reign of law and justice obtains, prosperity is sure to come to them. While they thus obey the primary laws of civilized society they may rest assured that they will be treated by us in a spirit of cordial and helpful sympathy. We would interfere with them only in the last resort, and then only if it became evident that their inability or unwillingness to do justice at home and abroad had violated the rights of the United States or had invited foreign aggression to the detriment of the entire body of American nations. . . . In asserting the Monroe Doctrine . . . we have acted in our own interest as well as in the interest of humanity at large.[24]

In this speech, Roosevelt established a policy that built on the principles espoused in the Monroe Doctrine. He gave notice that the Western Hemisphere was the responsibility of the United States and that the United States would use military force if necessary to protect its interests there. In effect, he laid out the conditions under which the United States would intervene in Latin America, and he also made it clear that the United States would take military action should any country engage in activities that could be seen as detrimental to U.S. interests. The United States was replacing European imperialist intentions in Latin America with its own, and its own foreign policy was being driven by a realist perspective backed up with its use of hard power.

Roosevelt's term in office was characterized by further U.S. expansion and involvement internationally. By the time Roosevelt became president in 1901, U.S. interests in Asia had been furthered by the Open Door policy that encouraged free and open trade rather than running the risk of having China divided into spheres of influence that might deprive the United States of its opportunity in this new market. In another assertion of U.S. interests in Asia, in 1905 Roosevelt helped negotiate the end to war between Russia and Japan, making sure that Russia would help balance the growing power of Japan. While Roosevelt won a Nobel Peace Prize for these efforts, they were driven in no small measure by Roosevelt's fear that if Japan got too strong, it could threaten U.S. markets and commercial interests in the Far East.

Consistent with Roosevelt's desire to dominate the Caribbean, which was seen as within the U.S. sphere of influence, he supported building a canal across the isthmus of Panama that would connect the Caribbean with the Pacific Ocean. The canal would also allow the U.S. navy to move quickly from the Atlantic to the Pacific, making it possible to have one, rather than two, navies to protect U.S. interests.[25] Building the canal was made possible because of Roosevelt's intervention on behalf of Panama's rebellion against existing Colombian rulers. The success of that rebellion allowed the United States to acquire the land through which the canal would be built.

As noted above, the Roosevelt Corollary to the Monroe Doctrine and the building of the Panama Canal are but two examples of growing U.S. involvement internationally. William Howard Taft, Roosevelt's successor, continued the policies started under Roosevelt. Taft pushed U.S. businesses to invest abroad as a way to further solidify U.S. interests. However, the expanding reach of the United States and its businesses meant that greater military involvement was necessary to protect them. Hence, Taft sent U.S. forces into Nicaragua and Honduras in 1910 and 1911, respectively, in order to protect U.S. lives and interests. In 1912, U.S. forces were deployed to Honduras, Panama, Cuba, and China, all in the name of "protecting U.S. interests." A detachment of marines was sent to Nicaragua in 1912 to "protect U.S. interests" and "to promote peace and stability," with a small group remaining until 1925. While some Americans opposed the United States' imperialist adventures, their voices largely went unnoticed. U.S. foreign policy and the place of the United States in the world had changed dramatically.

March to World War I

By 1900 the international economic as well as geopolitical picture had changed. As one historian explains it: "80 percent of world industrial output came from Europe and the United States, with Japan contributing another 10 percent; China contributed 7 percent and India 2 percent, totaling 99 percent of all industrial production. Thus the one hundred years from 1800 to 1900 saw a great reversal, with Europe and the United States taking the pride of

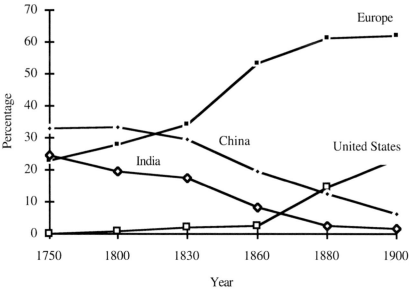

FIGURE 2.2
World Industrial Output. Originally published in Robert B. Marks, *The Origins of the Modern World: A Global and Ecological Narrative* (Rowman & Littlefield, 2000). Data derived from Paul Kennedy, *The Rise and Fall of the Great Powers* (New York: Vintage, 1987), 149.

place previously held by India and China" (see figure 2.2).[26] Industrialization had allowed the United States to become a major power.

Within the United States, the era of industrialization brought both economic and social changes. The period from 1900 until the outbreak of World War I was a time of reform known as the Progressive Era. Not only did this change the face of labor and business, but it was also a time when the United States continued its international involvement, justified at least in part by the need to support U.S. business interests. The resulting changes in foreign policy were characterized broadly as "dollar diplomacy," in recognition of the importance of business and trade.

Woodrow Wilson, who was elected president in 1912, continued the policies set by his predecessors. The United States was actively engaged in those regions and parts of the world that had been defined as within its sphere of influence and critical to national interest, primarily Latin America and the Pacific. Wilson broadened the rationale for U.S. involvement so that U.S. assistance (and intervention if necessary) was extended to helping other peoples and countries become democratic. Wilson's idealism and commitment to democratic values would characterize his administration and become the basis for active U.S. engagement in the war that would rage in Europe.

Wilsonian Idealism and U.S. Foreign Policy

Wilson outlined the ideals that he valued in and for the United States in his first inaugural address, delivered March 4, 1913:

> Nowhere else in the world have noble men and women exhibited in more strik-ing forms the beauty and energy of sympathy and helpfulness and counsel in their efforts to rectify wrong, alleviate suffering, and set the weak in the way of strength and hope. We have built up, moreover, a great system of government, which has stood through a long age as in many respects a model for those who seek to set liberty upon foundations that will endure against fortuitous change, against storm and accident. . . .
>
> . . . This is the high enterprise of the new day: To lift everything that concerns our life as a Nation to the light that shines from the hearthfire of every man's conscience and the vision of the right. It is inconceivable that we should do this as partisans; it is inconceivable we should do it in ignorance of the facts as they are or in blind haste. We shall restore, not destroy.[27]

Initially, U.S. interests in the first years of Wilson's administration centered on Asia, Latin America (primarily Mexico), and the Caribbean. Consistent with his broadened interpretation of national interest, Wilson deployed U.S. military forces to those areas to help protect or maintain order (e.g., in Haiti, China, Dominican Republic) rather than just to protect U.S. interests.

Shortly after Wilson took office, Europe went to war. Wilson's goal was to keep the United States out of that war if possible. On August 4, 1914, he pro-claimed the United States *neutral* in the European conflict. On May 7, 1915, the British passenger ship *Lusitania* was sunk by a German torpedo, resulting in the deaths of more than a thousand passengers and crew, including 124 Americans. In response, Wilson had the secretary of state deliver a note to the German ambassador in which the United States reiterated its neutrality but also gave warning that Germany should "not expect the Government of the United States to omit any word or any act necessary to the performance of its sacred duty of maintaining the rights of the United States and its citizens and of safeguarding their free exercise and enjoyment."[28]

In November 1916, Wilson was reelected president, in part because of his campaign slogan that he had kept the United States out of the European war. But ongoing trade with Britain, one of the belligerent nations, was drawing the United States into the conflict. The United States provided Britain and its allies with munitions, food, and raw materials, and it extended loans when the countries could not pay. During the first two years of the war (1914–1916), U.S. trade with Britain and its allies went from $800 million to $3 billion.[29]

Despite Wilson's intentions, he could not keep the United States out of the European war. German forces sank another British passenger ship, the *Arabic*, and then a French steamer, *Sussex*, and more American lives were lost. On January 22, 1917, as he was starting his second term in office, Wilson addressed the U.S. Senate and called for a "peace without victory." Specifically, he called for an end to the war on terms "which will create a peace that is worth guaranteeing and preserving, a peace that will win the approval of mankind, not merely a peace that will serve the national interests and immediate aims of the nations engaged." And he warned that "victory would mean peace forced upon the loser, a victor's terms imposed upon the vanquished. . . . Only a peace between equals can last."[30] In that prediction he was prescient, for the peace that was ultimately imposed on Germany contributed to the humiliation and economic devastation that fostered the rise of Hitler and Nazism and ultimately another war. Nonetheless, Wilson was not successful at either ending the war or keeping the United States out of it.

The resumption of German unrestricted submarine warfare in February 1917 and attacks on U.S.-flagged merchant ships made U.S. involvement inevitable. On April 2, 1917, Wilson went before a joint session of Congress and asked for a declaration of war against Germany, which was granted.

As the United States moved inextricably toward war, Wilson justified U.S. involvement in the most idealistic terms. "The world must be made safe for democracy. Its peace must be planted upon the tested foundations of political liberty."[31] In other words, the United States was going into this war for high-minded reasons and against an aggressive government that had violated international law.

Wilson's understanding of national interest and the ways in which he chose to implement American foreign policy represented a marked departure from the direction that the United States previously had taken. Whatever the actual reasons the United States had for going to war in Europe, Wilson put the decision into idealistic and moralistic terms. Further, his foreign policy in general was tied to a desire to actively extend democracy, thereby changing the U.S. policy posture from one that was unilateralist to one of active engagement internationally.

Wilson's Fourteen Points

On January 8, 1918, about ten months before World War I ended, Wilson again addressed the Congress, giving what has become known as his Fourteen Points speech. Driven in part by his desire to avoid war in the future, the

Fourteen Points outlined Wilson's vision to assure justice for all countries and peace in the future by creating an "association of nations . . . for the purpose of affording mutual guarantees of political independence and territorial integrity to great and small states alike."[32] The concept of uniting all states—large and small, powerful and those with less power—into one organization that would allow all of them to work together to thwart the imperialist or expansionist intentions of any one nation was a relatively new idea. Wilson's ideal notion of "collective security" was not to come to fruition, nor could the concept prevent another major war. Nonetheless, it provided the seeds that would eventually grow into the United Nations.

An armistice signed in Paris in November 1918 ended World War I. Wilson, Prime Minister Lloyd George of Britain, Premier Clemenceau of France, and Prime Minister Orlando of Italy negotiated the Treaty of Versailles. In a series of "secret" agreements, each of the allies was granted additional territory that was taken from the defeated countries. The German colonies were parceled out among the allies. New countries—Poland, Czechoslovakia, and Yugoslavia—were created as the existing European empires were disbanded. The treaty imposed reparations on Germany, that is, payments that had to be made to the allies to compensate for the damage caused by the war. The treaty also included provisions for the creation of the League of Nations that would embody many of the principles espoused by Wilson.

Unfortunately, U.S. domestic politics intervened and thwarted Wilson's plans. With an election coming up in 1920, the issue of the League of Nations became highly politicized. The Republican majority in the U.S. Senate opposed the creation of the League, as did the Republican candidate for president, Warren G. Harding. This was one of the first times to date that the Congress asserted its will on a foreign policy issue, thereby overriding the president's priorities. An indication of the growing power of the United States was that, without U.S. presence, the League of Nations could not succeed.

Although some of Wilson's goals for American foreign policy were defeated in the face of domestic opposition, many of his ideals and ideas influenced subsequent presidents and resurfaced periodically long after his death.[33]

U.S. Involvement in Russia

In March 1917, while World War I was raging, a revolution in Russia toppled the government of Czar Nicholas II. Some months later, in November 1917, the Bolsheviks, a communist faction led by V. I. Lenin, overthrew the provisional government. Virtually all the European countries sent troops, allegedly to help Russia form a new stable government, although many of the Western leaders hoped to stop the nascent Bolshevik (communist) movement. Hoping to encourage the anti-Bolshevik forces, Wilson sent U.S. troops, which remained in Russia from 1918 through 1920, after World War I ended; nonetheless, the communist forces prevailed.

This involvement by the United States proved to have long-term implications. It planted seeds of mistrust between the communist forces and the Western powers that would continue to fester, finally emerging full blown in the Cold War that followed World War II. The leaders of the Soviet Union did not forget the way in which the Western countries, especially the United States, did not hesitate to intervene in their civil war, including sending troops to their country. In turn, the leaders of the West were already defining the conflict as an ideological one that pitted the forces of democracy against those of communism. While the Soviet Union was an ally of the United States during World War II, the relationship was clouded.

Domestic Issues: The Executive and Legislative Branches

As we review the foreign policy of the United States from the founding through World War I, one of the patterns that becomes most apparent is the dominance of the president in setting foreign policy priorities. Consistent with the beliefs of the early founders of the country, a strong executive was seen as the critical policy-maker and the one who set the priorities, with Congress playing largely a "balancing" role. As history shows, that generally was the case. Foreign policy was made by the president, working with other members of the executive branch (e.g., the secretary of state). While the Congress played a role, it was largely secondary and compliant, with congressional attention more focused on enacting legislation for the growing and industrializing country.

One of the first, and perhaps most dramatic, examples of a departure from this pattern came in the Republican resistance to the League of Nations that was being pushed by Wilson. Article 10 was the heart of the League of Nations treaty; it stipulated that an attack on any member of the League was to be regarded as an attack on all members, and therefore that all should be prepared to go to war in response.[34] Republican opposition to the League was rooted in the concern that Article 10 would bind the United States too closely to other countries in opposition to the country's national interest and policy of unilateralism. The fear was that if the United States were to agree to the terms of the League, then the country could be plunged inevitably into foreign wars, whether or not it would be in the country's interest to do so.

Given congressional resistance, and knowing that entering into the League would require a two-thirds vote of the Senate, Wilson took his case to the

American people, making it part of the presidential campaign of 1920. Harding, the Republican candidate, opposed the League, and his election meant that the United States would not join. Ultimately it was members of the Senate who asserted their feelings in opposition to the League, thereby assuring its defeat, regardless of Wilson's desires.

While an assertion of congressional opposition to presidential priorities was rare at the time, it would become more common later in the twentieth century, setting the stage for ongoing battles between the two branches about the making and implementation of U.S. foreign policy.

The Shifting National Interest

Although the dominant foreign policy pursued by the United States in the early years of the country was one of unilateralism, it did not take long for that concept to be reinterpreted in light of changing perceptions of national interest. While trade, commerce, and economic relationships were necessary to U.S. growth and prosperity, the founders of the country also saw political and military aloofness from other countries as essential to U.S. well-being. Gradually, however, U.S. prosperity was tied to the country's "manifest destiny" to expand across the continent. In many cases, this meant displacing those who were already on the land, whether European colonial powers or the Native Americans who had been there long before western exploration. Sometimes U.S. expansion was peaceful, as in the case of the Louisiana Purchase. At other times, the desire to grow brought the United States into direct conflict with other countries (e.g., Mexico and Spain) or with the native peoples. In each case, the United States justified that aggression because of national interest.

As the country grew and prospered, U.S. business and investment became more international or global in scope. This also changed the direction of U.S. foreign policy, as the country had to protect those interests, militarily if necessary, when they were threatened. By 1900, not only had the United States become a major industrial power, but it was emerging as a major political and military force to be reckoned with as well. By that time, U.S. territory had expanded beyond the Western Hemisphere into parts of the Pacific and Asia. Still under the same general foreign policy framework, the United States kept its involvement focused only on those parts of the world defined as being in its national interest. The Spanish-American War of 1898 represented a change in U.S. foreign policy, as the country aggressively declared war on Spain for dubious reasons. Nonetheless, the victory over Spain helped solidify the U.S. position in the world.

Until 1915, the United States remained largely within its own sphere of influence geographically, becoming more actively engaged militarily in the regions it defined as important. As president, Wilson added yet another dimension to the conduct of U.S. foreign policy by injecting ideals and morality as valid and legitimate reasons for intervention; U.S. involvement in World War I was justified in part by high-minded principles espoused by Wilson. These were further articulated in his Fourteen Points and in the creation of a League of Nations that was designed to make war less likely in the future.

By the end of World War I, the United States had established itself as a major power not only in the Western Hemisphere, but in Europe as well. Further, U.S. involvement in the Russian Revolution set the stage for the mistrust that would follow. However, if U.S. involvement in World War I is measured against Wilson's "lofty" goals, it proved to be a failure; the war neither ended war forever nor established a universal democratic system. But it did change the role of the United States in the international system, although in many ways the leaders of the country did not realize or acknowledge this for some time. In fact, it set the stage for active U.S. engagement during and following World War II.

Walter Russell Mead notes: "With fewer casualties than any other great power, and fewer forces on the ground in Europe, the United States had a disproportionately influential role in shaping the peace." But Mead also notes: "The United States was the only true winner of World War I. . . . World War I made the United States the world's greatest financial power, crushed Germany—economically, America's most dangerous rival—and reduced both Britain and France to a status where neither country could mount an effective opposition to American designs anywhere in the world."[35]

Following World War I, the highest priority of the Harding administration was a "return to normalcy," which meant changing priorities and focusing inward and away from international engagement. This also meant the creation of new laws restricting U.S. immigration and the passage of other laws that limited freedom for anyone thought to be associated with a communist organization. Under existing laws, American women who married foreigners lost their citizenship and could even be deported if they or their husbands were found to be suspect.[36]

By the 1930s, as fascism was growing in Europe, the dominant feeling in the United States was a desire for isolationism in the truest sense. After World War I, although the United States was a stronger and more powerful country internationally, the priorities—the national interest—were again focused inward. While the United States tried to remain outside the politics and problems of Europe and focus again on domestic priorities, it did not take long for the United States to engage internationally once again.

Applying Foreign Policy Concepts:
The Spanish-American War

Earlier in this chapter, we asked the following questions: why did the United States choose to declare war against Spain, a European country? How did this serve the national interest? There are a number of factors that need to be considered in order to answer these questions.

Clearly, we now have a more complete understanding of the impact of the Spanish-American War on the United States. However, not all the information that we now have was available in 1896 when William McKinley was elected president. If you were an advisor to President McKinley and you knew then what we know now, what would you have advised him to do?

In order to determine this, you need to be able to identify the critical players at the time (e.g., role of Congress, the media, the public, business interests), what position or positions each of them took on this issue, and what you think was in the national interest at the time. This all must be put into the framework of U.S. foreign policy direction (unilateralist versus expansionist) as well as your own understanding of resources available to the United States, specifically, the use of hard versus soft power. Put another way, would you pursue a realist versus idealist policy?

With that background, what is your analysis of the Spanish-American War, and what would you have done?

The Case

William McKinley was elected president in 1896 on a pledge to protect American business. American businesses, which had already invested millions of dollars in Cuban sugar, were pushing the government to do something about the instability on the island of Cuba. Doing so would mean confronting Spain, which had been using repressive measures to battle an independence movement in Cuba. Within the Republican Party, Theodore Roosevelt and Senator Henry Cabot Lodge were already agitating for intervention, as this fit within their ideals for the United States, as were members of the press and some Democrats opposed to Spain's brutal methods. Lodge and Roosevelt were among a group of "expansionists" who met regularly to discuss national and international politics. (Roosevelt was an assistant secretary of the navy in the McKinley administration, before he became vice president in 1900.) These men believed strongly in "national greatness" and that the United States needed to assert its greatness globally. Ultimately, they realized this would mean that the United States would have to expand across the Pacific. This desire was consistent with the goals of American business, which saw the Pacific as a potential market. "By the mid-1890s," according to Judis, this "merged into a single powerful case for an American imperialism."[37]

To appease his critics who were calling for action, McKinley sent the battleship *Maine* to Havana as a show of force. On February 15, 1898, the *Maine* blew up in Havana harbor, resulting in the deaths of 266 Americans. Although later investigations suggested that the explosion was most likely the result of a shipboard accident, the leading newspapers of the time fueled what become known as "war fever." There were divisions within the government as to what the United States should do.

As president, McKinley was reticent to take the country to war. However, McKinley also faced pressure from his own party (Lodge and Roosevelt, for example) as well as the American public, who had been churned up by the press into calling for war. McKinley was further concerned about the impact of the political uncertainty on the domestic economy. Finally, under mounting political pressure, McKinley went to Congress in April 1898 and asked permission to intervene in Cuba, which was granted.

The Spanish-American War lasted three months and was a clear victory for the United States. The Treaty of Paris that ended the war granted Cuba its independence from Spain and gave Guam and Puerto Rico to the United States. The United States also purchased the Philippines from Spain for twenty million dollars. "The victory itself transformed American opinion and laid the groundwork for the McKinley administration's turn toward an imperial foreign policy."[38] The war showed that the United States could confront one of the major European powers and win.

The U.S. success in the war converted McKinley to a "new imperialist." Over the objections of the anti-imperialists, he decided to put a military governor in place in the Philippines. While the anti-imperialists warned of the danger of imposing American rule on the Philippines, the imperialists dismissed the concerns, reporting "that there was no 'nationalist sentiment'" and that the Americans "would be welcomed as liberators."[39] The anti-imperialists proved to be correct.

In the Philippines, a liberation army had been fighting against the Spanish for years before the Americans arrived in 1898 and was ready to fight the Americans. When the United States refused to grant independence to the Philippines, war broke out. Fighting continued in the Philippines; it lasted until 1916 and the passage of the Jones Act, "committing the United States to independence as soon as the Filipinos could establish a 'stable government.'"[40] The Philippines was given full independence in 1946 following World War II.

During the insurrection, the United States used brutal tactics against the Filipinos, which only fueled resentment and even hatred of the United States. Nonetheless, Roosevelt and the other imperialists never doubted the wisdom of the war against Spain, nor of taking the territory that it did for the United States. For this was all part of the destiny of U.S. national greatness.

What Would You Do If . . .

The time is 1898. McKinley has been president for two years. His highest priority is economic well-being for the country, which means ensuring the success of big business. But the primary foreign policy orientation of the country since its founding has been unilateralist. To this time, that meant intervening internationally only in those cases where it would directly benefit business and commerce. It also meant staying removed from wars with Europe. A group within the Republican Party (McKinley's party) has been agitating for a more imperialist stance for the United States, while others have been clamoring for intervention in Cuba on humanitarian grounds.

What would you do if you were a close advisor to President McKinley and he looked to you for recommendations about whether or not to go to war with Spain? Given what you know now, including the consequences (both intended and unintended), would you recommend war, and why? Are there other options you would recommend exploring to satisfy the domestic pressures as well as address prevailing foreign policy issues? What would be in U.S. national interest at that time?

3

The Interwar Years
through World War II

THE UNITED STATES EMBRACED A POLICY of *isolationism* during the period between the two world wars (roughly 1920 through 1941). If the foreign policy during the early years of the country was characterized by unilateralism and creeping engagement with other countries, the interwar period was a time when the United States really was isolationist in its policies, preferring to retreat inward and to remain removed from the international system as much—and as long—as possible.[1] Policies in the 1920s reflected the domestic political priorities of the time: a commitment to big business and economic growth, as well as the desire to shield the United States from the outside world. This was done by passing laws limiting who could enter the country and through policies that the leaders in Washington hoped would keep the United States out of another European war. As economic depression gripped the country in the 1930s, the highest priority was on domestic recovery rather than international engagement. Nonetheless, the United States found itself involved with the rest of the world, although initially this engagement was limited in scope. While the United States hoped to stay out of the conflict that later escalated into World War II, this proved to be impossible.

This chapter begins with a brief description of the interwar years and the relationship between domestic and foreign policies. The focus will then be on World War II, concluding with the bombing of Hiroshima and Nagasaki, which brought the United States—and the rest of the world—into the new "atomic age" that changed the conduct of international relations and foreign policy. Shortly after World War II ended, a new era—the Cold War—started that would dictate U.S. foreign policy for the next fifty years.

Interwar America

Although U.S. attention was focused inward in the 1920s and 1930s, the reality was that the country was one of the most powerful nations in the world. Since the Monroe Doctrine, the United States had established its primacy over Latin America. The United States also had a dominant place in Asia and the Pacific as early as the turn of the century, and subsequent policies ensured that it would retain that position. Where Europe was devastated by World War I, the industrial strength of the United States grew substantially, fueled in part by the industrial needs of its European allies who were at war. The combined military and industrial power of the United States meant that it had surpassed even the European countries, who looked to the United States not only for military help (which was limited in the First World War) but for economic support.[2]

In addition, building on the precedent set by Wilson, U.S. global dominance was not just military and economic but political and ideological as well. The ideals espoused earlier by Wilson continued to guide U.S. foreign policy. Even subsequent administrations, while more pragmatic than idealistic, pursued a foreign policy that was idealist in nature, tied to the desire to negotiate agreements and bring countries together to find ways of avoiding war to settle their differences rather than through armed conflict.

When he was elected president in 1920, Warren Harding inherited a country disillusioned by world war and whose attention was focused inward. Isolationism guided foreign policy, albeit with U.S. involvement externally when it was perceived to be in the national interest. The main priority of the Harding administration was economics and commerce, which continued under Calvin Coolidge. Before he was elected president in 1928, Herbert Hoover served as secretary of commerce and at that time declared: "The dominant fact of this last century has been economic development. And it continues today as the force which dominates the whole spiritual, social and political life of our country and the world."[3] This was the attitude that predominated during the 1920s through the administrations of Harding, Coolidge, and Hoover.

The 1920s on the whole was a period of economic prosperity and consumerism within the United States; the average income rose by over 25 percent between 1920 and 1929. The increase in income coupled with a drop in prices for many luxury items meant that Americans were buying products that they could not have afforded earlier. There were poor and unemployed in the country, but they were largely lost amid the prevailing sense of well-being.[4]

Consistent with the priority to look inward, and fearing an influx of foreigners who could disturb the domestic economic balance that existed, Congress passed a series of immigration acts that severely limited the number of people allowed to enter the United States from countries in eastern and southern Europe, especially Russia, Poland, and Italy. In 1921 national quotas for immigrants were imposed; the 1924 Immigration Act further restricted the number of people allowed to enter the country. Not only did the Immigration Act favor those countries with earlier emigration patterns (e.g., northern and western Europe), but it barred all Chinese, Japanese, and people from other Asian countries.[5] In many ways the act was a reaction to a growing nationalist/nativist sentiment within the United States that sought to "protect" the country from foreigners and to ensure that "undesirables," such as communists, could not enter the country. It was also consistent with isolationism and the desire to be removed from interaction with others.

Within the United States, this period also was marked by an increase in tensions between the races, with riots breaking out in many of the major cities. According to one historian, this was exacerbated by the 1924 Immigration Act, which was "deliberately designed to be both racist and discriminatory."[6] The Ku Klux Klan, which had been dormant, reemerged. This time its message of hate was not limited to blacks but was extended to include Jews, Catholics, and anyone else deemed a "foreigner."

This was also the era of prohibition and temperance, as the country looked for ways to control the increasing alcohol consumption, greed, gambling, organized crime, and political corruption that many believed were undermining the values of society. The imposition of prohibition only exacerbated these vices as trade in liquor became a new source of wealth and power for organized crime.

Women's suffrage was among the social advances made during this period. The passage of the Nineteenth Amendment in 1920 gave American women who were U.S. citizens the right to vote. The international nature of the First World War, coupled with recognition of the role that women played to help the war effort, ensured support of the amendment by Wilson and then its passage through the Congress in 1919. By 1920, it was ratified by the necessary thirty-six states.

During the 1920s, the primary emphasis of the Republican administrations was on helping and supporting big business, which had foreign policy implications. Congress imposed tariffs to protect American goods, raising duties on farm goods up to 28 percent. However, Europeans retaliated by raising their own tariffs on American goods, thereby making it harder to sell American products abroad. Congress reduced taxes on the wealthiest Americans from 65 to 50 percent and passed the Budget and Accounting Act, thereby giving itself greater oversight over the budget process, consistent with its constitutional responsibilities.

Thus, the early part of the decade was one in which the United States reveled in its prosperity and consumption and largely ignored growing economic, social, and political problems, both domestic and international. By the end of the decade, circumstances changed considerably.

U.S. Foreign Policy, 1920–1930

Although the United States was one of the major powers after World War I, its foreign policy did not reflect that status. Instead the United States followed a more limited foreign policy. Despite both the movement toward isolationism and emphasis on domestic economic growth, the Harding administration did not completely abandon the internationalism or idealism of the previous Wilson administration. However, Harding's focus internationally was limited largely to participation in disarmament conferences in the belief that a desired outcome of limiting the growth of weapons would help minimize the chances of war. Clearly, this would be in the best interest of the United States.

In fall 1921, Harding convened a conference in Washington, D.C., to find ways to control the size of countries' navies (especially Japan's) and to limit a possible military buildup that could potentially affect the United States by deflecting its economic growth. The Washington conference resulted in a series of agreements that encouraged all countries involved to respect one another's possessions in the Pacific, and that also limited the size and number of naval vessels they could build.[7] One flaw in these agreements was that they could not be enforced (an important lesson in any arms control agreement). For example, Japan secretly built up to and ultimately exceeded the treaty limits while simultaneously building its air power as it moved toward militarism and aggression. However, the agreements provided at least some sense of stability for the next decade.

Harding died suddenly in 1923 and was replaced by Calvin Coolidge, who completed Harding's term and then won reelection as president. Like Harding, Coolidge's main priority was domestic economic stability, especially in areas like farming that had not yet recovered from the downturn following the war. And, like Harding, Coolidge was willing to engage internationally in a limited way specifically to pursue the desired outcome of keeping the United States out of another war.

In August 1928, representatives of the United States and France coauthored the Kellogg-Briand Pact, idealistically designed to outlaw war. The leaders who signed the pact did so aware of "their solemn duty to promote the welfare of mankind." And they were "persuaded that the time has come when a frank renunciation of war as an instrument of national policy[8] should be made to the end that the peaceful and friendly relations now existing between their peoples should be perpetuated." Most important, the signers of the pact agreed that "the settlement or solution of all disputes or conflicts of whatever nature or of whatever origin they may be, which may arise among them, shall never be sought except by pacific means."[9]

In many ways, the Kellogg-Briand Pact reflects the idealism of the Wilson years and the goals of Wilson's Fourteen Points, which encouraged countries to find ways to avoid war. The pact was signed by sixty-five countries, virtually all that were then in existence, and was ratified by the U.S. Senate.[10] U.S. Secretary of State Frank Kellogg won a Nobel Peace Prize for this effort. Unfortunately, though, it did not result in ending war as a means of settling disputes between and among nations.

In 1930 another naval conference was convened, this time in London, which brought together the United States, France, Great Britain, Italy, and Japan specifically to extend the limits that they had agreed on at the Washington Conference of 1921. However, the international situation had changed since the earlier conference. Both France and Italy, concerned that the agreement would limit their military power, refused to sign. The London Conference also included an "escalator clause," allowing a country to build more ships if it felt threatened by another country, thereby opening the door to an arms buildup. Despite the optimistic belief that international security could be assured with arms control and arms limitation agreements, war was brewing in Europe.

Escalation to World War II: 1930–1941

Despite international idealism and desire to avoid war, World War II was on the horizon. By the early 1930s, fascism was growing in Germany, Italy, and Japan, all of which harbored militaristic and expansionist goals. In 1931, in direct violation of the Nine Power Treaty to respect the integrity of China, Japan conquered the province of Manchuria and created the puppet state of Manchukuo. This was done by a group of Japanese military officials, without the backing of the Japanese government. The United States sent a note of protest in response and invoked the Kellogg-Briand Pact in condemning Japan's aggression. In January 1932, Japan bombed the city of Shanghai, another direct violation of China's sovereignty. However, the United States did not intervene—this was outside what was perceived as its direct national interest at the time, and not intervening reflected U.S. desire to stay removed from international conflicts. And without unanimous action and absent United States participation, the League of Nations was powerless to do anything. In fact, facing censure for its invasion of Manchuria, Japan withdrew from the League, as did Italy following its takeover of Ethiopia in 1935–1936. This sent an important signal that collective security, as it was constructed at that time, would not succeed in preventing war.

Simultaneously, the world fell into deep economic depression. Although the warning signs were apparent earlier, they were largely ignored until the crash of the New York stock market in October 1929. Economic downturn in Europe and throughout Europe's colonies quickly followed. In 1931, Japan suffered poor harvests, and severe economic dislocations resulted. These economic conditions fueled the fascist movement already growing in Japan, and Germany followed a similar pattern.

The U.S. presidential election of 1932 reflected the disillusionment of the American people and the desire for change. Franklin D. Roosevelt headed the Democratic ticket and defeated incumbent Herbert Hoover by 472 electoral votes to 59. Roosevelt used his first inaugural address on March 4, 1933, to reassure the American people, stating that "the only thing we have to fear is fear itself—nameless, unreasoning, unjustified terror which paralyzes needed efforts to convert retreat into advance."[11] And, at that point, the American people had a lot to fear. As one historian points out, "In 1932, at the height of the Depression, 13 or 14 million Americans, a quarter of the workforce and mainly men, were out of work. Industrial output [which had fueled the U.S. economy] was down by 60 percent."[12] The price of livestock and agriculture (crops) had fallen, which had a devastating effect on the farmers in the country. Given the level of discontent, there was fear that the country might be heading for domestic unrest or even a revolution.[13]

Because of the deteriorating economic situation, Roosevelt's highest priority was domestic needs such as putting people back to work, creating and unifying existing "relief" (social welfare) agencies, and stricter supervision of the banking industry in order to guarantee that the crash of 1929 and the run on the banks that followed would not be duplicated. In his inaugural address, Roosevelt stated: "Through this program of action, we address ourselves to putting our own national house in order." It was only after he outlined his domestic "program of action" (which was to become the New Deal) that Roosevelt addressed international issues. Even then his attention was not to the war brewing in Europe. Instead he expressed concern about the ways in which a change in "international trade relations" affected the United States.

Noting the interdependence that was already evident among nations, Roosevelt talked of the need to "spare no effort to restore world trade by international economic adjustment."[14] He alluded to the situations in Europe and the Pacific, both of which were moving toward war, and to the need for the United States to face the crisis if national interests were threatened. To meet these joint crises, domestic and international, Roosevelt also informed the American public that he was "prepared under my constitutional duty to recommend the measures that a stricken nation in the midst of a stricken world might require."[15] And while he asked for the help of the Congress to take whatever actions were necessary (as specified in the Constitution), he also made it clear that he would invoke his executive power should that become necessary.[16]

In this inaugural address, Roosevelt foreshadowed a number of themes that became more prominent in his administration, and as the United States headed toward war. First was the priority to focus inward and address the devastating economic situation facing the country. In his speech, when Roosevelt addressed the international situation, he did so in a way that made it clear that U.S. national interest was affected negatively because of the decline in international trade. By asking for the help of Congress, Roosevelt showed that he understood the relationship between the president and the Congress. However, he also raised the possibility of acting outside the bounds of Congress should that become necessary. This was the statement of a strong executive, which made it possible for Roosevelt to do what he outlined as being in the best interest of the country.

Given domestic priorities, it is not surprising that during Roosevelt's early years the United States tried to continue a policy of isolationism not only regarding Europe and the Pacific but toward Latin America as well. Many of the countries in that region similarly were suffering from economic disruption and inflation along with political instability as economic conditions worsened. Rather than get involved in Latin America, traditionally an area of U.S. interest, Roosevelt's approach was to assure the countries to the south that they would be treated as equals and with respect. Roosevelt pledged that the United States would be a "good neighbor," but he retreated from involvement in Cuba and Mexico, two countries that had been defined earlier as within the U.S. sphere of influence.[17]

Neutrality Acts

The outbreak of war between Italy and Ethiopia in May 1935 prompted Congress to pass a series of laws that prohibited the United States from providing arms or money to the belligerents or from sending U.S. ships into harm's way. Congress hoped that these "neutrality acts" would keep the United States out of the European war.

In 1937 war broke out between Japan and China, which threatened U.S. interests in China. The United States sent a note of condemnation, claiming that this was in violation of existing agreements, including the Open Door policy and the Washington Conference. Japan responded that because of changing circumstances, the Open Door was no longer applicable, in effect putting the United States on notice that Japan would not comply with any existing agreement.

In September 1938, in an attempt to stop German aggression without going to war, the leaders of Britain and France met with Hitler in Munich and agreed that Germany could annex part of Czechoslovakia in exchange for the promise of peace. One year later, and despite his pledge, Hitler attacked Poland. Britain and France, both of which had promised to support Poland, declared war on Germany. War in Europe was inevitable; the lesson learned was that appeasement would not work.

During this period Roosevelt continued to appeal for peace internationally. He sent letters to Hitler and to Mussolini in Italy in September 1938 and in 1939, trying to persuade them to seek peace and affirming U.S. neutrality in the situation in Europe. In November 1939, Congress passed another neutrality act but this time amended it to allow the belligerents to purchase war munitions and materials from the United States as long as they paid cash and carried the purchases in their own ships. "That was as far as American public opinion would go at that point; it was a step away from complete isolation, but a long way from intervention in Europe's quarrels."[18] Nonetheless, the United States was creeping toward involvement in the European war.

From Neutrality to Nonbelligerency

On June 10, 1940, Roosevelt spoke at the University of Virginia in Charlottesville and outlined a subtle shift in U.S. foreign policy from "neutrality" to "nonbelligerency." He said that the United States subsequently would pursue "two obvious and simultaneous courses: we will extend to the opponents of force the material resources of this nation; and, at the same time, we will harness and speed up the use of those resources in order that we ourselves in the Americas may have equipment and training equal to the task of any emergency and every defense." While he made it clear that "we still insist on the need for vast improvements in our own social and economic life," he also warned that the United States would gear up for a war footing should it become necessary.[19] One year later, it would.

The presidential election of 1940 was hard fought. Roosevelt's opponent, Wendell Wilkie, accused Roosevelt of trying to drag the country into the war. Nonetheless, the two candidates were not as far apart on foreign policy as it first appeared. Wilkie supported Roosevelt's policy to get the country on a war footing and to aid ally Great Britain. Both men favored instituting a draft, which Congress passed in September. But as the election got closer, Wilkie's campaign rhetoric appeared to become more extreme. He warned about the dangers of sending American men into a foreign war. He implied that the United States had no direct interest in the war and, therefore, that Americans should not fight and die in Europe. Ultimately, though, Roosevelt defeated Wilkie and won an unprecedented third term as president. According to one historian, Roosevelt believed that "in the interests of the United States, Great Britain had to be supported both up to the limits his own public support and the law of neutrality would permit."[20] Roosevelt began to prepare the country for the possibility of war.

In his message to Congress on the "state of the union" in January 1941, Roosevelt spoke of the "four freedoms," which became a call to the American public to go to war if necessary. Roosevelt reminded the American public why the country went to war in the past, "for the maintenance of American rights and for the principles of peaceful commerce," and that the war then raging on four continents was for the "armed defense of democratic existence." He reminded the country that "thinking of our children and their children, we oppose enforced isolation for ourselves or for any part of the Americas." And he presaged the U.S. reaction to the Japanese attack on Pearl Harbor when he warned: "As long as the aggressor nations maintain the offensive, they—not we—will choose the time and the place and the method of their attack."

Roosevelt ended this speech with a call for personal sacrifice so that all Americans could respond to the call of "a world founded on four essential freedoms." These were freedom of speech and expression, freedom to worship God in one's own way, freedom from want, "which will secure to every nation a healthy peacetime life for its inhabitants," and freedom from fear—all to be guaranteed "everywhere in the world." Then, drawing on the idealism and appeal to moral virtue that had permeated much of American foreign policy since Wilson, Roosevelt called for a moral world order characterized by "cooperation of free countries, working together in a friendly, civilized society."[21] Hence, almost one year before the United States formally became involved in World War II, Roosevelt set the stage for U.S. involvement by asking the American public to sacrifice and by reminding them that the United States had a unique role to play in the world.

Two months later, in March 1941, Congress passed the Lend-Lease Act, allowing the United States to assist countries whose defense was seen as vital to the United States by lending or leasing them war supplies, equipment, or material. In August 1941, Roosevelt met with British prime minister Winston Churchill off the coast of Newfoundland, Canada, and issued the Atlantic Charter, affirming common principles "for a better future for the world." In this document, the two leaders reiterated many of the principles that Roosevelt had already laid out in his Four Freedoms speech, but they also echoed many of the ideas and ideals originally articulated by Wilson.[22] This statement moved the United States even closer to war.

War

U.S. entry into the war became inevitable when the Japanese attacked Pearl Harbor on December 7, 1941. On December 8, Roosevelt went to Congress and asked for a declaration of war against Japan. He began his message with the now famous words that December 7, 1941, would be "a date which will live in infamy" as "the United States of America was suddenly and deliberately attacked by the naval and air forces of the Empire of Japan."[23] Three days later, Germany and Italy declared war on the United States. The United States was at war in both Europe and the Pacific theater.

Although it took the bombing of Pearl Harbor for the United States to enter the war officially, it is clear that the country had been moving toward involvement for some time. Roosevelt's speeches for at least one year prior to the attack were preparing the country for what appeared to be inevitable. In addition, U.S. policies—gearing up industrially to help the war effort, assuring that the United States was prepared should it become necessary to go to war, moving from neutrality to nonbelligerency—were all designed to get the United States ready to enter the war. In many ways, the United States had no choice. It was one of the major powers in the world; by 1938, it had overtaken Britain and Germany as the greatest manufacturing producer.[24] The United States had been inching past isolationism, and Roosevelt was building public support for war, including warning the American people of the sacrifices they would have to endure for important reasons. The United States was once again going to fight the forces opposing democracy and freedom.

The Legacy of World War II

In many ways, the Second World War was a product of the twentieth century because of the role technology played; the surprise attack by Japanese aircraft on the naval base at Pearl Harbor was a reminder that all countries were suddenly vulnerable to such surprise attacks. Further, the war ended with the decision to use the newest technology, the atomic bomb. The emergence of these new technologies not only changed the way war was fought but also set the stage for the Cold War that would follow.

It is not the purpose of this book to describe the course of the Second World War. Suffice it to say, the United States became fully mobilized for the war effort, which led to some important changes domestically. Because men were drafted, women had to take on new roles domestically, including going to work to keep industry going. As women accepted these new roles, they were given more responsibility and proved themselves as professionals and corporate leaders, which had repercussions in the decades following the war. African Americans lobbied for greater integration, especially in light of a controversy that emerged during the election of 1940 about the segregation of the army. This push for integration also had important—and long-term—social implications for civil rights.[25]

This period was also characterized by one of the most inhumane policies seen in the United States. On February 19, 1942, President Roosevelt signed Executive Order 9066 authorizing the evacuation of more than 112,000 Japanese living on the West Coast to "relocation centers," where they spent the remainder of the war.[26] Many of these people were American citizens, and some had family members serving in the U.S. military. This policy was indicative of the fear that pervaded the country. The United States had been attacked by Japan, which was translated into a potential threat from the Japanese (and Japanese Americans) within the country.

The war also created strange, if fleeting, international alliances. It was not surprising that the United States joined with Britain and France, two traditional allies, to fight Nazi Germany. However, a new alliance was created when the Allied forces joined with the Soviet Union's communist leader, Joseph Stalin, to fight against Germany. Although the alliance with the Soviet Union was a necessary part of the war effort, Roosevelt and especially Churchill were suspicious of Stalin's motives as well as his ideology. This alliance lasted until the war ended and Germany was defeated.

By 1944, when it was clear that the Allied forces would win the war, one of Roosevelt's priorities was to start to prepare for peace. In January 1944, he again faced the Congress and the American public to describe "the state of the union." This time, however, his speech dealt with both winning the war and the need "to maintain a fair and stable economy at home." To assure both of these priorities, Roosevelt made a number of recommendations that he claimed would amount to a new bill of rights, appropriate for the time. These included the right to a good education, the right to a decent home, and the right to protection in case of illness and in old age. Roosevelt concluded his speech by noting:

> All of these rights spell security. And after this war is won we must be prepared to move forward, in the implementation of these rights, to new goals of human happiness and well-being.
>
> America's own rightful place in the world depends in large part upon how fully these and similar rights have been carried into practice for our citizens. For unless there is security at home there cannot be lasting peace in the world.[27]

In this speech, Roosevelt not only predicted the end of war but prepared the country for a return to postwar normalcy, with an emphasis on domestic issues once again.

Technology and World War II

Pearl Harbor was a wake-up call about the role of technology in redefining a country's security. When oceans could only be breached by ship, surprise attack was difficult because of the time involved. Pearl Harbor made clear what air power could do and mean. Suddenly, the United States and other countries were vulnerable, as this new technology could be used to attack in a way that had not been seen before. The role of air power changed the nature of warfare as well. Unlike World War I, where much of the war was fought on the ground and in the trenches, during World War II all countries depended on aerial bombing. This did not totally erase the need for ground or sea battles, as the history of World War II shows. Instead, it offered the belligerents more and different opportunities and ways to fight the enemy.

For example, the Battle of Britain in 1940 was an ongoing attack by German bombers sent to bring destruction on Britain. This part of Hitler's strategy of attrition against Britain was made possible by air power. British bombers attacked Germany as early as 1941, joined by U.S. air forces in 1942. The Germans responded with V-1 and V-2 flying bombs and rockets against Britain. While the Allies tried to confine their attacks to industry and "high-value" targets such as railroads, it was inevitable that civilians were killed and cities destroyed. Similarly, the German bombing of London did not differentiate between military and civilian targets. This showed both the strengths and weaknesses of the new technology: while it allowed countries to attack one another in the homeland, where they were most vulnerable, the risk to civilians increased and, with that, the number of noncombatant casualties. The allied bombing of Dresden, Germany, and the firebombing of Tokyo, Japan, are also examples of the destructive power of air attacks, which virtually leveled both cities and resulted in the deaths of hundreds of thousands of civilians.[28]

In June 1944, with the Germans apparently on the run, the Allies crossed the English Channel, landed on the beach at Normandy, France, and began the ground attack that would bring the war in Europe to a close. The fighting intensified in fall 1944, and the war was the primary campaign issue in the U.S. presidential election in November. President Roosevelt and his running mate, Harry Truman, were elected overwhelmingly. In December, one month after the election, the final defeat of Germany began with the Battle of the Bulge. On May 8, 1945, not quite one month after the death of President Roosevelt, Germany signed the terms of unconditional surrender. However, fighting continued in the Pacific, leaving it up to President Truman to end that war.

The Decision to Bomb Hiroshima and Nagasaki

As president, Roosevelt was aware of the role of technology and the importance of dominating technologically. In May 1942, to make sure that the United States retained an edge, Roosevelt authorized the creation of the Manhattan Project, which brought together some of the greatest scientists of the time. The team's goal was to determine whether it was possible to split the atom and create a chain reaction that would result in the release of energy. If this energy could be harnessed and controlled, as some of the physicists thought, then the United States would be able to create a new and very powerful weapon.

On July 16, 1945, the new weapon was tested successfully in the desert near Alamogordo, New Mexico. The project was so secret that even Vice President Truman was unaware of its existence. Yet, when he became president, Truman was the one who had to make the decision to use the weapon. With the war in Europe over, U.S. forces were concentrated in the Pacific, and the Americans stepped up their bombing of Japanese cities, resulting in hundreds of thousands of civilian deaths.

On both military and moral grounds, scholars have thoroughly debated the decision to drop the atomic bombs, especially since Japanese defeat appeared inevitable.[29] Nonetheless, Truman ultimately made the decision to use the atomic bomb to force a quick end to the war, thereby minimizing further American casualties. On August 6, 1945, the *Enola Gay* dropped an atomic bomb, dubbed "Little Man," on the city of Hiroshima, Japan, killing more than 70,000 people. Three days later, on August 9, a second bomb, called "Fat Boy," was dropped on the city of Nagasaki. The atomic age had begun.

On August 6, the White House issued a press release: "With this bomb we have now added a new and revolutionary increase in destruction to supplement the growing power of our armed forces. In their present form these bombs are now in production and even more powerful forms are in development." The release continued: "It is an atomic bomb. It is a harnessing of the basic power of the universe. The force from which the sun draws its power has been loosed against those who brought war to the Far East."[30]

In this release, the White House noted the role of technology and how it had changed the face of warfare. "Before 1939, it was the accepted belief of scientists that it was theoretically possible to release atomic energy. But no one knew any practical method of doing it. By 1942, however, we knew that the Germans were working feverishly to add atomic energy to the other engines of war with which they hoped to enslave the world. But they failed."[31]

On September 2, 1945, Japan surrendered. In retrospect, it is clear that more than simply military reasons affected the decision to drop the atomic bombs. Influencing that decision was the desire to send a signal to the Soviet Union about U.S. military supremacy.[32] Once the war—and the need for the alliance—ended, the suspicion that characterized the relationship between the United States and the Soviet Union returned. The seeds of the Cold War that would follow World War II were already planted.

The United Nations: Defining the Postwar World

The horrors of World War II reinforced the importance of preventing such catastrophes in the future. Planning for the creation of an organization that could bring countries together with that goal began before World War II ended. President Roosevelt and Prime Minister Churchill worked together to bring this idea to fruition.

As a vice presidential candidate in 1920, Franklin Roosevelt supported the need to approve a "general plan" of the League of Nations.[33] Over time, however, it was perceived that "the organization's inherent structure and its rules of procedure were grossly inadequate to the basic task of safeguarding peace and preventing war."[34] Roosevelt supported the basic idealistic philosophy on which the League was structured, but he believed that an organization such as the League could not succeed if it required unanimous action by all member states. In other words, while he agreed with the values of cooperation and collective security in principle, he also understood the importance of power and of the need to inject realist thinking if such an organization were to succeed.

The principles embodied in the short document called the Atlantic Charter, which Roosevelt and Churchill negotiated in August 1941, ultimately led to the creation of the United Nations.[35] The two leaders sent the text of the charter to Stalin for his endorsement, but he saw it as an attempt at Anglo-American domination. Stalin told British foreign secretary Anthony Eden that the charter seemed directed against the Soviet Union.[36] The idealistic visions of a world that could avoid war were counterbalanced by the schism growing between East and West.

Creation of the United Nations

Despite Stalin's reservations, on January 1, 1942, representatives of the Soviet Union and China joined President Roosevelt and Prime Minister Churchill in signing the Declaration of the United Nations. The following day, twenty-two other countries signed as well, all of which were countries then at war with the Axis powers. They also agreed to remain united and not to sign any peace agreement individually with the Axis countries. Although the idea of a "united nations" then referred to the Allied countries, it quickly grew into the skeleton for an international peacekeeping and collective security organization. Planning for the nascent organization continued with an eye toward learning the lessons of the League of Nations so that its weaknesses would not be repeated. Planners recognized the need for countries to work together in opposition to any aggressor nations (i.e., idealism) balanced against the use of power and military might if and/or when necessary (i.e., realism).

One of the highest priorities was finding funding for the new organization. The planners (primarily the British and Americans) also had to address the problem of assuaging Soviet suspicions as well as the fears of smaller countries that they would be overwhelmed by the power of the larger ones. During these early years (1942 through 1943) in the midst of war, the mood within the United States was changing and becoming more international in outlook. This aided Roosevelt in his task to build domestic support for the new United Nations while also planning for the postwar order, although he still had to overcome the objections of isolationists, such as Senator Arthur Vandenberg of Michigan.

As world leaders Roosevelt, Churchill, Stalin, and Chiang Kai-shek of China[37] met to discuss the war effort, they also talked about the postwar United Nations. When Roosevelt addressed the U.S. public on December 24, 1943, he referred to the "Big Four" nations and declared that peace would be secure as long as they worked together to achieve that goal. But he also noted that "force and the willingness to use it were the keys to lasting peace."[38] In other words, Britain, Russia, China, and the United States all were prepared to use force if necessary to keep peace in the future.

By the summer of 1944, formal talks on the new organization were well under way. The organization would consist of a Security Council, a General Assembly, an International Court of Justice, and a Secretariat, with other agencies to address specific issues (especially economic and social) to be brought in as needed. The primary purposes of the organization were to maintain peace (using force if necessary) and to foster cooperation among all nations, leading to the common good. The leaders agreed that all countries should be bound by the decisions of the new organization, but they had questions about how best to achieve this. The structure of the Security Council would include permanent members, each of which would have a veto in recognition of the power that each held, both politically and militarily. But this structure also acknowledged the reality that any action would require them to act in unanimity, and therefore ideally would foster cooperation among them. The General Assembly would be composed of all member nations and would be vested with broad authority, in contrast with the Security Council, which was primarily charged with peacekeeping.

Negotiations on the details continued through 1944. The four major powers issued a statement following a conference at Dumbarton Oaks in Washington, D.C., entitled "Proposals for the Establishment of a General International Organization." The proposals included expanding the Security Council to five permanent members (the big four countries plus France) and six rotating members elected by the General Assembly. In addition to the International Court of Justice, the new structure would include an Economic and Social Council and a Military Staff Committee to direct the forces that would be employed in the event of a UN military action.

On April 25, 1945, less than one month after Roosevelt's death, delegates from forty-six nations gathered in San Francisco for a conference on the UN. The basic structure of the organization agreed to at that time was the one negotiated at Dumbarton Oaks. Despite ongoing political issues, the goals of the organization were paramount, and the delegates approved the charter of the UN. President Truman submitted it to the Senate, which voted to ratify the charter on July 28, 1945.

The UN was to embody the lessons of the League of Nations, and in many ways, it was successful. But, as history has shown, no organization could successfully ensure that war would be avoided. Although optimistically and idealistically the new organization would force the United States and the Soviet Union to work together, the tensions of the Cold War were already in place.

On the whole, the American public supported the notion of an organization that would help deter or avoid war. By the end of World War II, the American people had also come to the realization that the United States could no longer resort to isolationism or even unilateralism in its foreign policy. Rather, the United States would have to become actively engaged in the international system. (See the case study of the creation of the United Nations at the end of this chapter.)

The End of Isolationism

The period following World War I was a time when the United States turned inward once again, reverting to an isolationist foreign policy. Yet the decade following the war was one in which the United States was engaged diplomatically, initiating the Kellogg-Briand Pact and convening the Washington Conference, in the idealistic belief that negotiations and agreements could avoid conflict and war in the future. It did not take long for this premise to be questioned. Once Japan invaded China and Hitler began his relentless drive for power, no international agreement would stop them. Furthermore, even the League of Nations, which had specifically been created as an instrument of collective security, proved to be powerless unless all countries agreed to work together to stop the aggression of any one.

Under a succession of presidents, the highest priority of the United States was to remain removed from the conflicts escalating in the Pacific and Europe. Yet, as Roosevelt saw, that would be impossible. The best he could do was justify the reasons for U.S. involvement in these foreign wars and prepare the American public for the sacrifices they would have to make once the country went to war. The bombing of Pearl Harbor made U.S. involvement inevitable. The surprise attack also gave notice to all nations of the dangers inherent in new technology.

The way that World War II was conducted was important for a number of reasons. The advent and use of new technology made it clear that whatever country had the best and most advanced technology would be in a position of power internationally. This meant that even before World War II ended, the rush to technological dominance that characterized much of the Cold War had begun. During the war, the United States feared that Germany would be the first country to get new technology and then use it against the Allies. This drove the development of new weapons by the United States. The fact that the United States was able not only to build but also to use atomic weapons made an important point both during and after the war.

By the end of World War II, the international order had changed. The United States emerged from that war as the major power and was well positioned internationally. War had not been fought on its mainland, so unlike the European countries and Japan, it had an intact industrial base. The U.S. economy was thriving. The United States was the dominant military power as well, with a close relationship that had developed between the economy and the military sector, or what Eisenhower would later call "the military-industrial complex." Further, the United States was instrumental in creating a structure that would define the postwar world, embodied internationally in the United Nations.

Domestically, the country faced a number of challenges. The return of men in uniform displaced women who had been in the workforce and who had taken on greater roles both in their homes and in society. Following the war there was a return to a more "traditional" family that was fostered by the growth of the new suburbs. Nonetheless, within twenty years, women were fighting for access to jobs, status, and pay equal to that of their male counterparts. African Americans, who had fought in the war, returned home only to face discrimination, and they, too, felt that a promise had been broken. This led directly to the civil rights movement that started in the 1950s and really took hold early in the 1960s.

The period following World War II was difficult as the United States adjusted to a changing international order as well as these domestic issues. It would be up to Harry Truman to lead the country through these many domestic and international issues.

Applying Foreign Policy Concepts:
Realism versus Idealism in International Organizations

As noted in the discussion of the League of Nations in chapter 2 and the creation of the United Nations in this chapter, both were born from the idealist emphasis on the importance of cooperation and countries working together to ensure the common good, including a peaceful world. Yet one of the lessons of the League was that cooperation was not necessarily effective unless it was backed up by the use of hard power. This was a very hard lesson for the United States to learn at this particular point in time.

Furthermore, President Roosevelt, in working with Prime Minister Churchill to frame what would become the UN, also understood that if this new organization was going to succeed, it would have to get the support of Joseph Stalin, who was not trusted by either of the two men. We now know that they were right not to trust Stalin, but we also know that the organization would not have been put into place without his support. And, at that time, creating the UN as a framework for the world that would exist after the Second World War was important enough for them to work with Stalin, as they had worked with him as a way to fight Hitler. Roosevelt also knew that the UN would be doomed to the same fate as the League of Nations unless he could sell the idea to the Congress and the American public.

With these factors in mind, what is your understanding and analysis of the creation of the UN, and what would you have done?

The Case

The signing of the Atlantic Charter in August 1941 by Franklin Roosevelt and Winston Churchill outlined some important principles for the international system. Even though the United States was not yet formally at war, through programs such as Lend-Lease it was supporting its allies and moving inextricably toward war. The Atlantic Charter itself is quite short and reaffirms "certain common principles in the national policies of their respective countries on which they based their hopes for a better future in the world." Central to these principles was "the abandonment of the use of force."[39]

This idea of countries affirming certain basic principles was embodied in a Declaration of United Nations signed by twenty-six countries on January 1, 1942. But each of the countries thereby also acknowledged that they were "engaged in a common struggle against savage and brutal forces seeking to subjugate the world," and each government then pledged "to employ its full resources, military or economic, against those members of the Tripartite Pact; and its adherents with which such government is at war."[40]

Ultimately the principles that held these united nations together led to the creation of a formal international organization that would bring together countries for the pursuit of collective security backed up by the use of force if necessary. To Roosevelt and Churchill, this new organization balanced the idealism of cooperation and collective security with the reality of the need to use military force if and/or when necessary. President Roosevelt understood that getting the support of the American public and the Congress would be essential to the success of this undertaking. The lessons of the League of Nations are clear: without the United States, such an international organization cannot succeed, and the Congress must accept and buy into the premises for this organization if that body was to ratify the treaty.

Going into World War II there was a group within the United States who wanted the country to remain isolationist and removed from the wars in Europe, as evidenced by the passage of the neutrality acts. Isolationist senator Arthur Vandenberg, a Republican from Michigan and the "acknowledged but unofficial spokesman of Senate Republicans on foreign policy matters," prior to the bombing of Pearl Harbor "advocated strict neutrality and a rigid arms embargo to prevent American involvement in the war."[41] He proved to be prescient when he wrote that "we have thrown ourselves squarely into the power politics and power wars of Europe, Asia, and Africa. We have taken the first step upon a course from which we can never hereafter retreat."[42] Ironically, Vandenberg had been a supporter of the attempt to establish a League of Nations "but drifted toward isolationism after a visit to Europe in 1935 convinced him that war was inevitable."[43]

For Roosevelt and his advisors, the United Nations that he envisioned with Churchill was an opportunity to build on the idealism embodied in the League of Nations while also compensating for the flaws that led ultimately to its failure. But, again learning from the lessons of the League, Roosevelt had to make it palatable enough for even staunch isolationists like Vandenberg to support. At a time when the United States was engulfed in war in both Europe and the Pacific, Roosevelt's challenge was to convince the members of the Congress as well as the American people that the United States not only would benefit from participating in this organization but would suffer great losses politically and perceptually should it choose *not* to join.

It is important to bear in mind that Roosevelt had to present this idea at a time when the United States was in the midst of war that was costly in terms of lives and money. Yet it was also a period in which the United States was clearly solidifying its place as a world leader. The challenge facing Roosevelt was how to put forward, during the war, a framework for this international organization that would help to avoid such wars in the future.

What Would You Do If . . .

The time is 1943. The United States is in the midst of a major war; peace seems like a distant dream at this point. The idea of advocating for the creation of an international organization that would work for international peace in the future seems like a futile gesture. Yet throughout his presidency, Roosevelt had prepared the country for the possibility of war, long before the United States became a belligerent nation, and he also knew that during the war was the time to begin to prepare for the peace. While virtually no one doubted the wisdom of, nor necessity for, going to war after the attack on Pearl Harbor, clearly there were some within the Congress, like Vandenberg, who remained committed to the idea that the United States needed to remain faithful to its own national interest even if that meant staying aloof from the affairs of other countries.

What would you do if you were an advisor to President Roosevelt and he looked to you for recommendations about how to present this idea of participating in an international organization for collective security to the American public and the Congress? How would you frame the approach? What would be the balance of idealism versus realism? And why and how would participating in such an organization be in the national interest of the United States at that time?

For the record, in fall 1943 both the Senate and the House of Representatives "approved resolutions calling for United States involvement in an international peacekeeping organization to be established after the war."[44]

4

The Cold War

Two countries emerged in positions of global power at the end of World War II: the United States, which came out of the war with its homeland intact, its economy strengthened by the war effort, and its military unsurpassed technologically, and the Soviet Union, which had joined with the United States and the Western allies against Germany, but which was also charting its own course. One of the unintended consequences of World War II was that it set the stage for the Cold War that followed by pitting these two "superpowers," as they came to be called, against each other. Neither of these two countries specifically wanted nor sought this power; in fact, in the 1920s and 1930s, each had pursued an isolationist foreign policy, preferring to focus on domestic priorities rather than trying to secure a place of power internationally. Yet World War II thrust both countries into positions of international leadership that became even more important after the war ended. The Soviet Union emerged from the war as one of the most powerful countries in Europe, while the United States was the only country strong enough to "balance" that power, and it was in the United States' interest to do so.[1]

In contrast, the relative power of those countries that had been dominant before World War II (e.g., the countries of western Europe—France, the United Kingdom, and Germany—and Japan) receded as they were forced to look inward, rather than outward, in order to recover from the devastation of the war. The result was a restructuring of the international system into a bipolar world in which the forces of democracy and free-market capitalism, embodied by the United States and its allies, faced the Soviet Union and its allies, the forces of communism.

Rather than the traditional "hot war," where countries fought one another directly on the battlefield, this was a "cold war," or a period of ongoing tensions played out in a number of arenas. First, the Cold War was a war of *ideology*, which assumed that the two divergent approaches (democracy and communism) could not coexist peacefully. Therefore, one side would have to emerge as dominant.

One of the misconceptions that guided U.S. foreign policy during the Cold War was the belief that communism was a single monolithic force. This suggested that *all* communist countries, whether China or Vietnam or even some of the left-leaning movements in Africa and South America, were loyal to and supported (and were, in turn, supported by) the Soviet Union. This belief gave rise to the domino theory that ultimately led to U.S. involvement in Southeast Asia. According to the domino theory, if one country in Southeast Asia became communist, then the other neighboring countries would fall like a row of dominoes and similarly become communist. Hence, any incursion of communism had to be stopped before it spread.

The Cold War was also a *political* war in which the two approaches were seen as antithetical to each other, leading inevitably to conflict. The belief in the expansive political nature of communism had not only foreign policy implications for the United States but important domestic ones as well. The growth of McCarthyism and the Red Scare created a domestic atmosphere that supported U.S. foreign policy priorities.

The Cold War involved *military* confrontation. While no war was fought directly between the United States and the Soviet Union, the two sides fought each other indirectly through "proxy wars." The battleground on which Cold War conflicts were fought expanded dramatically to include countries in Latin America and Africa as well as Asia. Often the Soviet Union and sometimes the People's Republic of China backed communist-led insurgencies and communist-leaning leaders, and the United States backed virtually any government or force that was not communist. These proxy wars made it possible for the two superpowers to avoid a direct military confrontation that could, potentially, lead to nuclear holocaust. The outcome was the same—victory for the forces of democracy or communism—but the danger to the rest of the world from nuclear weapons was diminished. What neither side seemed to consider (especially in the early years) was the desire of other countries, such as India and Pakistan, to acquire nuclear weapons so that they could better deter—or if necessary fight—their own enemies.

Finally, the Cold War was a war of *economics*. The United States and its allies were steeped in capitalist free-market economics. In contrast, the Soviet Union followed a communist economic system, where the state planned the economy and owned the means of production. Although the conflict between these two systems appeared to be secondary to political, military, and ideological competition, in reality, as during the formation of this country, economics pervaded many of the foreign policy decisions that the United States made, especially in the early years of the Cold War. For example, the Marshall Plan to aid Europe had its roots in the U.S. desire to expand markets for its own goods and the need for stable trading partners that would not be tempted to turn to communism. This made economic tools important elements of the U.S. foreign policy of containment and set the precedent of using foreign aid (i.e., money) as an instrument of foreign policy.[2]

The Cold War was an especially important time in the evolution of U.S. foreign policy. As we shall see in this chapter, domestic and international policies and priorities came together once again as the United States revised and strengthened not only its military but its decision-making apparatus to support the goals and needs of this new "cold" war. It was a time when domestic and international politics merged through movements like the Red Scare, which helped build support among the American public for policies that were seen as necessary for success in the Cold War. We see the role of a strong executive as a series of presidents—starting with Harry Truman—provided the guidance and direction for a new course of action. Then, in the belief that presidents had overstepped their powers, we see Congress asserting its constitutional authority and oversight role. And, most important, we see the creation of a framework for American foreign policy that is rooted in unapologetic internationalism and engagement. Not only did the United States move beyond unilateralism or isolationism, but it did so in a way that left no doubt about the country's belief in itself and its dominance in the new world order. The concept of national interest changed dramatically after World War II, and all aspects of U.S. policy during the Cold War were designed to promote the "new" national interest.

The Early Years of the Cold War

In many ways, the origins of the Cold War can be traced to 1917 and the Russian Revolution. As noted in chapter 2, U.S. troops remained in Russia from 1918 through 1920 to fight against the Bolsheviks (communists). This action, specifically the fact that the United States sent troops to fight against the communist forces in what was a civil war, was not forgotten by subsequent Soviet leaders and was part of the reason for suspicion and mistrust. On the other hand, the United States and its allies (primarily Great Britain) harbored their own suspicions of Stalin and his intentions. Although it was in all sides' interest to fight together against the Germans during World War

II, it was not long after the war ended that a chasm emerged between the former allies.

Germany surrendered in May 1945. In July, the leaders of the three major victorious wartime powers (Truman, Churchill, and Stalin) met in Potsdam, Germany, to address the postwar order in Europe. Germany was divided among the four powers (the three plus France), which together ultimately decided the future of that country. Berlin, the capital of Germany, was similarly divided among the four. Physically it was located in the heart of what was to become the Soviet sector of East Germany, so Berlin, more than any other place, became a barometer of the level of Cold War tensions.

Just as Roosevelt prepared the American people for participating in World War II before the United States officially entered the war and then started preparing them for the peace before the war ended, so Truman began setting the stage for the Cold War before it started. In October 1945, he gave a major foreign policy address in New York City that became known as the "Fundamentals of American Foreign Policy." This was his first major statement on the topic after Potsdam. In this statement he outlined twelve points that he said would guide U.S. foreign policy. Some of the points are reminiscent of Franklin Roosevelt's Four Freedoms speech, in which he pledged to support the basic freedoms to which all people are entitled.[3] For example, Truman stated his belief that all peoples "should be permitted to choose their own form of government by their freely expressed choice," and he spoke of the need for the establishment of "freedom from fear and freedom from want."

Truman also used this statement to send a signal, especially to Stalin, about U.S. intentions in the emerging world order. For example, he made it clear that the United States had "no plans for aggression against any other state, large or small. We have no objectives which need clash with the peaceful aims of any other nation." And, as he warned Stalin and any other potential aggressor, "We shall approve no territorial changes in any friendly part of the world unless they accord with the freely expressed wishes of the people concerned." He also foreshadowed some of the major postwar programs: "By the combined and cooperative action of our war Allies, we shall help the defeated enemy states establish peaceful democratic governments of their own free choice."[4]

The tenuous nature of the World War II alliance became even more apparent in 1946 when Joseph Stalin gave a speech in which he spoke of "the inevitability of conflict with capitalist powers" and the need for the Soviet people "to strengthen and defend their homeland."[5] In other words, although World War II was behind them, Stalin was telling the people of the Soviet Union that war was not over yet. For those nations predisposed to be concerned about Soviet intentions, this speech reinforced the belief that a confrontation between the two sides was inevitable.

George Kennan and Early Cold War Policy

The policies that the United States pursued during the Cold War had their origins in 1946 and 1947. Within a short time after the end of World War II, it was clear to the United States that the next battle would be between the United States and the Soviet Union. In order to understand the evolution of U.S. Cold War foreign policy, it is important to examine in some detail the critical events and ideas that framed the policy decisions that the United States made.

The assessment of George Kennan, a U.S. diplomat stationed in Moscow, reinforced the beliefs about a fundamental clash between the two countries and ideologies. In February 1946, Kennan sent a document to Washington that became known as "the Long Telegram." This document and Kennan's subsequent article "The Sources of Soviet Conduct" (the X Article), published in 1947, helped crystallize the thinking of U.S. policy-makers and changed the course of U.S. foreign policy.[6] Both warned the American public about an aggressive Soviet Union and the need for the United States to be prepared to counter that aggression anywhere in the world. For the analyses he put forward and the impact that he had, Kennan has become known as one of the critical architects of U.S. Cold War foreign policy, especially the policy of containment.

The Long Telegram

Kennan sent the Long Telegram from Moscow on February 22, 1946, describing the Soviet threat as he saw it. The document, intended as information for the president and secretary of state, was in five parts and began with the statement that the "USSR still lives in antagonistic 'capitalist encirclement' with which in the long run there can be no permanent peaceful coexistence." Kennan saw the Soviet leadership as defining a world in conflict because "Internal conflicts of capitalism inevitably generate wars" that are "insoluble by means of peaceful compromise." And based on the premises that he put forth, he concluded that "Relentless battle must be waged against socialist and social-democratic leaders abroad." Hence, Kennan made clear that the United States would face an ongoing battle that would pit the United States against the Soviet Union.

In part 2 of the telegram, Kennan documented how he arrived at his conclusions and drew a distinction between the outlook of the Russian people, who are "friendly to outside world, eager for experience of it . . . eager above all to live in peace and enjoy fruits of their own labor," and the attitudes of the Soviet leadership. In his analysis, the Communist Party line made peaceful coexistence impossible.

Part 3 offered Kennan's assessment of what the Soviet outlook meant on a practical level, that is, for future Soviet policy. In this section Kennan outlined his view of the Soviet Union's drive for power and for "increasing in every way strength and prestige of Soviet state." He also painted a grim picture of a country that will do whatever it takes to achieve that end, including taking advantage of the parts of Europe seen as being "of immediate strategic necessity," and where the Soviets sensed "strong possibilities of opposition to Western centers of power."[7] Part 4 of the telegram identified the ways in which these policies might be played out via "unofficial" organs, such the Russian Orthodox Church.

In part 5, "Practical Deductions from Standpoint of U.S. Policy," Kennan prescribed what U.S. policy should be to counter the Soviet intentions, beginning with the need to recognize the nature of the enemy and to prepare the United States to fight against it. To that end, Kennan concluded that "much depends on health and vigor of our own society. World communism is like malignant parasite which feeds only on diseased tissue. *This is point at which domestic and foreign policies meet.* Every courageous and incisive measure to solve internal problems of our own society . . . is a diplomatic victory over Moscow" (emphasis added). According to Kennan, the United States "must formulate and put forward for other nations a much more positive and constructive picture of sort of world we would like to see. . . . It is not enough to urge people to develop political processes similar to our own. Many foreign peoples, in Europe at least, are tired and frightened by experiences of past, and are less interested in abstract freedom than security." And he warned that the United States "should be better able than Russians to give them this. And unless we do, Russians certainly will."[8] In other words, the Soviet Union will press for an advantage in Europe, and unless the United States intervenes, the Soviet Union will "win." It is instructive to note that about six months later, the Soviet ambassador to the United States, Nikolai Novikov, sent a cable from Washington to Moscow in which he painted a similar portrait of the United States.[9]

The X Article

One year later, in 1947, Kennan published an article entitled "The Sources of Soviet Conduct" in the journal *Foreign Affairs* under the pseudonym "X." This article went further than the Long Telegram in outlining ideas for the future U.S. foreign policy of containment. By publishing in *Foreign Affairs*, a respected journal read by policy-makers and others, Kennan made his points publicly. In fact, one of the most important aspects of the article was that it was directed at the American public, or at least those members of the public who studied and cared about foreign policy (i.e., "the attentive public"). In doing so, Kennan built support for the policies he believed would be most important for the United States to win the emerging Cold War.

In the article, he reprised themes outlined in the Long Telegram, such as "the innate antagonism between capitalism and socialism." And he warned that out of the antagonism "flow many of the phenomena that we find disturbing in the Kremlin's conduct of foreign policy: the secretiveness, the lack of frankness, the duplicity, the wary suspiciousness, and the basic unfriendliness of purpose." From that he concluded: "This means that we are going to continue for a long time to find the Russians difficult to deal with." As he outlined the characteristics that influence Soviet behavior, he also noted that the "cumulative effect of these factors is to give to the whole subordinate apparatus of Soviet power an unshakable stubbornness and steadfastness in its orientation. This orientation can be changed at will by the Kremlin but by no other power."

Kennan then put forward his prescription for the United States: "In these circumstances it is clear that the main element of any United States policy toward the Soviet Union must be that of a long-term, patient but firm and vigilant *containment* of Russian expansive tendencies" (emphasis added). With that, Kennan articulated the basic tenets that would guide U.S. foreign policy for the next fifty years, premised on an expansionist and aggressive Soviet Union and the need for the United States to contain those tendencies. He also described some of the ways that the United States could contain the USSR: "The Soviet pressure against the free institutions of the western world is something that can be contained by the adroit and vigilant application of counter-force at a series of constantly shifting geographical and political points."[10]

While Kennan made it clear in this article that he thought the Soviet Union was far weaker than the United States and the West, he also warned that the Russian leaders were dedicated to the success of their cause and that they had the patience to wait and continue their fight. He was prescient when he noted that "Russia, as opposed to the Western world in general, is still by far the weaker party, that Soviet policy is highly flexible, and that Soviet society may well contain deficiencies which will eventually weaken its own total potential." (This would not happen until approximately forty-four years later, when the Soviet Union imploded in August 1991.) But, for the short term, Kennan argued it was up to the United States to do whatever it had to do to contain the Soviet Union.[11]

The X article not only outlined the containment policy that was the framework of American foreign policy during the Cold War, but it also sowed the seeds for the U.S. alliance system that followed by encouraging the United States to align with countries surrounding the Soviet Union in support of the common goal of containing the USSR. While this strategy helped contain Soviet expansion by making it clear that if the USSR went into any of those countries it would have to deal with the United States, it also sent a signal to the Soviet Union, which perceived that it was being surrounded by hostile countries. The result was to exacerbate the cycle of mistrust and suspicion that characterized much of the Cold War.

1947: The Truman Doctrine and the Marshall Plan

A series of communist takeovers in countries of Eastern Europe followed World War II. Bulgaria and Yugoslavia elected communist majorities in 1945, and communist governments were created in Hungary, Poland, and Romania in 1946. In addition, the Soviet Union retained its control of the Baltic republics of Latvia, Lithuania, and Estonia after World War II. Not only did these lead to the creation of a "Soviet bloc" in Eastern Europe, but they validated Kennan's warnings of an expansionist Soviet Union (see figure 4.1).

The situation in Greece, engaged in civil war since 1945, grew very serious from the perspective of the United States. Britain had been sending money and troops to Greece in support of the forces defending the monarchy against communist insurgents. However, by 1947 it could no longer afford to do so. Instead, it would be up to the United States to pick up the slack. Similarly, unrest in Turkey and Soviet pressure on that country furthered U.S. concerns about Soviet intentions regarding Europe.

Thus, by 1947 the world was divided into two basic camps centered on the United States and the Soviet Union: West versus East. Drawing on the warnings put forward in the Long Telegram and outlined in the X article, Truman delivered a speech to the U.S. Congress in March 1947 outlining what became known as the "Truman Doctrine." In this speech, Truman formalized the policies that the United States would pursue, as well as the reasons behind them. It was a clear articulation of U.S. policies and intentions at the start of the Cold War.

In his speech, Truman specifically identified Greece and Turkey as two major areas of concern to the United States. Regarding Greece, Truman laid out the background of the ongoing war and the fact that the Greek government had asked the United States for assistance. Truman noted that "Greece must have assistance if it is to become a self-supporting and self-respecting

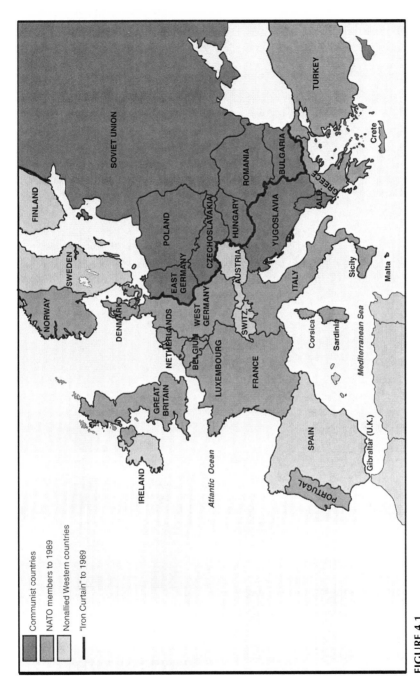

Communist countries

NATO members to 1989

Nonallied Western countries

"Iron Curtain" to 1989

FIGURE 4.1
Cold War Europe.

democracy. The United States must supply this assistance. . . . There is no other country to which democratic Greece can turn. No other nation is willing and able to provide the necessary support for a democratic Greek government."

Truman continued: "The British government, which has been helping Greece, can give no further financial or economic aid after March 1 [1947]. *Great Britain finds itself under the necessity of reducing or liquidating its commitments in several parts of the world, including Greece*" (emphasis added). The importance of this statement cannot be underestimated. Not only did Truman make the case for U.S. assistance to Greece, but he also made it clear that the United States would take on the global role that the British had played earlier and could no longer afford to continue. Thus, the power balance shifted from Europe in general and Britain in particular to the United States. It also set the United States on a particular course of action not only in Greece but in other parts of the world as both Britain and France withdrew from their colonial commitments and the United States replaced them as the major power. With that relative change in status, it was the United States that emerged as the major imperial power in the West.

Truman also noted that "Turkey now needs our support. Since the war Turkey has sought additional financial assistance from Great Britain and the United States for the purpose of effecting that modernization necessary for the maintenance of its national integrity. That integrity is essential to the preservation of order in the Middle East." And, once again, Truman argued that the United States had to step in because Britain could "no longer extend financial or economic aid to Turkey."

Leading to the call for the Congress to act, Truman uttered the words that have often been quoted: "I believe that it must be the policy of the United States to support free peoples who are resisting attempted subjugation by armed minorities or by outside pressures. I believe that we must assist free peoples to work out their own destinies in their own way. I believe that our help should be primarily through economic and financial aid which is essential to economic stability and orderly political processes."[12] To support these beliefs, Truman asked Congress to authorize four hundred million dollars in assistance to Greece and Turkey. Congress authorized the funds, and the role of the United States as the defender of countries fighting communist aggression was established. The United States was now firmly committed to using its hard power, economic and military, as well as its soft power (i.e., its influence) to support its allies and in opposition to communism.

The Truman Doctrine had a number of other important foreign policy implications. It established the precedent of using foreign aid and economic assistance as an instrument of foreign policy, something that continued through the duration of the Cold War and continues to the present (post–Cold War) period. It also made clear to the Soviet Union and to all other countries that the United States would use military force not only within its own hemisphere (Monroe Doctrine) or when democratic ideals were threatened (Wilsonian perspective) but in support of any country fighting communism anywhere in the world.

The National Security Act of 1947

When Truman outlined a new and more muscular direction in U.S. foreign policy, he also needed to create a structure that would ensure its implementation. The bureaucratic structure for the conduct of U.S. foreign policy had been in place virtually since the creation of the country, when the foreign policy orientation was very different. That structure no longer was appropriate for a world in which the United States was going to be playing a dominant role. With the advent of the Cold War, the military became an important and overt instrument of U.S. foreign policy; the success of U.S. foreign policy was tied directly to military might. For the United States to play a major world role, not only did it have to have a credible military force, but it had to be perceived as willing to use that force in support of its foreign policy goals. Therefore, the country needed a structure that more firmly linked the military to the civilian sides of policy-making.

President Truman designed the National Security Act to create a structure that would accomplish these various goals, all of which were seen as necessary for success in the Cold War. Until the creation of the Department of Homeland Security in November 2002, the National Security Act of 1947 was the most sweeping change made to the military and foreign policy apparatus since the country was created.[13]

The National Security Act of 1947[14] did a number of things. The War and Navy Departments were merged into a single Department of Defense (DoD), which was more appropriate for the new direction in U.S. foreign policy. The DoD was to be headed by a civilian, and each military service would be headed by a civilian secretary who reported to the secretary of defense.[15] It authorized the establishment of a Central Intelligence Agency (CIA) headed by a director of central intelligence; the ability to keep track of the Soviet Union and other adversaries was seen as essential to preparing for and winning the Cold War. The act provided for the creation of a National Security Council (NSC) charged with coordinating domestic, military, and foreign policies relating to national security. The membership of the NSC would consist of the secretaries of state and defense with other officials (such as the director of the CIA and the chair of the Joint Chiefs of Staff) serving as advisors as needed. Initially, the president hired a small NSC staff to coordinate foreign policy options from among the various agencies. Starting in 1953, under President Eisenhower, the staff was headed by an assistant for national security. Initially, this job involved little more than serving as secretary to the NSC; however, over time, and as U.S. foreign policy became more complex, the role of national security advisor grew so that now that position serves as one of the most important advisors to the president.

With the passage of the National Security Act, the United States was better equipped militarily as well as from a policy-process perspective to wage the Cold War.

The Marshall Plan

As Congress debated the Truman Doctrine, in June 1947 Secretary of State George C. Marshall delivered a commencement address at Harvard University outlining the basic principles for the postwar recovery of Europe. Marshall proposed a specific plan for European economic recovery to be implemented over the next several years in the belief that only if Europe were strong economically could it withstand any attempt at communist insurgency. But it also put the burden on the Europeans to determine their own needs: "Before the United States Government can proceed much further in its efforts to alleviate the situation and help start the European world on its way to recovery, there must be some agreement among the countries of Europe as to the requirements of the situation and the part those countries themselves will take in order to give proper effect to whatever action might be undertaken by this Government. It would be neither fitting nor efficacious for this government to undertake to draw up unilaterally a program designed to place Europe on its feet economically. This is the business of the Europeans."[16]

In response, Britain and France took the lead and invited twenty-two European countries, including the Soviet Union and its Eastern European allies, to a conference to draw up an outline for European reconstruction that could be presented to the United States. While the USSR and members of the Eastern bloc refused to participate, virtually all the countries of Western Europe did, and on September 23, 1947, they submitted a report to the United States on general European needs.

On April 3, 1948, President Truman signed into law the European Recovery Act—widely known as the Marshall Plan. It provided for $5.3 billion specifically for European economic recovery for the following year. During the period from 1948 through 1950, the United States spent $12 billion in economic aid for Europe, more than half of which went to Britain, France, and West Germany. This infusion of money gave those countries the impetus they needed to begin to recover from the war. And, as planned, they became major trading partners of the United States (and, through the European Union, remain so today).

The Marshall Plan was a critical success to the nations that it helped the most. It not only strengthened the economic systems of those countries, but by doing so, it helped stabilize their political systems as well. By forcing the countries of Europe to work together, it actually created the early framework for what would later grow into the European Union. It tied the United States more firmly to Western Europe, and it solidified the role of the United States as global leader. But it also exacerbated the divide between Western Europe and the countries of Eastern Europe, which were pulled more firmly into the Soviet orbit.

By 1947, just two years after World War II ended, the United States had secured its place as a "superpower" politically, militarily, and economically. Further, it had transformed its foreign policy into one that was unapologetically international and engaged, and its foreign policy–making process was restructured to support that perspective. And Congress and the American public supported this direction for the country.

The Escalation of the Cold War: Berlin to Korea

A coup in Czechoslovakia in 1948 brought a communist government to power and furthered U.S. concerns about an expansionist Soviet Union. Those fears were made even more real in June 1948, when the Soviet Union closed all roads through East Germany into Berlin, blocking land access to the city. The United States saw this as an act of Soviet aggression against an ally and felt that it had to respond. The United States led a massive airlift that lasted one year. During that period, all necessary supplies, including food, clothing, and medicines, were brought into West Berlin by air (see figure 4.2). Stalin lifted the blockade in June 1949, but this would not be the last time that Cold War tensions were played out in this divided city.

The Creation of NATO

The Berlin blockade reinforced the importance of U.S. military involvement in Europe as well as the critical role of the United States in deterring the Soviet Union. The desire by the United States and Europe to formalize their relationship as well as to build on the need to contain communism contributed directly to the creation of the North Atlantic Treaty Organization (NATO) in April 1949. At the heart of the North Atlantic Treaty is Article 5,

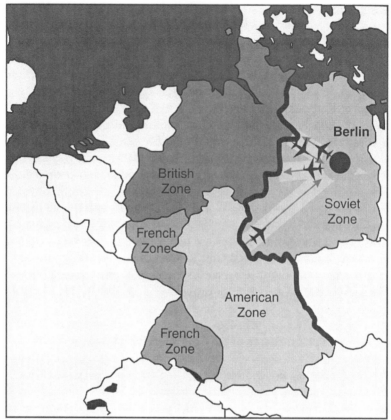

FIGURE 4.2
Germany after World War II Showing Allied Airlift to Berlin.

which unequivocally links the United States and Europe with its statement of collective security and mutual support.[17] In many ways, this statement of collective security/defense is similar to the one outlined in Article 10 of the League of Nations charter, that the collective power of nations working together would be sufficient to deter any aggressive nation.[18] In contrast to the earlier League of Nations, what made the NATO alliance credible was the link between the United States and its allies in Western Europe and, as evidenced by the Berlin blockade, the willingness of the United States to use its military power to support its allies when necessary.

The NATO treaty contains other components that were—and remain—important politically, if not necessarily militarily. For example, Article 2 specifically references the "further development of peaceful and friendly international relations by strengthening their free institutions. . . . They will seek to eliminate conflict in their international economic policies and will encourage economic collaboration between any or all of them."[19] While this made it clear that these like-minded countries (democratic and capitalist) would work together and cooperate, it further divided East and West.[20] In general, NATO represents one of the clearest, and also most enduring, examples of the U.S. postwar alliance system designed to contain communism.

The End of the Decade

Two other events occurred in 1949 that served as harsh reminders to the United States about the dangers of the Cold War. In September 1949 the Soviet Union tested an atomic bomb, making it the second country to acquire these new weapons of mass destruction. This happened years before the United States anticipated that the Soviets had the technology to do so. With that test, the world really was bipolar, and the United States could no longer count on technological domination to assure the defeat of the USSR.

Then, in October 1949, after years of civil war, Mao Tse-tung (Mao Zedong) proclaimed the creation of the People's Republic of China (PRC), a communist state. Despite the fact that Chinese and Soviet communism were different and that each country was pursuing separate goals,[21] to U.S. policymakers the creation of the PRC was another indication of the spread of communism, which they believed was monolithic and out for world domination. This perception colored many of the foreign policies that they made during the Cold War.

By 1950 the United States was established as a major power in European affairs. Further, it had started to play an active role in the Middle East when it supported the creation of the state of Israel in 1948. (The United States was the first country to recognize the creation of Israel.) In 1953 the United States cemented its place in that region when it supported the overthrow of Prime Minister Mohammed Mossadiq in Iran. Eisenhower wanted a pro-U.S. leader in Iran because of its strategic location bordering the Soviet Union as well as its supply of oil (which Mossadiq had nationalized). Thus, Eisenhower ordered the CIA to work with the Iranian military to overthrow Mossadiq. With the help of the United States, Shah Mohammed Reza Pahlevi was restored as leader of Iran following a coup in August 1953, regaining the role he had had before Mossadiq took power two years earlier. Iranian resentment toward the United States grew because, as one scholar noted, the shah was seen as "holding the American proxy in the Persian Gulf—as the protector of America's interests."[22] Those feelings would come to a head during the Iranian revolution of 1979 and the seizure of the U.S. embassy in Tehran.

NSC 68

In the 1950s, the United States was flexing its muscles globally. The National Security Act established the structure necessary for the United States to act as a global superpower. The Truman Doctrine and Marshall Plan outlined clearly the active role that the United States would take in Europe, and the creation of NATO reinforced the ties between the United States and its European allies. And the United States was willing to play an active role in parts of the world, such as the Middle East, in which it had not been involved before. However, all of these actions were guided by the strong belief in the need to contain communism led by the Soviet Union.

In April 1950, two months before the outbreak of war in Korea, the NSC issued a report to President Truman known as "NSC 68: United States Objectives and Programs for National Security." This document laid out the bipolar nature of the Cold War world and, like the Long Telegram, reinforced the belief that the goal of "those who control the Soviet Union and the international communist movement is to retain and solidify their absolute power, first in the Soviet Union and second in the areas not under their control." And because the United States is the "principal center of power in the non-Soviet world and the bulwark of opposition to Soviet expansion [it] is the principal enemy whose integrity and vitality must be subverted or destroyed . . . if the Kremlin is to achieve its fundamental design."[23]

The analysis put forth in NSC 68 (which was classified until 1975) led to the conclusion that the United States had to build up its military forces (conventional and nuclear) in order to meet its commitments and confront—and deter—the Soviet threat. Any questions about Soviet intentions were laid to rest in June, when war broke out in Korea.

War in Korea

By the time that war broke out in Korea in June 1950, the United States had been involved in Asia for about a century. However, it was the U.S. occupation of Japan following the end of World War II that made the United States a major presence in that region. When civil war broke out on the Korean peninsula, precipitating invasion by the Soviet-backed North into the U.S.-backed South, Truman felt that the United States had to act on behalf of its ally, South Korea.

Truman asked Secretary of State Dean Acheson to bring the issue before the United Nations Security Council, which condemned the invasion as a breach of the peace agreed to at the end of World War II. Voting when the Soviet ambassador was absent (and therefore could not veto the action),[24] the Security Council agreed to call for an end to fighting and required the invading armies of the North to withdraw to the thirty-eighth parallel, an arbitrary dividing line that had been established earlier. When this did not happen, on June 27 the UN Security Council called on member states to aid South Korea, created a special military command, and invited the United States to lead it.

Truman did not ask Congress for a formal declaration of war. Since this was not an act of war but merely a "police action" in support of the United Nations, he used his power as commander in chief and issued a statement consistent with the Security Council request: "I have ordered United States air and sea forces to give the Korean Government troops cover and support." He concluded the statement by asserting: "I know that all members of the United Nations will consider carefully the consequences of this latest act of aggression in Korea in defiance of the Charter of the United Nations. A return to the role of force in international affairs would have far-reaching effects. The United States will continue to uphold the rule of law."[25]

Initially under the leadership of U.S. General Douglas MacArthur,[26] the Korean War continued until an armistice was signed between North Korea and the United Nations on July 27, 1953. The armistice drew the dividing line between North and South Korea at the thirty-eighth parallel (where it had been before the war broke out) and established a demilitarized zone, patrolled by UN forces, to separate the two sides.

The Korean War, where approximately thirty-five thousand Americans lost their lives, was the first example of active U.S. military engagement under the new Cold War framework. The military was an important instrument of U.S. foreign policy and was used directly to support the foreign policy and ideological goals of confronting communism, a clear commitment to realist political thinking backed up by the use of hard power. The war was fought on the basis of President Truman's power to commit forces, and without a congressional declaration of war. It was a clear assertion of U.S. global superiority. But given the tenuous relationship between the United States and the Soviet Union, both of which had nuclear weapons, it was also a reminder of how fragile the peace could be as well as the dangers of war between the superpowers.

The Cold War at Home

To be successful, foreign policy needs the support of the American public, which is often unsophisticated about the details. Hence, the U.S. leadership simplified the policy into a depiction of democracy versus communism or "good" versus "evil." Truman helped draw the lines in some of his speeches, but actual events coupled with the coverage of those events reinforced the notion of a divided world. It was the rise of Senator Joseph McCarthy and the subsequent Red Scare that brought the Cold War home.

In February 1950, McCarthy gave a speech in which he charged that there were more than two hundred communists in the State Department. He followed this with speeches on the floor of the U.S. Senate, where he talked about "loyalty risks." Although many viewed him as an extremist and a demagogue, his attacks got the attention of the press and the public. McCarthy spoke in terms that the "average" American could understand, and his charges resonated. The Senate held investigations and hearings to look into McCarthy's allegations. Ultimately, the Senate censured him, and both McCarthy and the charges he made were discredited, but not before the damage was done and many innocent people suffered. Nonetheless, McCarthy and the Red Scare created the atmosphere at home that contributed directly to building support for U.S. military and foreign policy during the Cold War.

The Domino Theory

North Korea's invasion of South Korea exacerbated America's fears of communism and gave ammunition to those in Washington who felt that the United States was not doing enough to contain communism. Journalist Stewart Alsop wrote: "We are losing Asia fast" (referring not only to Korea but to China as well). He went further when he warned that after China, "the two pins in the second row are Burma and Indochina. If they go, the three pins in the next row, Siam, Malaya, and Indonesia, are pretty sure to topple in their turn. And if all of Asia goes . . . magnetism will almost certainly drag down the four pins of the fourth row, India, Pakistan, Japan and Philippines."[27] This belief, that if one country were to fall to communism others would follow, became the rationale for increasing support to South Korea, and it was the basis for the domino theory that contributed directly to the U.S. decision to get involved in Vietnam.

Eisenhower

The decade of the 1950s was characterized by brinkmanship and ongoing tensions between East and West. Both the United States and Soviet Union arrived at policies that each felt would solidify its own power as well as send signals to the other country. This suggests that foreign policy and military decisions made by the United States during this period not only were designed to further those policies deemed to be in the national interest but also were based on a perception of the ways in which each country viewed the other. We will examine the policies and decisions made during this period from those multiple perspectives.

In 1952 the United States elected Dwight Eisenhower president based in part on his pledge to "bring the boys home from Korea." In June 1953, about six months after Eisenhower took office, the Korean War ended with the signing of an armistice. The United States deployed troops to help patrol the border between North and South Korea and reaffirmed its commitment to protect its allies against communism. With the war in Korea, the United States expanded its reach and demonstrated that it would use military force when necessary to contain communist aggression.

The United States made some of its foreign policy decisions during this period in reaction to external events over which it had no control. For example, Stalin's death in 1953 just before the Korean War ended had a direct impact on U.S. policies. So much of U.S. foreign policy was tied to *perceptions* about the Soviet Union that Stalin's death led to uncertainty about who would succeed him and what that would mean for Soviet decision-making. In 1956, after three years of unclear leadership, Nikita Khrushchev came to power. He used a "secret" speech at a session of the twentieth congress of the Communist Party of the Soviet Union to denounce Stalin and declare that "coexistence" would become the goal of Soviet foreign policy.[28] The speech was widely covered and, taken together with announcements of Soviet reductions in armaments, might have signaled a significant change in international relations. This was not to be; the Soviet army quickly quashed the Hungarian revolution of 1956, which served as a reminder not only of Soviet military power but of its willingness to use it.

Committed to containment, Eisenhower's foreign policy built on the recommendations of NSC 68 as well as the advice of "cold warriors" such as Secretary of State John Foster Dulles. Eisenhower shifted U.S. foreign policy to rely more heavily on weapons of mass destruction as the primary deterrent against Soviet aggression. With the advent of the hydrogen bomb and apparent technological superiority, the United States had a credible threat that if this country or its allies were attacked by the Soviet Union (or China), the response would be overwhelming. This was the doctrine of "massive retaliation." However, the success of this strategy was premised on U.S. military superiority.

That assumption was put to rest in October 1957 when the Soviet Union launched a satellite, known as *Sputnik*, using a rocket that had a range of five thousand miles (capable of hitting the United States). The fact that the Soviets had this capability came as a surprise to the United States, which had not yet tested its own long-range rocket (the ICBM) successfully. As a result of *Sputnik*, there was a fundamental shift in the perceived balance of power between the United States and the Soviet Union; the Soviet Union had apparently surpassed the United States.[29] This came at a time when U.S. foreign policy was premised on the idea of military balance or even U.S. superiority, and it contributed to the acceleration of the arms race that had already started.

The Eisenhower years were characterized by international tension and a tenuous balance of power. The Suez Canal crisis of 1956 disrupted the delicate balance that existed in the Middle East. It also caused strains between the United States and France and Britain, its closest European allies. Precipitated by Egyptian president Nasser's nationalization of the Suez Canal, Britain and France conspired with Israel to overthrow the Egyptian leader. Israel invaded Egypt in October 1956, allegedly to destroy bases that had been used against Israeli settlers. As agreed, the British and French governments immediately claimed that the war would put passage through the Suez Canal in danger and called for a cease-fire. When Nasser rejected this, the two countries launched an attack against Egypt. Britain, France, and Israel all denied that they had colluded, and with U.S. pressure, the UN negotiated a cease-fire. All sides suffered as a result of this adventure. The British prime minister resigned, and the British government lost prestige within the British commonwealth. The attack by Israel fueled the hatred between Israel and the Arab peoples. The United States was angered that it had not been told of this plan by three of its allies. And to many in the United States and Western Europe, Suez was an unnecessary distraction during a time of Cold War tension.

The U-2 Incident

In May 1960, Eisenhower was looking forward to a summit meeting with Khrushchev in Paris that was to be his final diplomatic act before he stepped down as president. However, just before that meeting, the Soviet Union shot down a U.S. U-2 spy plane that had been flying over the USSR.[30] Even more embarrassing to Eisenhower, the pilot, Francis Gary Powers, was captured.[31] A series of events followed, starting with Eisenhower's claims that a "weather plane" had been lost. When the Kremlin published a photograph of the plane along with the claims that the pilot was alive, Eisenhower faced a dilemma: admit that he lied about the plane, or say that he was unaware of its mission. Either way, the outcome would not be good for Eisenhower and perceptions of the United States, and it virtually guaranteed that the summit would fail. As reporter James Reston wrote in the *New York Times*, "This was a sad and perplexed capital tonight, caught in a swirl of charges of clumsy administration, bad judgment and bad faith."[32]

In many ways, this event set the tone for the election of 1960. The Cold War to date had been a delicate balancing act that included not only military might, as defined by actual numbers of weapons, but also perceptions. The U-2 incident and the subsequent failure of the Paris summit held in August

1960 were further indicators that the perception of balance had shifted in favor of the Soviet Union. It is little wonder that one of John F. Kennedy's major election themes was a "missile gap" and that the United States was losing the arms race to the USSR.

The Kennedy Years

John F. Kennedy defeated Eisenhower's vice president, Richard Nixon, in the election of 1960 and became president. While the American public saw Kennedy as youthful, handsome, and energetic, the Soviet Union perceived him as young and inexperienced. Here, too, perceptions became reality as that image of Kennedy played into the decisions that the Soviet Union made during Kennedy's brief tenure in office; the foreign policy decisions made by Kennedy defined the direction of U.S. foreign policy for the next decade.

In August 1961, after he had been in office about seven months, Kennedy faced a crisis over Berlin. The Soviets demanded that the Western powers evacuate West Berlin, and Khrushchev threatened to sign a peace treaty with East Germany, a move that would have further isolated the Western sector of the city. When Kennedy refused to comply with Khrushchev's demands, the Soviets sealed East Berlin from the West by erecting a wall. That wall became a symbol of the Cold War divisions between East and West; when the wall came down in 1989, it was a tangible sign that the Cold War was over.

Berlin was an early crisis for the Kennedy administration. But Kennedy faced other areas of crisis and even conflict that further defined U.S. foreign policy under Kennedy and beyond. Two specific areas that had long-term implications for U.S. foreign policy were Cuba and Southeast Asia—specifically Vietnam.

Cuba

Since the Monroe Doctrine and the Roosevelt Corollary, the United States defined Cuba as being within its sphere of influence. Therefore, the United States initially welcomed Fidel Castro when he overthrew Cuban dictator Fulgencio Batista in 1959, believing that Castro would create a democracy on the island. However, in 1960, when Castro turned to the Kremlin for aid and support, the United States became concerned about the danger of creeping communism in its own hemisphere.

When Kennedy became president, he inherited and accepted a plan drawn up by the Eisenhower administration for a CIA-backed invasion of Cuba, executed with the help of Cuban exiles in the United States. The plan assumed that once the Cuban exiles landed in Cuba and the Cuban people learned about the invasion, they would rise up and overthrow Castro. But the Bay of Pigs invasion in April 1961 was a disaster. Not only did the people of Cuba not rise up, but virtually every member of the invading force was either killed or captured.

Kennedy gained respect domestically when he spoke to the American public and took responsibility for what happened. "There's an old saying that victory has a hundred fathers and defeat is an orphan. I am the responsible officer of the government," he said.[33] In contrast, the failed invasion undermined his credibility internationally by reinforcing the perception that he was inexperienced and not up to the task of managing U.S. foreign policy. At a time when perceptions mattered, this sent an important signal to the Soviet Union that, no doubt, helped prompt the other big crisis in Cuba during Kennedy's term.

The Cuban Missile Crisis of October 1962 was a critical turning point in the course of the Cold War. There are many reasons why the Soviet Union chose to put missiles in Cuba: the United States had invaded the island the year before, and the Soviet Union wanted to protect its client state; it was an assertion of Soviet superiority designed to send a signal to China[34]—Khrushchev wanted to demonstrate leadership domestically by taking a bold step internationally. But there is little doubt that the Soviet Union did so at least in part in the belief that, as a result of what happened at the Bay of Pigs, Kennedy simply was not strong enough to stop them.

The Cuban Missile Crisis undoubtedly was the most dangerous confrontation of the Cold War, a time when the two superpowers were indeed "eyeball to eyeball." President Kennedy and his closest advisors reviewed a range of options and, as tensions grew, opted for a naval blockade of the island of Cuba coupled with "back-channel" diplomacy. In retrospect, it was the decision to pursue both courses of action simultaneously that made a peaceful resolution of the crisis possible.

Countless volumes have been written about the Cuban Missile Crisis.[35] Suffice it to say, the successful—and peaceful—resolution of the conflict led to an increase in stature internationally for both Kennedy and the United States and a concomitant diminishment of both Khrushchev's and the Soviet Union's prestige. At a time when perception of balance was relative (in that a relative increase in one side came at the expense of the other), this was an important shift. In part as a result of this gamble in Cuba, Khrushchev was removed from power shortly thereafter.

In 1992, thirty years after the missile crisis, former U.S., Soviet, and Cuban officials met in Havana to discuss and explore the circumstances of the event. Following that conference Robert McNamara, who had been Kennedy's secretary of defense, revealed that "the two nations were much closer to nuclear conflict than was previously realized."[36] McNamara also disclosed that he had learned at the conference that Soviet officials "had sent Havana short-range nuclear weapons and that Soviet commanders there were authorized to use them in the event of American invasion. . . . The short-range nuclear weapons were in addition to medium-range nuclear weapons that would have required authorization from Moscow to use." Given the new information, McNamara concluded, "The actions of all three parties were shaped by *misjudgments, miscalculations* and *misinformation*," and that "in a nuclear age, such mistakes could be disastrous" (emphasis added).[37]

Nonetheless, the outcome of the Cuban Missile Crisis changed the momentum of the Cold War by shifting the balance back in favor of the United States.[38]

Vietnam

The other area of tension growing at this time that affected U.S. foreign policy far beyond the Kennedy administration was Vietnam, in Southeast Asia. During the presidential transition, Eisenhower warned the newly elected president about the dangers in Southeast Asia from communist-backed insurgencies in Vietnam and Laos. The French colony of Vietnam gained its independence after defeating France at Dien Bien Phu in 1954. This victory was followed by an agreement signed in Geneva to divide Vietnam at the seventeenth parallel until elections could be held two years later. The United States did not sign the agreement but promised to abide by its terms, pledging support to the government of Ngo Dinh Diem in the south. The northern part of the country was controlled by communists under Ho Chi Minh, who had led the fight for independence against the French. The elections were not held in 1956, and unrest continued to fester.

The seeds for protracted U.S. involvement in Southeast Asia were sown under Eisenhower when he sought congressional approval for limited U.S. involvement in the region. Congress then made clear its opposition to unilateral U.S. involvement to replace France, which had withdrawn after its defeat in 1954. Referring to the popularity of Ho Chi Minh, then-senator John F. Kennedy, according to one historian, "warned that no amount of military aid could conquer 'an enemy which has the support and covert appeal of the people.'"[39]

At the time, Laos was in the midst of an uprising led by communist Pathet Lao forces allied with the Vietnamese communists (Vietminh). Eisenhower felt that Laos, rather than Vietnam, would be the trouble spot, and he warned Kennedy that the conflict in Laos was potentially destabilizing to the region.

Eisenhower said of the communist insurgency that it was "the cork in the bottle . . . whose removal could threaten all of Southeast Asia." And in late 1960, as he was leaving office, Eisenhower warned: "We cannot let Laos fall to the Communists, even if we have to fight—with our allies or without them."[40]

Shortly after he took office, in March 1961, Kennedy made a statement on Laos echoing Eisenhower's concerns: "The security of all of Southeast Asia will be endangered if Laos loses its . . . independence. Its own safety runs with the safety of us all. . . . I want to make it clear to the American people, and to all the world, that all we want in Laos is peace, not war."[41]

However, it was Vietnam, not Laos, that proved to be the real dilemma. International negotiations settled the conflict in Laos in 1962 with an agreement reached that guaranteed neutrality for the country of Laos.[42] At the same time, the unrest in Vietnam grew, led by popular leader Ho Chi Minh, who continued to gain strength against the despised (and U.S.-backed) Diem. The Kennedy administration was very concerned about "losing" Vietnam to communism. Kennedy was also concerned about what such a loss (or even continued conflict) might mean for the rest of Southeast Asia, including Laos and Cambodia, both of which were neutral nations. To assuage this concern, in 1961 Kennedy authorized sending about four hundred U.S. special forces to Vietnam and one hundred military advisors to aid Diem in the South. Diem was overthrown and assassinated on November 2, 1963, and the civil war in Vietnam escalated. By the time of Kennedy's death three weeks later on November 22, 1963, there were twenty-three thousand Americans in the country.[43] The United States clearly was committed to Vietnam, and the president had yet to seek authorization from Congress.

Johnson: Vietnam and the Great Society

After Kennedy's assassination, Vice President Lyndon Johnson became president and inherited the problem of Vietnam. Johnson had had a long career in Congress, first in the House of Representatives and then in the Senate, where he served as majority leader from 1955 until he became vice president in 1961. That experience influenced the ways in which Johnson made decisions and especially his understanding of the need for congressional support for those policies that he thought were important.

Johnson came into office committed to making change domestically by enacting a series of laws to promote what became known as "the Great Society." However, Johnson also was aware that an unpopular and costly war in Vietnam could put his domestic policies at risk. A Congress that was pressured by constituents because of the war would be far less likely to compromise or support presidential initiatives in other (domestic) areas.[44] The policies of the Johnson administration illustrate clearly the confluence of domestic and international politics and how one can easily affect—and derail—the other.

The Tonkin Gulf Resolution

By 1964 domestic turmoil within the United States was increasing. The civil rights movement was growing in strength, as was the women's movement. Leaders like Martin Luther King, Jr., energized the black community, and the Vietnam War became a rallying cry as minorities were disproportionately being asked to fight—and die—there. Johnson knew that there was a direct relationship between what would happen in Vietnam and domestic politics.

In 1970, after he was out of office, Johnson reflected on the dilemma that he faced as president, trying to balance the escalating war effort and domestic reforms. At that time Johnson told historian Doris Kearns Goodwin: "If I left the woman I really loved—the Great Society—in order to get involved with that bitch of a war on the other side of the world, then I would lose everything at home. All my programs. All my hopes to feed the hungry and shelter the homeless. All my dreams to provide education and medical care to the browns and blacks and the lame and the poor. But if I left that war and let the Communists take over South Vietnam, then I would have been seen as a coward and my nation would be seen as an appeaser and we would find it impossible to accomplish anything for anybody anywhere on the entire globe."[45] Hence, Johnson believed that the United States would have to continue to fight in Vietnam, regardless of the costs.

The war in Vietnam escalated slowly, and still Johnson did not have official congressional authorization to send troops into combat. Johnson knew that he needed congressional backing and domestic support for the war effort. His opportunity to get these came in August 1964 when two U.S. destroyers, the *Maddox* and the *Turner Joy*, were allegedly fired on in the Gulf of Tonkin. The first attack against the *Maddox* came on August 2; a second one, two days later, was questionable, however. The commander of the *Maddox* later admitted that he did not think they were fired on at all. Rather, he indicated that "weather effects" and "overeager" sonar operators were probably to blame rather than an attack by the North Vietnamese. Nonetheless, the incident gave Johnson the excuse to seek congressional support for the war.

On August 5, 1964, Johnson sent a message to Congress. The thrust of his public statement was the need for the United States to honor its commitments to meet communist aggression in Southeast Asia under the terms of the Southeast Asia Collective Defense Treaty (SEATO), approved in 1955 as part of the Cold War alliance system.[46] Johnson asked Congress "to join in affirming the national determination that all such attacks will be met, and that the United States will continue in its basic policy of assisting the free nations of the area to defend their freedom."[47]

On August 7, 1964, Congress passed a joint resolution as Johnson requested. (The text of the resolution had been drawn up months earlier.) The heart of the resolution, and the power that Johnson sought, is found in Section 1: "The Congress approves and supports the determination of the President, as Commander in Chief, *to take all necessary measures* to repel any armed attack against the forces of the United States and to prevent further aggression" (emphasis added). Section 3 keeps the resolution active until "the President shall determine that the peace and security of the area is reasonably assured . . . *except that it may be terminated earlier by concurrent resolution of the Congress*" (emphasis added).[48]

Congress debated the resolution for two days before the House passed it on a 416 to 0 vote, and the Senate by a vote of 88 to 2. One of the two members of the Senate who voted against the resolution was Oregon Republican Wayne Morse, "who objected to the resolution on the basis of his belief that the resolution was indirectly a declaration of war and that it violated Article 1, Section 8, of the U.S. Constitution."[49] The other was Democratic Senator Ernest Gruening of Alaska, who called the resolution "a predated declaration of war."[50]

The Tonkin Gulf Resolution is significant for a number of reasons. First, it gave Johnson virtually open-ended permission to take whatever actions he deemed necessary in Vietnam. Second, it left the timing open ended so that the resolution (and the powers that went with it) would remain in force until either the president determined that the circumstances had changed or Congress terminated it, which it did in January 1971. And third, it clearly shifted the policy-making balance of power. Despite questions of constitutionality, when Congress passed the Tonkin Gulf Resolution, it gave the power to initiate military action to the president (Congress would reassert itself and take some of that power back under President Nixon). In remarks made when he signed the resolution into law on August 10, 1964, Johnson said that it stood "squarely on the corners of the Constitution," and "confirms and reinforces powers of the Presidency."[51]

After the resolution passed, Johnson escalated the war in Vietnam. By 1966, 450,000 American troops were in Vietnam, and General William Westmoreland, commander of U.S. forces in Vietnam from 1965 through 1968, requested an increase to 542,000 by the end of 1967.[52] By mid-1967, according to one historian, "Westmoreland conceded that if his request for an additional 200,000 men was granted, the war might go on for as long as two years. If not, he warned, it could last five years or even longer."[53] In other words, the United States was in the midst of what came to be known as a quagmire. Fighting intensified during this period, and so did battle deaths; the number of Americans killed in action rose to 13,500 by late 1967.[54] In order to keep the war effort going, draft calls increased as well. The increase in number of men drafted coupled with growing American casualties and no end in sight to the conflict contributed to opposition to the war at home.

The Great Society

While Johnson was dealing with the Vietnam War, domestically he continued to push his Great Society policies. In 1964 in response to the civil rights movement, Congress passed the Civil Rights Act, outlawing discrimination in public accommodations and in the use of federal funds and giving more protection in voting rights. Passage of this bill also carried a powerful message that change is possible when the voice of the people is heard in Washington, a message that would be applied a few years later by war protesters. In 1965, under Johnson's direction, Congress passed the Medicare Bill, a housing bill, the Voting Rights Act, an Economic Opportunity Act to fight the "war on poverty," a Clean Air Act, and measures to create a new Department of Housing and Urban Development and National Foundations for the Arts and Humanities. Between 1965 and 1968, Congress passed five hundred reform laws, made possible in part by Johnson's understanding of and ability to work with the legislative branch.

While these represented a great success for Johnson's domestic priorities, the war in Vietnam continued to escalate and was taking a toll economically. In order to continue to pay for the war effort, ultimately Johnson had to cut back on spending for the domestic programs that he had fought so hard to enact. The size of the federal deficit rose, as did taxes. And public discontent over the course and conduct of the war was growing.

In January 1968, the situation in Vietnam worsened. During the cease-fire in place for the lunar new year—the Tet holiday—the forces of the North launched a major surprise offensive. The Tet offensive lasted about one month, and even though the South "won," defined by a greater number of North Vietnamese troops lost than South Vietnamese or U.S. forces, it was a propaganda victory for the North. The media played and replayed images of North Vietnamese and Viet Cong troops attacking the South, including the U.S. embassy in Saigon, which raised questions in the minds of the public about who really was winning the war. Walter Cronkite, the anchor of CBS nightly news and known as "the most trusted man in America," having recently returned from Vietnam, concluded his broadcast on February 27, 1968, with a commentary in which he said: "To say that we are closer to victory today is to believe, in the

face of the evidence, the optimists who have been wrong in the past. To suggest
we are on the edge of defeat is to yield to unreasonable pessimism. To say that
we are mired in stalemate seems the only realistic, yet unsatisfactory, conclusion."[55] This further fueled the antiwar movement at home.

In March 1968, at the time of the first Democratic primary contest for
the presidency, Johnson's approval rating had dropped to 26 percent. When
peace candidate Eugene McCarthy (Democratic senator from Minnesota)
won 42 percent of the vote in the New Hampshire primary, it sent a strong
signal to Johnson about how the public felt about his performance.[56] On
March 31, Johnson announced "a unilateral halt of all United States air and
naval bombardment of most of the populated areas of the north." He called
on the North Vietnamese government to join peace negotiations that would
bring an end to the war.[57] And then he announced: "I shall not seek, and I will
not accept, the nomination of my party for another term as your President."[58]
He later said that he had had enough: "I felt that I was being chased on all
sides by a giant stampede coming at me from all directions. On one side, the
American people were stampeding me to do something about Vietnam. On
another side, the inflationary economy was booming out of control. Up ahead
were dozens of danger signs pointing to another summer of riots in the cities.
I was being forced over the edge by rioting blacks, demonstrating students,
marching welfare mothers, squawking professors, and hysterical reporters."[59]

Johnson learned an important lesson in American foreign policy: it doesn't
matter how successful a president is domestically because an unpopular war
will make a difference at the polls. While Americans generally vote economics
and "pocketbook" issues, when the country is fighting a war that involves the
deaths of Americans in a country far away and with a dubious relationship to
national interest, foreign policy will become a more important issue.

Nixon

Richard Nixon defeated Vice President Hubert Humphrey in the 1968 election and became president in January 1969. He inherited the war in Vietnam
as one of his foreign policy issues. The Vietnam War was fought against the
backdrop of the Cold War; one of the most important foreign policy legacies
of the Nixon administration was the way he handled two of the major communist adversaries of the United States, the Soviet Union and China, while
also trying to extricate the country from Vietnam. Guided in part by Henry
Kissinger, who served first as national security advisor and then as secretary
of state, Nixon pursued a policy of détente, or reconciliation, with the Soviet
Union and began the process that resulted in opening diplomatic relations

with China. These two competing trends, fighting communism in Southeast Asia on the one hand and reconciliation with major communist powers on the other, are among the most interesting facets of the evolution of U.S. foreign policy in the period.

Escalation in Vietnam

The Vietnam War escalated during the Nixon years. As opposition to the war grew domestically, Nixon changed the strategy for fighting that war by reducing the number of troops on the ground and relying more heavily on air attacks. In 1969, in an assertion of congressional authority, Congress passed a nonbinding "Sense of the Senate" resolution that told the president he could not commit additional troops or encumber funds for the war without the express permission of that body. Although this did not have the force of law, it sent the important message that Congress was not pleased with the conduct of the war and that its members were "hearing" their constituents. It also made it clear that Congress would assert its constitutional powers, especially those aspects regarding declaring war, that it had given to the president, or that a series of presidents had taken. In April 1970, Nixon informed the country that over the next year he authorized the withdrawal of more than one hundred fifty thousand ground troops from Vietnam.

However, by the end of the month, the public was shocked to learn that U.S. forces had entered Cambodia, which was neutral in the conflict. This led to outrage and protests across the country. Public anger grew when on May 4, 1970, National Guard troops shot and killed four students who were protesting at Kent State University in Ohio. Many college and university campuses across the country suspended classes so that students and faculty could protest the war and the policies of the Nixon administration. Protestors went to Washington to demand that Congress take action to bring the war to an end.

Congress debated the wisdom of the Tonkin Gulf Resolution and the power it had given to the president, and opposition to the "blank check" given through the resolution grew. In response to the growing concerns about the conduct of the war, as well as the president's virtually unchecked ability to escalate it, on January 12, 1971, Congress repealed the Gulf of Tonkin Resolution.

By 1970, eager to find a way to end the war, Kissinger began "secret" peace negotiations. Meanwhile, Nixon continued to authorize bombing Vietnam and Cambodia. In 1972, even with the troop withdrawals, there were more than forty thousand Americans stationed in Vietnam.[60] On January 27, 1973, a cease-fire agreement was signed in Paris, and in 1975 Vietnam was unified as a communist country. Approximately fifty-nine thousand Americans had died in Vietnam.

War Powers

Repeal of the Gulf of Tonkin Resolution in 1971 was the first step in the assertion of congressional authority to regain some control of the foreign policy process and to begin, once again, to enforce the checks and balances between the two branches outlined in the Constitution. As the war went on with no end in sight, and as protests grew, Congress came under increasing pressure to limit what was seen as the abuse of presidential power regarding the ability to commit the United States to war. The impetus to do something was pushed further by the Watergate scandal and by questions about the integrity of the president. In response to these growing concerns, on November 7, 1973, Congress passed Public Law 93-148, known as the War Powers Resolution, over Nixon's veto.

The War Powers Resolution states that its purpose is "to fulfill the intent of the framers of the Constitution of the United States and insure that the collective judgment of *both* the Congress and the President will apply to the introduction of United States Armed Forces into hostilities, or into situations where imminent involvement in hostilities is clearly indicated" (emphasis added).[61] The law clearly asserts that any time U.S. forces will be sent into hostile or even potentially hostile situations, the president must consult with and report to Congress. It also specifies the need for consultation between the president and Congress before introducing troops into hostility, and it contains the provisions under which the president must report to Congress "in the absence of a declaration of war." The resolution clearly was designed to limit the possibility of giving any subsequent presidents the blank check that Johnson and Nixon had to commit the United States to conflict and to escalate that conflict without a formal declaration of war. It also was designed to make it very difficult for Congress to once again cede all its war-powers authority to the president.[62]

Nixon vetoed the bill and questioned its constitutionality, as have subsequent presidents (who have generally complied with it), but Congress overrode the veto. Specifically, presidents have questioned the provisions in Section 5, "Congressional Action," under which the president must end the use of force within sixty days unless Congress authorizes otherwise (Section b) and which require that forces be removed "if the Congress so directs by concurrent resolution" (Section c). Critics argue that these provisions usurp the president's constitutional power as commander in chief. And there are always questions of enforcement.[63] Nonetheless, the War Powers Resolution had the desired effect of putting the president on notice that he should report to Congress before deploying U.S. troops. That puts the burden on Congress to determine how to respond. In that sense, the law helped reaffirm the balance in roles and responsibility between the executive and legislative branches.

The Soviet Union, Détente, and Arms Control

As the war in Vietnam was growing, so were the number of nuclear weapons worldwide and expenditures for defense.[64] The vast number of nuclear weapons formed the basis of "mutually assured destruction"—or MAD—the deterrent allegedly keeping the United States and Soviet Union from attacking each other or their allies. To help get spending and weapons proliferation under control, the Soviet Union and United States entered into a process of discussion and negotiation designed to limit the spread of nuclear weapons.

The arms control process started in 1969 and was part of détente, defined by Henry Kissinger as "an environment in which competitors can regulate and restrain their differences and ultimately move from competition to cooperation."[65] One of the things that make this policy and the arms control process in general so intriguing from the perspective of American foreign policy is that it is an idealistic approach (the notion of cooperation) employed by a decision-maker (Kissinger) who, in many ways, was the ultimate realist. The process resulted in a successful agreement, the Strategic Arms Limitation Treaty (SALT I), signed in 1972, and set the stage for subsequent agreements. More important, it made relations between the United States and the Soviet Union more *predictable* by establishing an ongoing forum for discussion and conversation that continued through the duration of the Cold War. Regardless of the level of tension between the two countries, the discussion and negotiation process continued in the belief that it was in the national interest of both.

SALT I satisfied the immediate needs of both countries. "The Soviet Union gained recognition of its status as the United States' equal; the United States gained a commitment from the Soviet Union to moderate its quest for preeminent power in the world."[66] SALT I did not stop the arms race. Rather, it set limits for specific nuclear weapons, providing a ceiling up to which both sides could build, and then allowed both sides to channel additional resources into other weapon systems. At a time when both countries had enough nuclear delivery systems to obliterate each other, this was seen as an important step.

China and Normalization

As was the case with arms control and détente with the Soviet Union, in many ways only an administration known for its virulent anticommunist position could begin the process of normalizing relations with China.[67] The United States did not recognize the PRC, referring to the Nationalist government of Taiwan as "China." But in 1971, Nixon sent Kissinger to Beijing to begin the process of "normalization." The desire for rapprochement between the two countries was born of *pragmatism*, not idealism. For China, closer relations with the United States would serve as an important balance to its growing antagonism with the Soviet Union. For the United States and for Nixon in particular, stronger relations with China would allow him to play China against the USSR, appear to weaken China's ties to Hanoi at a time when the course of the Vietnam War was not going well, and help Nixon politically by allowing him to run for reelection in 1972 stressing what he had done to help achieve a more peaceful world, rather than by having the Vietnam War as the main foreign policy focus.

In 1972, President Nixon visited mainland China, the first American president to do so. At the end of the trip, Nixon issued a statement known as the Shanghai Communiqué, that has defined U.S. policy toward China and Taiwan since that time. Using language that had been negotiated earlier, the document states: "The United States acknowledges that all Chinese on either side of the Taiwan Strait maintain there is but one China and that Taiwan is part of China. The United States does not challenge that position. It reaffirms its interest in a peaceful settlement of the Taiwan question by the Chinese themselves." This phrase articulates the "one China" policy that remains in place today. In the document the United States also declared: "With this in mind, it [the United States] affirms the ultimate objective of the withdrawal of all U.S. forces and military installations from Taiwan. In the meantime, it will progressively reduce its forces and military installations on Taiwan *as the tension in the area diminishes*" (emphasis added).[68] Thus the United States will maintain forces and serve as a protector to Taiwan as long as it perceives there is danger of armed attack by China and forceful attempt to take over the island, that is, until the status quo changes. Because of this initiative, seven years later, in 1979 under President Carter, the United States established full diplomatic relations with China.

Nixon, the quintessential realist politician, had successfully orchestrated rapprochement with the Soviet Union and China, thereby easing Cold War tensions and shifting the balance of global international relations. By putting a process into place for ongoing negotiations between the United States and the Soviet Union, he ensured that the two sides would continue to talk, which would also help minimize tensions. And he negotiated an end to the war in Vietnam, although belatedly. Nonetheless, by the time of his resignation in 1974, his foreign policy successes were lost in the face of deep domestic divisions and political scandal.

When Nixon resigned in August 1974, he was succeeded by his vice president, Gerald Ford. Ford's primary goal was to restore the faith of the American people in government in general and in the presidency in particular. But he also inherited an economy with rampant inflation (up to 12 percent in 1974) and a growing recession.

Carter

Jimmy Carter defeated Gerald Ford in the election of 1976. Carter believed in the need to restore the perception of integrity to the government and he ran as an "outsider" who could bring a new tone to Washington. He also wanted to help the country recover from the "Vietnam hangover" that made the United States hesitant to get involved in any international conflict.

In his campaign and early in his presidency, Carter brought back to foreign policy the idealist perspective advocated by Woodrow Wilson, and he vowed to make the fight for human rights the centerpiece of his foreign policy agenda. In March 1977, Carter addressed the UN General Assembly and reiterated that commitment to global human rights. While the Carter administration pursued the foreign policy perceived as consistent with the basic tenets on which the United States was founded (freedom and liberty for all), it also angered many of the international leaders who saw this as a direct attack on their domestic policies. For example, Carter angered the Soviet Union by praising Soviet dissidents who had dared to speak up against the government.

The Carter years (1977–1981) were marked by a series of both dramatic successes and notable failures in foreign policy. The successes included the Camp David accords signed in March 1979, the first major agreement between Israel and an Arab nation (Egypt), which resulted in Israel's withdrawal from the Sinai (and President Carter subsequently won a Nobel Peace Prize for this accomplishment). He also successfully negotiated the treaties returning the Panama Canal to the control of Panama and making the canal a neutral waterway open to all shipping traffic after 1999. The United States was given the permanent right to defend the waterway and its neutrality.

The Panama Canal treaties resulted in a fight between the president and Congress. Given an increasingly assertive Congress that did not see why the treaties were to the advantage of the United States, Carter had to fight for their passage at great political cost. He successfully negotiated the SALT II treaty with the Soviet Union, thereby continuing the arms control process started by Nixon. But in the wake of the Soviet invasion of Afghanistan in December 1979, and in the face of a hostile Congress, Carter never submitted it for ratification, although he did commit the United States to abide by its terms.

Perhaps the most spectacular foreign policy failure of the Carter years was the Iranian revolution and the way in which Carter handled the taking of American hostages at the embassy in Tehran.[69] Day after day nothing happened as network news anchors, such as Walter Cronkite, began each broadcast with an announcement about how many days the hostages had been held. This contributed to an undermining of public confidence in Carter, and when he finally did authorize a rescue attempt, it was over the objections of members of his cabinet such as Secretary of State Cyrus Vance, who resigned in protest. The rescue attempt on April 24, 1980, was a dismal failure, and the entire experience on top of four years of economic recession, high gas prices, unparalleled inflation, and other domestic economic woes contributed directly to Carter's defeat at the polls in November 1980 by Ronald Reagan.

Carter's administration is instructive in the course of American foreign policy. In part, Carter inherited the economic problems that were the result of years of war as well as domestic ills and bad decisions. But he chose to pursue a foreign policy based on values and idealism at a time when pragmatism and realism probably would have been more successful. He saw issues in black-and-white terms and presented them to the American public and to the world in that way. While this encouraged and empowered some, it also inflamed and alienated others, both at home and abroad. Implementing foreign policy successfully requires domestic support as well as international cooperation, and Carter was not able to get either. It was only after the Cold War ended, and years after he stepped down as president and took on the role of "elder statesman," that Carter came to play an important role internationally in pursuit of peace and human rights and won a Nobel Prize for his efforts.

Growing Engagement

United States foreign policy evolved significantly between the end of World War II and the election of Ronald Reagan. The early Cold War years were defined by a foreign policy of realism and power politics, and every aspect of the policy-making apparatus was aligned to achieve its foreign policy and military goals. The United States was the unchallenged leader of the West, and its vision created and guided the international order for much of the Cold War.

U.S. engagement in Vietnam changed much of that. Involved initially as part of the global fight against communism, in Vietnam the United States learned that a superior military fighting force, created to deter or if necessary fight a war against another major power, is basically useless in the type of guerrilla war it fought in Vietnam. Further, U.S. decision-makers learned that a war cannot be fought (and won) without the ongoing support of the

American public, and that support can come only from a clear articulation of why the war is necessary and its relationship to national interest.

By the end of the Carter administration, the United States was suffering from "Vietnam hangover" and national self-doubt. It was these negative forces that Ronald Reagan came into office determined to fight. For Reagan, the United States was still a superpower, and it had to start acting like one again.

Applying Foreign Policy Concepts:
The Tonkin Gulf Resolution and the Lessons of Vietnam

When Johnson went to the Congress with the Tonkin Gulf Resolution in August 1964, the result was an escalation of the war in Vietnam. Johnson knew that he would need congressional approval to send in combat troops and to stage the military buildup that he thought would be necessary for the United States to win that war. What he did not know then and could not have anticipated was the fact that the United States would not win that war and that Vietnam would be unified as a communist country.

In May 1975, approximately one month after the fall of Vietnam, then-secretary of state Henry Kissinger drafted a memo to President Gerald Ford outlining what he saw as the major lessons of the war. Although the memo was never sent nor signed, it is now available publicly and has some important insights. Among the lessons Kissinger notes are "the importance of absolute honesty and objectivity in all reporting, within and from the Government as well as from the press." Another lesson is "a dedication to consistency," in terms of the reasons given for going to war, and then for seeing that war through." And he speaks in this memo of the need to "ask ourselves whether it was all worth it, or at least what benefits we did gain."

If they had been applied by Johnson in 1964, those lessons and others that Kissinger articulated in this memo might have changed the decisions that Johnson made and altered the course of the war.[70]

The Case

By early 1964, President Lyndon Johnson realized that he needed to do something to address the growing conflict in Vietnam. President Kennedy had sent special forces units into that country, but he had not taken the issue to Congress. For the most part, the American public was largely ignorant about the war brewing in Southeast Asia.

Johnson was a product of the Congress and understood the often difficult relationship that exists between the executive and legislative branches of government. Although he was not asking for a formal declaration of war, politically he knew that it would be in his best interest to seek congressional approval to escalate the war in Vietnam. Not doing so would mean running the risk that Congress would deny support for the domestic programs that he was working on, collectively known as "the Great Society."

Johnson faced a dilemma. Once he went to Congress to ask for congressional approval to escalate the war, it would be critical that the United States win the war. The United States had little experience fighting the type of guerrilla warfare such as the one growing in Vietnam, and the French, America's allies, had lost to the Vietnamese ten years earlier. And Johnson knew that he would have to make the case to the American people that fighting this war on the other side of the world was in the U.S. national interest.

Anticipating the need to go to Congress, Johnson drafted a resolution justifying the escalation of the war. In August 1964, he was given the opportunity to use that resolution. Two U.S. naval ships, the *Maddox* and the *Turner Joy*, were allegedly fired on in the Gulf of Tonkin. Although the circumstances surrounding the attacks were murky, Johnson wanted to take advantage of them to ask Congress for permission to meet such attacks with military force. Congress gave that permission along with support for the president to "take all necessary measures to repel any armed attack against the forces of the United States and to prevent further aggression."[71]

The Gulf of Tonkin Resolution allowed Johnson to do what he wanted to do and escalate the war. The United States ended its involvement in Vietnam in 1973, and North and South Vietnam were unified two years later as a communist country, but 59,000 Americans lost their lives in that war. Domestically, opposition to the war put enough pressure on Lyndon Johnson so that he decided not to run for reelection in 1968. A growing peace movement reached its climax in 1970, following the deaths of four students who were protesting the war at Kent State University and had been shot by the National Guard. In response, colleges and universities around the country closed as students and faculty protested the war and held "teach-ins" about it. In January 1971, Congress repealed the resolution, and two years later it passed the War Powers Resolution to rein in the power of the president to engage the United States in foreign conflicts or war without congressional approval.

It took many years for the United States to recover from the "Vietnam hangover." The perception of U.S. weakness as a result of its defeat clouded the ways in which other countries viewed the United States, which affected its foreign policy options. Veterans returning home from the war were shunned as domestic opposition to the war became confused with hostility toward those who fought it. The domino theory proved not to be true, as the creation of a communist government in Vietnam did not lead to communism sweeping the rest of the region. And the peace movement melded with the women's and civil rights movements, resulting in major social upheaval and later change within the United States.

What Would You Do If . . .

The time is 1964. President Johnson has been president for just over one year, and he inherited a war in Southeast Asia. His highest priority was his domestic agenda, but he knew that that could be held hostage to an unsuccessful war in Vietnam. Johnson knew that he needed to make some critical choices that would affect not only his administration, but his legacy and U.S. policies in general for years to come.

What would you do if you were a close advisor to President Johnson and he looked to you for recommendations on what to do about Vietnam? You have just received word that two U.S. ships may or may not have been fired on in the Gulf of Tonkin. But the details of the alleged attacks are sketchy at best. Given what you know now, including the consequences (both intended and unintended), what would you recommend that President Johnson do, and why? In your assessment, you will need to address what course would be in the U.S. national interest at that time and why.

5

Beyond the Cold War

Reagan through Clinton

T HUS FAR, WE HAVE IDENTIFIED A NUMBER of broad themes that help explain the direction of U.S. foreign policy from the nation's founding through the Cold War, as well as some of the decisions that were made and why. Under the leadership of a series of strong presidents, with domestic and congressional support, and as a result of changing international conditions, the United States became a major power, militarily, politically, and economically. President Truman altered the foreign policy decision-making apparatus (i.e., the bureaucracy) to allow the government to implement more effectively the policies of a "superpower" during the Cold War, which lasted about forty-five years. The structure, framework, and approach that were then in place made it more difficult for the country to make the adjustments required for a post–Cold War world.

The 1980s started with the election of Ronald Reagan, who early in his administration referred to the Soviet Union as "the evil empire." He promoted building a weapons shield to protect the United States from incoming Soviet missiles, and he increased spending for defense and the military. In other words, he did everything that a Cold War president needed to do. And just as President Kennedy stood next to the Berlin Wall in 1963 to proclaim "Ich bin ein Berliner,"[1] in 1987 President Reagan told Mikhail Gorbachev, the leader of the Soviet Union, to "tear down this wall."[2] Two years later, in 1989, that would happen. If Cold War tensions could be measured by policies regarding Berlin, then the fall of the Berlin Wall was the best indicator that the old order literally was crumbling. It would take two more years for the Soviet Union to fall. After years of waiting for this to happen, was the United States ready for it when it did?

When Reagan's vice president, George H. W. Bush, was elected president in 1988, the Cold War international order was disintegrating. Democratic revolutions were sweeping Eastern Europe. One after another the communist governments fell and were replaced by democratically elected leaders who believed in capitalist market economies. President Bush proclaimed the creation of a "new world order," as distinguished from the "old" Cold War order.

After decades of proclaiming that the West would inevitably win the Cold War, it did. Yet it happened so suddenly that all the United States could do was react to international events that quickly became priorities in the absence of the Cold War framework: wars in the Middle East, ethnic strife and genocide in Yugoslavia and Africa, and an apparent increase in terrorism. Divisions arose between the United States and its closest allies about what policies to follow in each of these cases. While hints of these issues were present during the Cold War, they were either ignored or dealt with as "sideshows" to the more important issue of U.S.-Soviet relations. The Cold War goal of containing communism (broadly defined) provided the focus for all aspects of U.S. policy since 1945. After 1989,[3] the United States had new and different challenges to face. And without the Cold War framework as its guide, U.S. foreign policy often appeared rudderless.

This chapter focuses on the period from 1981 and the start of the Reagan administration through the administration of Bill Clinton (2000) with a focus on what the changing international order meant for U.S. foreign policy without the Cold War framework to guide it. We begin here with the prelude to the end of the Cold War and address the fall of the Berlin Wall, the implosion of the Soviet Union, and the democratic revolutions that swept the countries of the former Eastern Bloc. In this chapter, we also address the plethora of ethnic and nationalist conflicts that emerged following the Cold War and the challenges that they posed to American foreign policy-making.

From Cold War to Democratic Revolutions

"On the day of Mr. Reagan's inauguration as president in 1981," writes one historian, "the Iranians released their American hostages. That closed a humiliating and frustrating episode."[4] One can speculate as to why Iran chose to release them on that day; suffice it to say, it provided a powerful start to the Reagan administration. Whereas Jimmy Carter's administration ended in apparent failure, Ronald Reagan came into office the image of American strength. No longer would U.S. foreign policy be based on "soft" ideas, such as human rights, but it would once again be tied to strength and power.[5] While the American public might have yearned for such a change, it came at a price.

Reagan's election signaled a return to a strong executive whose administration defined the policies and the priorities of the nation at that time. And, for the most part, despite its earlier assertions of oversight, Congress complied with and approved Reagan's domestic policies and priorities, even though they resulted in budget deficits. In what became known as "the Reagan Revolution," Reagan focused his attention on domestic issues, especially the economy. He cut taxes across the board and, concomitantly, slashed social programs, many of which had been in place since the New Deal. He focused on "supply-side economics" that promised prosperity by putting more money into the hands of people who would spend it, thereby stimulating the economy. He blamed the recession that hit the country in 1981 and 1982 on residual effects of Carter's policies (as opposed to the impact of Vietnam), and when the economy started to recover before the congressional elections of 1984, he took the credit. And Reagan authorized an increase in spending for defense in order to counter what he had called "America's weakened defense" during the election campaign.

Reagan successfully energized the American public and instilled a sense of pride in the country once again. The United States returned to the policies of "us versus them," good versus evil, democracy versus communism, that were tempered under Carter. However, Reagan's hard-line rhetoric, such as his "evil empire" speeches in June 1982 and March 1983,[6] reawakened Cold War fears in the Soviet Union as well as within many in the United States.

The hostile rhetoric put the Soviet Union on warning that the Cold War was not over. In response, the Soviet leadership once again denounced the United States. In the words of one historian, "Matters were not helped when, within a few months of Mr. Reagan's inauguration, America's nuclear force was twice in one week activated following erroneous computer warnings that Soviet missile attacks were on the way."[7] Hence, U.S. foreign policy during at least the first years of Reagan's eight years in office was characterized by increasingly hostile rhetoric, an arms buildup, and a sense that the United States was reliving the policies of decades earlier, before détente and arms control.[8]

When the Berlin Wall fell in 1989, then-president George H. W. Bush as well as Reagan took the credit. Yet the end of the Cold War was the result of the confluence of many factors; Reagan just happened to be president when a series of critical events started to unfold. Shortly before he left office, when asked about the role he had played in facilitating the end of the Cold War, Reagan referred to himself as "a supporting actor." When asked at a press conference who deserved the credit for the changes in the Soviet Union that ultimately led to the end of the Cold War, Reagan replied that "Mr. Gorbachev deserves most of the credit, as the leader of this country."[9]

There is little doubt that Reagan's policies of increasing spending for defense and ratcheting up the hostile rhetoric pushed an already significantly diminished Soviet Union to the brink. The priority of Mikhail Gorbachev, who became general secretary of the Communist Party of the Soviet Union in 1985 just as Reagan was beginning his second term in office, was to demilitarize the Soviet Union so that much-needed resources could be diverted to the depleted economy. Further, since he came of age in the post-Stalin era, Gorbachev had a different perspective on the West than previous leaders, and he saw Europe and Russia as sharing a "common home." In Gorbachev's first meeting with a Western leader, Prime Minister Margaret Thatcher reported that she was impressed and described Gorbachev as someone she could work with. Further, Gorbachev articulated his apparently forward-looking ideas about glasnost (openness) and perestroika (economic restructuring away from a command economy) in his book *Perestroika*, which was published in the West and was readily available.[10]

Reagan also was receptive to Gorbachev's ideas and was willing to work with him on implementing new policies. Reagan believed that a change in the direction of the Soviet Union would be in the best interests of the United States and therefore modified his own approach over time, becoming less "cold warrior" and more the diplomat whose primary goal was to encourage Gorbachev to continue down the new path that he had chosen. Doing this required personal contact, and the two leaders met periodically to outline areas of common interest. Reagan was so successful that by the time his administration ended, the Cold War was on a course to its inevitable end.[11]

Reagan and Gorbachev actively pursued arms control talks as part of their mutually beneficial policy agenda. The meeting between the two men in Reykjavik, Iceland, in 1986 appeared to be a failure, yet it led directly to the INF Treaty limiting intermediate-range nuclear weapons signed in December 1987. This treaty specified the destruction of all land-based missiles with a range of between 500 and 5,500 kilometers (which could strike from Europe into Soviet territory and vice versa), with specific provisions for on-site inspection. Not only was this treaty seen as important because it eliminated a certain type of weapon system, but it laid the groundwork for further arms control agreements leading to the destruction of other types of weapons. As was the case with Richard Nixon, whose anticommunist stance made it possible for him to negotiate with both the Soviet Union and China without charges that he was "selling out" the country, Ronald Reagan, another "cold warrior," was able to negotiate successfully with Gorbachev.

Iran-Contra

In the West, Reagan was celebrated for helping to bring about the fall of communism. But the Iran-Contra affair was a different type of foreign policy situation that also defined this administration. "Iran-Contra" refers to a complex set of policies and actions that led to congressional hearings and a federal commission to explore what really happened. One outcome of Iran-Contra was a clear statement of presidential responsibility. It is also another example of the assertion of congressional oversight regarding the executive branch. And it raised—and then clarified—some important points about who holds ultimate responsibility for making and implementing U.S. foreign policy, something that had become fuzzy over time.

A revolution in Nicaragua in 1980 resulted in the overthrow of the Somoza regime, which had been supported by the United States. It was replaced by the left-leaning Sandinista government, which the Reagan administration saw not only as communist but also as a potential threat to U.S. influence in Latin America. Hence, overthrowing the new Sandinista government by supporting a group of rebels, known as the Contras, became a U.S. policy priority. However, within the United States, public opinion polls indicated that the American people did not support military involvement in Nicaragua, which led the government to try to conceal any possible involvement in the conflict. In 1984, in response to CIA actions to mine the harbors of Nicaragua, Congress passed the Boland Amendment, making it illegal to support "directly or indirectly, military or paramilitary operations in Nicaragua." This was one of three amendments limiting U.S. action in Nicaragua. Ignoring this prohibition, members of the National Security Council (NSC) staff devised an undercover operation to aid the Contras secretly, through third-party support.[12]

In 1986, stories surfaced that the United States had secretly sold weapons to Iran, an enemy of this country since the revolution of 1979, with the profits from the sale funneled to the Contras. Further, in exchange for getting the weapons, Iran promised to ensure the release of hostages being held in Lebanon. When asked about the reports of this linkage, Reagan denied the basic facts. But critical questions remained unanswered, and the president convened a special commission to investigate. As a result of the commission's investigations and findings, most of the blame fell on Robert (Bud) McFarlane, Reagan's former national security advisor, and NSC staff member Colonel Oliver North, who was found guilty of lying to Congress in hearings about the incident. It was clear that the whole scheme was set up in a way that sheltered the president and vice president by keeping the details from them. (During the Watergate hearings, this approach was known as "plausible deniability.")

Although neither President Reagan nor Vice President Bush was charged with or indicted on any specific crime related to Iran-Contra, the uncertainty about whether they were—or were not—involved raised important questions about who is responsible for making and implementing U.S. foreign policy, and what responsibility the president does or should have when illegal actions are committed by members of the administration in the name of foreign policy or "national interest."

The Tower Commission and Report

The special review board convened to look into Iran-Contra was headed by former Republican senator John Tower. The other two members were former Democratic senator and secretary of state Edmund Muskie and Brent Scowcroft, a retired air force general who had been national security advisor to President Ford (and who would become George H. W. Bush's national security advisor). The goal of the Tower Commission was to look into the allegations and then issue a report on what happened. It was this report, published in 1987, that provided the clearest picture of Iran-Contra. But the report did something else; it clarified, once again, the relationships among the various actors who make foreign/national security policy (for in this case they were interchangeable) for the country, and it made it clear that ultimate responsibility rests with the president.

> Ours is a government of checks and balances, of shared power and responsibility. The Constitution places the President and the Congress in dynamic tension. They both cooperate and compete in the making of national policy. . . .
>   The Constitution gives both the President and the Congress an important role. The Congress is critical in formulating national policies and in marshalling the resources to carry them out. But those resources . . . are lodged in the Executive Branch. As Chief Executive and Commander-in-Chief, and with broad authority in the area of foreign affairs, it is the President who is empowered to act for the nation and protect its interests.[13]

The report is even more blunt in its recommendations: "The primary responsibility for the formulation and implementation of national security policy falls on the President." The authors, all of whom had experience with the executive and legislative branches, warned that "The departments and agencies—the Defense Department, State Department, and CIA bureaucracies—tend to resist policy change." This makes it even more incumbent upon the president to "bring his perspectives to bear on these bureaucracies for they are his instruments for executing national security policy. . . . His task is to provide them leadership and direction."[14]

After years in which it appeared that a strong president was leading the country, the Tower Commission report served as a reminder about the difficulties and complexities of making foreign policy. It also provided a warning of how easily the system can go awry when the president is not really in control of nor taking responsibility for those who work under him.

George H. W. Bush and the "New World Order"

Despite Iran-Contra, Reagan left office a popular president. He was succeeded by his vice president, George H. W. Bush. But the world in which Bush took office in January 1989 was changing quickly. The country of Yugoslavia was disintegrating and on the path to ethnic conflict. The government of Somalia was collapsing, leaving the country in a state of chaos and clan warfare. The border between the East (Hungary) and West (Austria) was opened, and on November 9, 1989, the Berlin Wall came down. The Solidarity Party, led by Lech Walesa, gained power in Poland, and by Christmas the (communist) Polish People's Republic was replaced by the democratic Republic of Poland. Other countries in the Soviet Eastern European bloc started the process of removing their communist leaders and replacing them with democratically elected governments. And the Soviet economy was declining steadily, leading to the assumption that change in that country was inevitable.

In contrast to the optimistic changes taking place in Eastern Europe, in June 1989 the government of China brutally and violently cracked down on students calling for reform who were protesting in Tiananmen Square in Beijing. As many as 2,000 were believed killed in that incident. When democracy appeared to be sweeping most of the communist countries of Eastern Europe, government hold was tightened in China.

Amidst uncertainty about the direction of the Soviet Union or Eastern Europe, and unwilling to push too much, Bush pursued a tentative and status quo foreign policy, preferring to limit U.S. involvement internationally. Nonetheless, Bush also recognized the significance of the changes taking place. As international events were unfolding rapidly, President Bush spoke of the creation of "a new world order" that would emerge in the wake of communism. He coined the phrase in a speech on September 11, 1990, in which he used Iraq's invasion of Kuwait the month before to outline his vision for the future. At that time, he said: "At this very moment, they [American soldiers] serve together with Arabs, Europeans, Asians, and Africans in defense of principle and the dream of a *new world order*" (emphasis added).[15] In other words, in a rapidly changing world, old adversaries, such as the United States and the Soviet Union, could work together and share responsibilities that would make for a better future.

Unfortunately, while the Cold War was ending, other "hot wars" were emerging that would require the attention of the United States. The most immediate of these was Iraq's invasion of Kuwait.

The Persian Gulf War

On August 2, 1990, Iraq invaded Kuwait, which provided the impetus for the Bush administration to get involved internationally. Over the next few months, President Bush and members of the administration used the United Nations to build support for a military response to this act of aggression. On November 29, 1990, the Security Council passed Resolution 678 authorizing "member states . . . to use all necessary means to uphold and implement [all resolutions] and to restore international peace and security to the area." The Security Council also set a deadline of six weeks for Iraq to withdraw from Kuwait. Otherwise, the UN would authorize military force.[16]

As early as September 1990, shortly after the invasion, when it became apparent that the United States might get involved in an armed conflict, Bush knew that he would need approval from the Congress under the terms of the War Powers Resolution. According to his memoirs, Bush used the Gulf of Tonkin Resolution as a model so that he, too, could get the same kind of open-ended support from the Congress that President Johnson had been given in 1964.[17] In addition, Bush met with congressional leaders from both parties to build support for his position. In the meantime, UN Secretary General Javier Perez de Cuellar tried to resolve the situation peacefully to avoid armed conflict. On January 9, 1991, Secretary of State James Baker met with the Iraqi deputy prime minister, Tariq Aziz, in Geneva and warned him that the only way to avert war was for Iraq to comply with Resolution 678 and withdraw completely from Kuwait.

On January 10, Aziz made it clear that Iraq would not comply with the terms stated. At that time, joint resolutions were introduced into both houses of Congress authorizing the deployment of U.S. forces to Iraq under the terms of the UN resolution. On January 12, both houses of Congress voted to support the joint resolution; the House vote was 250 to 183, and the Senate vote was 52 to 47, "the smallest margin ever to vote for war."[18] The attack started early in the morning (Iraq time) on January 17, 1991.

The war lasted forty-three days and resulted in the defeat of Iraq and its withdrawal from Kuwait. Most notable about this effort is that "the coalition," as it was known, of military working with the United States was not tied to traditional alliances but rather was made up of forces drawn from a range of countries that came together in pursuit of a common outcome. For the first time since World War II, the United States and the Soviet Union cooperated and worked together on the same side—a remarkable event.

In addition, the Persian Gulf War was a true product of new technology both within the military and the media. While coverage of the Vietnam War earned it the moniker of "the first television war" for the nightly news coverage of battles and body bags, the Persian Gulf War was the first CNN war, leading to what has become known as "the CNN effect."[19] For the first time, the American people as well as the rest of the world got "live" coverage of what was happening in Baghdad and throughout Iraq and Kuwait. This changed expectations of what war coverage should be, something that would be taken even further during the presidency of George W. Bush, when reporters were "embedded" with troops to cover the 2003 war against Iraq.

The End of the Soviet Union

In August 1991, shortly after the Persian Gulf War ended, there was an attempted coup in the Soviet Union. With Mikhail Gorbachev under house arrest at his vacation home in the Crimea by hard-liners who had initiated the coup, it was Boris Yeltsin, then-leader of the Soviet republic of Russia, who faced the rebels. Standing on a tank in front of the "Russian White House," Yeltsin declared that he would be in charge of all security forces on Russian territory until order was restored. With that statement, as well as the forceful image of him facing down the troops, Yeltsin emerged as the de facto leader of the country. The end of the Soviet Union was near. On December 8, 1991, the leaders of the Soviet republics of Russia, Ukraine, and Belarus announced the end of the Soviet Union, leading to the creation of a new Commonwealth of Independent States (CIS). This was confirmed on December 21 at a meeting of representatives of eleven of the former Soviet republics. The end of the old Soviet Union was finalized on December 25, 1991, when Mikhail Gorbachev resigned as president of the USSR.

The dissolution of the Soviet Union, and with that the end of the Cold War, came as a surprise to the United States. While leaders of the United States and other Western countries had long called for this as well as for the victory of democracy over communism, the reality is that few actually thought it would happen. Since 1991, one of the questions that political scientists, historians, and policy-makers have asked is whether the United States was responsible for the end of the Soviet Union. But the death of the Soviet Union was the result of the confluence of a number of factors. These range from the perceived need to continue an arms buildup, which had a detrimental effect on the Soviet economy, to the democratic revolutions sweeping Eastern Europe, which clearly undermined the power of the Soviet government, to the liberalizing policies of Mikhail Gorbachev, which suggested that change was possible. As one historian noted: "Collapse, when it finally came, had come from within."[20]

The Balkans and Ethnic Conflict

Even with the euphoria surrounding the end of the Cold War, U.S. foreign policy remained unsettled. The existence of ethnic warfare and genocide in countries around the world became more prominent when not overshadowed by the Cold War. One of the areas that erupted as a crisis for the United States was Yugoslavia. The country had been artificially created after World War I, and its diverse groups (Serb, Croat, and Bosnian Muslim primarily) had been held together in part by the strength of the country's leader, Josip Tito. After his death in 1980, and with no designated successor, nationalist leaders emerged and called for independent states for each of the ethnic groups (e.g., "Serbia for the Serbs"). This meant that it was simply a question of time until the country dissolved into civil and ethnic warfare as each group vied for territory and power.[21]

On June 25, 1991, Croatia and Slovenia, two of the six republics that made up Yugoslavia, declared their independence.[22] Two days later, on June 27, the first of the wars that would wrack the Balkans for the next eight years began. The Yugoslav-Slovene War lasted ten days, until the UN negotiated a settlement. This falsely conveyed the idea that these "little" ethnic wars in the Balkans could be resolved quickly by negotiation. As the crisis grew and the conflict spread, the United States had to decide whether or how to deal with this situation. The dilemma facing the Bush administration was defining what was in the national interest. On the one hand, this was a war being fought in Europe, close to U.S. allies. This raised concerns that if the United States did not take action, the situation would escalate and the United States would no longer have a choice as to whether or not to get involved. On the other hand, the war was outside the formal NATO guidelines area, it was in a country with which the United States had little involvement, and therefore it would be a stretch to see it as directly relevant to U.S. national interest.

President Bush chose to deal with the situation using a combination of diplomacy (soft power) and threats (hard power). He sent Secretary of State James Baker to meet with Serbian leader Slobodan Milosevic to warn him not to take military action that would make the situation worse. On the whole, though, it fell to the Europeans to address the deteriorating situation in what remained of Yugoslavia, and the Bush administration was content to leave this "European problem" to the Europeans. But the problem would not go away; rather, it would be left to the Clinton administration to decide how to deal with it.

The administration of George H. W. Bush was a period of transition in U.S. foreign policy. Initially the victory in the Gulf War suggested that the post–Cold War period would be a time of shifting alliances created as necessary to meet specific threats. This suggested a flexibility in U.S. foreign policy that the Cold War had not allowed. Further, it indicated that Congress would be willing to grant to a president "permission" to use force against a specific enemy even when the United States was not directly threatened, as long as the case could be made that "national interest" was at stake. It also showed that the American public could and would support such a war, even in a distant country.

This new era in U.S. foreign policy also carried dangers that were not yet fully formed or understood. Ethnic conflict and genocide in other countries were threats to human rights but were difficult to articulate to the American public in a way that tied them to U.S. national interest. It was far more difficult to justify military involvement in a distant country on humanitarian grounds than on economic ones. In short, the concepts of "threat" and "national interest" were starting to have different meanings outside the context of the Cold War.

Going into the presidential election of 1992, war was under way in the Yugoslav republic of Bosnia; the Bush administration was debating what to do about the conflict in Somalia; and unrest was building in Haiti, a country directly within the traditional U.S. sphere of influence. But overshadowing these foreign policy issues was a faltering economy. President Bush's popularity had gone from a high of 89 percent in January 1991, as he was building support for the Persian Gulf War, to a low of 29 percent in July 1992, about four months before the election.[23] With the foreign policy victory in the Persian Gulf behind them, the American public wanted to know what President Bush would do to address the domestic economic situation. It was Bush's challenger Bill Clinton who seemed to have the answers.

The Clinton Years

To meet domestic concerns raised during the campaign, candidate Clinton focused on the economy and the recession that was sweeping the country. The budget deficits that had started under President Reagan were taking their toll domestically and Clinton, accusing President Bush of being out of touch with America, promised to "focus like a laser beam on the economy." Clinton's priority was going to be domestic politics, but like other presidents before him, once in office Clinton discovered that international events have a way of interfering.

Clinton suffered two foreign policy disasters early in his administration, in Haiti and Somalia, both of which affected his views on foreign policy and the role of the president. Those situations directly influenced his subsequent decisions about Bosnia and later Kosovo. And, in a clear example of the inter- action between domestic and international politics, a Republican-controlled Congress and questions about the president's conduct further limited his foreign policy options.

With the end of the Cold War, the United States was the last remaining superpower. This gave the United States a unique and important role in the international arena. Without the Cold War, the emphasis in foreign policy shifted once again; no longer would the focus be on using the military to deter a single (communist) threat. Instead, Clinton's acknowledgment of a globalized world meant recognition of the interdependence of countries and a return to trade and economic relations as a central component of foreign policy. While the military would still have to be prepared to fight two wars simultaneously (which was the established military posture), ideally it could also be used as a force for good in support of human rights and humanitarian missions. But many of these idealistic (i.e., Wilsonian) goals were derailed by domestic politics, specifically the conflict between President Clinton and the Congress, as well as by international political realities.

Although we cannot yet assess fully the foreign policy of the Clinton ad- ministration, it is possible to select some examples of foreign policy decisions that President Clinton made and provide a preliminary analysis of them. Looking at those cases is instructive for understanding the problems associ- ated with American foreign policy after the Cold War. The Clinton adminis- tration holds an important lesson about the impact of domestic politics and the ways in which domestic and foreign policy are intertwined. It also serves as a reminder that international events cannot be controlled by a president who is often forced to react to events and how, without the Cold War frame- work, international relations became unpredictable.

Somalia

U.S. involvement in Somalia predated President Clinton; it originated in a decision made by President George H. W. Bush in December 1992 (after he was defeated by Clinton in November) to send troops into Somalia on a humanitarian mission. This case serves as an example of how ill-prepared the United States was—and is—for the challenges that it would face after the

Cold War. It also shows the ways in which foreign policy decisions often are made in reaction to events.

The ouster of dictator Mohammed Siad Barre in 1991 resulted in instability and clan warfare in Somalia that, coupled with years of drought, led to widespread famine and internal chaos. Although in August 1992 Bush had ordered an airlift of food as a short-term solution, it became clear that more help was needed. The NSC held a series of meetings throughout November, after the U.S. presidential election, to determine what to do to address the situation, which was seen as a humanitarian crisis. In one meeting on November 25, Bush was given three possible options: "increased support for existing UN efforts, a U.S.-organized coalition effort without the participation of American ground troops, or a major U.S. effort to lead a multinational force in which U.S. ground troops took the leading role." Then-chair of the Joint Chiefs of Staff, Colin Powell, "expressed concern about the use of ground troops." After "a broad discussion," President Bush decided that if other countries would join the effort, "U.S. combat troops would lead an international force to Somalia."[24]

The United States deployed troops to Somalia in December 1992 on a humanitarian mission to ensure that food was distributed to those who needed it. The deployment was authorized with the promise that U.S. forces would be out by Inauguration Day in January 1993. U.S. diplomat Robert Oakley was sent to Somalia to try to negotiate among the various clan leaders in order to restore some stability to the country. Despite earlier promises, when Clinton came into office, U.S. ground troops were in Somalia with no end to their deployment in sight.

By the end of summer 1993, about six months after Clinton took office, the administration faced a series of issues regarding Somalia. First, there did not seem to be an easy diplomatic solution to the problem. Second, in what was becoming a pattern, Congress was asking questions and raising issues about the role of the U.S. forces in Somalia. Finally, Clinton was facing the possibility of U.S. intervention in the growing war in Bosnia, and he saw the two as related. Clinton told his advisors, "unless we can get the Somalia mission under control . . . it's going to be very hard to convince Congress to provide the forces to implement an agreement on Bosnia."[25] Nevertheless, U.S. troops had already been deployed to Somalia.

On October 3, 1993, U.S. forces staged a raid in the city of Mogadishu to capture the warlord Mohammed Farah Aidid and his top lieutenants, but the United States paid a high price. The battle fought on the streets of Mogadishu resulted in hundreds (perhaps thousands) of Somali casualties and the death of eighteen Americans. U.S. public opinion was directly affected by pictures of a dead American soldier being dragged through the streets of Mogadishu.[26] This battle, "the largest firefight Americans had been involved in since Vietnam,"[27] evoked strong reactions from the Congress as well as the public. Clinton addressed the American public to remind them of why U.S. troops were in Somalia, but he faced a dilemma. To leave would send a message about U.S. impotence in the face of nonstate actors, such as the warlords in Somalia. But staying would only put more U.S. soldiers in harm's way with an unclear objective. Clinton set a deadline of March 31, 1994, for a political settlement to be finalized so that U.S. troops could be withdrawn. The reaction to this solution among Republican members of Congress was especially hostile. For example, Senator Nancy Kassebaum stated: "I can think of no further compounding of the tragedy that has occurred there for our forces than to have them withdraw and see what started out to be a very successful, noble mission end in chaos."[28] Clinton also was criticized for sending troops into a mission that they were not prepared for and then for wanting them to withdraw in order to save more lives.

Clinton learned a lesson from this about sending U.S. troops to distant lands that were seen as removed from American national interests. As a result of Somalia, the Clinton administration chose not to interfere in the genocide that took place in Rwanda in 1994.[29] But perhaps more important, it helped frame the Clinton administration's perceptions regarding whether—and when—to intervene for humanitarian reasons.

Haiti

As Clinton was dealing with the situation in Somalia, another potential crisis was growing in Haiti. Half of the Caribbean island of Hispaniola, Haiti was well within the U.S. sphere of influence going back to the days of the Roosevelt Corollary. Consequently, instability in Haiti put Clinton into a position where he felt that he had to act. This military action also proved to be disastrous and further reinforced the administration's as well as congressional and public perceptions about the limits to U.S. military involvement.

President Clinton came into office a strong supporter of Jean-Bertrand Aristide. Aristide was Haiti's first democratically elected president, but he was overthrown in a military coup in 1991, eight months after his election. The United States brokered an accord between Aristide and Haiti's military rulers stipulating that Aristide would return to power on October 30, 1993. U.S. forces were then to be sent to Haiti as part of a UN contingent to train Haitians in engineering (such as building roads and other infrastructure) and to help serve as an internal police force.

In September 1993, the CIA reported that the Haitian leaders did not intend to keep the agreement. Nonetheless, some in the Clinton administration felt that the United States had to live up to its side of the agreement. Clinton authorized the deployment of a naval ship to Haiti carrying engineers and other forces to fulfill the U.S. commitment. When the ship arrived on October 11, 1993, it was met by a mob, many armed with guns and other weapons, while the police simply stood by. The Haitian leaders refused to guarantee the safety of the U.S. forces, and the ship anchored in the harbor, awaiting orders. On October 12, Washington ordered the ship to leave without allowing the forces to set foot in the country, and this became another foreign policy embarrassment for Clinton.

Clinton felt pressed to intervene in Haiti at least in part for domestic political reasons—to avert the possibility of an influx of Haitian refugees into the United States. Further, a significant African American constituency wanted to see the United States do something to help end the military dictatorship in Haiti. Despite his desire to respond to domestic concerns, Clinton learned quickly the limits of U.S. force in the face of civil unrest and without the support of the people and government that it was allegedly trying to help.

In addition, Clinton provoked the Congress by not seeking congressional approval to send troops to Haiti, arguing that he possessed "executive authority" to do so. In response, the Congress passed a resolution stating that "the President should have sought and welcomed congressional approval before deploying U.S. forces to Haiti."[30]

In 1994, with the situation in Haiti still unresolved, Clinton ordered a larger invasion force to the island. However, prior to their landing, former president Carter was able to negotiate a deal with rebel Haitian leader Cedras, allowing him to leave the island and authorizing American troops to come in to restore order.[31]

Clinton learned harsh lessons from Haiti, another foreign policy debacle that undermined his credibility. To the members of Congress, it was an abuse of the power of the president, which further exacerbated the strains that already existed between the two branches.

The Balkans

When candidate Clinton was campaigning for the presidency against George H. W. Bush, he condemned the then-president for not acting more forcefully to address the situation in the Balkans. By the time Clinton took office as president in January 1993, the siege of Sarajevo, which became the longest siege in modern history, was well under way, and stories of the genocide taking place throughout Bosnia were already hitting the American media. The issues were far from clear cut, and explaining to the American public why involvement in this area would be in U.S. national interest would be difficult.

As a result, Clinton called this "the most frustrating and complex foreign policy issue in the world today."[32]

Under Clinton, the United States pursued a bifurcated policy toward the Balkans. Policy was characterized either by an overwhelming desire not to get involved, which was the attitude of the administration toward the war in Bosnia in 1993 and into early 1994, or by the impulse to jump in and take a leadership role, which the United States did later in 1994. The former was the result of a number of factors: the harsh lessons of Somalia and Haiti of the difficulties of a humanitarian mission; the desire to let the Europeans take the lead under UN auspices (through the United Nations Protection Forces, or UNPROFOR); and concern about getting support of the Congress and the public at a time when Clinton's popularity was low.[33] The decision to take a leadership role in the Balkans was the result of a change in the political landscape so that once the administration decided it was time to act, it did so decisively, resulting in a negotiated end to the war.

One of the events that prompted the Clinton administration to act was the "Sarajevo Market Massacre" on August 28, 1995, which resulted in the deaths of thirty-seven civilians, with eighty-eight wounded. It prompted a public outcry that provided the political support Clinton needed. Pushed by the United States, NATO accelerated its air strikes against Serb targets. This helped provide the military cover necessary for the Bosnian and Croat forces on the ground to launch a major ground offensive in preparation for the start of negotiations that would bring an end to the war. Negotiations were held at Wright-Patterson Air Force Base outside Dayton, Ohio, under the leadership of Assistant Secretary of State Richard Holbrooke. The major political leaders of Serbia (Milosevic), Croatia (Tudjman), and Bosnia (Izetbegovic) participated in the discussion, and in November 1995, President Clinton announced that an agreement had been reached. The peace agreement was signed in Paris on December 14, 1995, and the war in Bosnia ended.[34] Unfortunately, that was neither the end of war in the Balkans nor of U.S. military involvement there.

Kosovo and the Clinton Doctrine

The 1997 report "National Security Strategy for a New Century" suggests that U.S. military intervention may be appropriate "to respond to, relieve, and/or restrict the consequences of human catastrophe."[35] The willingness to use military force in this way defines what has been called the "new interventionism," one of the foundations of the Clinton Doctrine that was central to justifying the operation in Kosovo in 1999. This doctrine has at its core many of the ideals that Jimmy Carter espoused when he spoke of the need to make human rights central to U.S. foreign policy, and it echoes the earlier ideas of Woodrow Wilson.

Kosovo was another foreign policy issue that Clinton faced, and he did so while he was also under attack domestically for his liaison with White House intern Monica Lewinsky. The Dayton Peace Accords that ended the war in Bosnia did nothing to address the ethnic violence growing in the Serb province of Kosovo. Kosovo had been declared an "autonomous province" in 1963. But it had few rights until the Yugoslav constitution of 1974 allowed the province to write its own constitution, thereby giving it the same status as the six republics of then-Yugoslavia. After Serbian leader Milosevic came to power in 1987, the Serb minority in Kosovo increasingly repressed the Albanian majority, imposing more and more restrictions on what they could and could not do. In 1997, violence erupted when a group calling itself the Kosovo Liberation Army (KLA) began a series of terrorist-type attacks against the Serbs. Under the auspices of the European Union, a negotiation was called to take place at Rambouillet, outside Paris, in the hope of averting armed conflict. The negotiators gave Milosevic an ultimatum: withdraw from Kosovo or risk NATO military action. When the talks failed, the United States and Europe had little choice but to follow through, and in March 1999, NATO began bombing Serbia.

Kosovo was a difficult situation for the United States in many ways. While there was little doubt that human rights abuses were taking place, there were also divisions among the NATO allies as to what form an intervention should take. Clinton made it clear that he would not authorize sending U.S. ground forces into Kosovo, which put him at odds with the allies, especially Britain, and it publicly sent a signal as to military limits; one official in the Clinton administration later claimed that to state this so publicly was a mistake.[36] Clinton did agree to support air strikes.

Clinton understandably was cautious about the deployment of U.S. military forces at this time. He had easily won reelection in 1996 because of domestic reasons. The economy was doing well, and despite a hostile Republican Congress, Clinton's public approval rating hit a high of 73 percent in December 1998.[37] In 1999, at the same time that he was facing decisions about Kosovo, he was under investigation for his affair with White House intern Monica Lewinsky. He was under additional scrutiny by Congress because he did not seek congressional approval for the earlier U.S. involvement in Bosnia and Kosovo, which he claimed had not been needed because these were NATO (as opposed to U.S.) missions. However, to the Republican-controlled Congress, this was part of a pattern of presidential disregard for congressional oversight.

With U.S. support, NATO made a decision to begin bombing Serbia; the attacks started in March 1999 and continued as a NATO operation tied to the need to assure international intervention when human rights abuses call for it or when it is in support of humanitarian goals. But Clinton came under scrutiny regarding the U.S. policy on Kosovo. On the one hand, there were those who felt that the United States should have become involved sooner because of the clear human rights abuses. On the other hand, there were questions about whether Clinton had overstepped his responsibilities by agreeing to deploy U.S. troops and aircraft without broad support by the Congress.

Domestically, a thriving economy took precedence over foreign policy situations, even perceived failures. As outgoing president in 2001, Clinton had an approval rating of 67 percent, "the highest of any outgoing president since modern polling began—even surpassing Dwight Eisenhower and Ronald Reagan."[38]

Economics: Trade and Globalization

In approaching foreign policy from a broad perspective, Clinton understood that the world was changing and becoming more interconnected economically, a phenomenon referred to as "globalization." The economic failure of one country could have repercussions for other countries, and therefore it was in the United States' national interest to be sure that the global economy was strong. Clinton also understood that technology altered the way international business was conducted. Just as détente with the communist countries was best achieved by conservative Republicans, so was free trade pursued more successfully by a president from the Democratic Party, which was traditionally aligned with labor and was seen as protectionist.

With bipartisan support and despite objections from the largely Democratic unions, which claimed that it would result in the loss of jobs, Clinton successfully enacted the North American Free Trade Agreement (NAFTA) in 1994, uniting the United States, Canada, and Mexico. NAFTA strengthened both economic and political ties among the three countries, and now, years after the agreement went into effect, there is little evidence that it resulted in a loss of jobs in the United States. In 1995, when Mexico was in financial crisis, the Clinton administration provided that country with a $12.5 billion loan. While this was seen as a significant risk at the time, it not only stabilized the country, but Mexico repaid the loan within two years. This further strengthened the ties between the two countries.[39]

It is now clear that Clinton had an understanding of some of the changes taking place in the international system and was able to use them to strengthen the United States economically. While he had his foreign policy failures, notably Haiti and Somalia, his understanding of economics, both domestic and international, can be seen as one area of success.

Terrorism

One of the hallmarks of the post–Cold War world was the emergence of nonstate actors playing a major role in the international system. At a time when politicians are debating the findings of the 9/11 Commission and how to increase the safety and security of the United States, a brief look at the pattern of terrorism during the Clinton years leading to the attacks of September 11 is instructive.[40] Perhaps the most important point is that "state-sponsored terrorism"—such as the acts perpetrated or supported by Libya, Syria, and Lebanon—has declined overall and is being replaced by a growth of independent organizations, many of which are seen as extremist and radical.[41] This pattern created a foreign policy dilemma for President Clinton and then George W. Bush of how to respond to attacks that are not tied to a nation-state. Since international relations and international law are based on and assume a nation-state (country) as the primary actor, there are few guidelines about how a country should interact with a nonstate actor.

After U.S. embassies were bombed in Kenya and Tanzania in 1998, terrorist attacks against the United States, U.S. property, and Americans in general became an even greater threat. Although there had been other such attacks during the Clinton administration, such as the 1993 bombing of the World Trade Center, Clinton felt that this time he had to take military action in response. He authorized a military attack directed at suspected terrorist facilities in Afghanistan and Sudan. Even though no terrorist leaders were caught, and there were questions about whether the facilities targeted were military or civilian, Clinton's popularity remained high.[42]

In September 1998, Clinton addressed the UN General Assembly, and global terrorism was one of the central points of his talk. At that time, he admonished the international community that "all nations must put the fight against terrorism at the top of our agenda." He warned that terrorism is not only an American problem, but "a clear and present danger to tolerant and open societies and innocent people everywhere." And he also said: "If terrorism is at the top of the American agenda—[it] should be at the top of the world's agenda." He then offered common solutions to the problem, especially the need for countries to work together to counter this threat. He concluded that "together we can meet it and overcome its threats, its injuries, and its fears with confidence."[43] Despite this optimistic call for international unity against a common threat, terrorist acts against Americans (and also U.S. allies) have increased.

In the aftermath of September 11, 2001, significant questions have been raised about what was then known about the terrorist cells acting in or against the United States, and whether the Clinton administration should have done more to stop Al Qaeda. Those questions might never be answered.

Rethinking Foreign Policy Prior to 9/11

By the end of the Clinton administration it was clear that U.S. foreign policy had no clear framework. Rather, each of the two immediate post–Cold War presidents, George H.W. Bush and Bill Clinton, was unsure how to address the emergence of ethnic conflicts and civil wars and the humanitarian and human rights crises that accompany them. The result was the emergence of policies that were inconsistent and often opaque. While the Bush administration showed little doubt about the need to send U.S. troops to the Persian Gulf in the wake of Saddam Hussein's invasion of Kuwait or to deploy troops to Somalia to aid the humanitarian crisis unfolding there, he was unwilling to send troops to the former Yugoslavia, preferring instead to leave that to the Europeans to deal with. Similarly, Clinton appeared to be aggressive in his deployment of U.S. troops to Haiti for a mission that became a foreign policy fiasco and raised questions about both his and the United States' intentions regarding the use of force.

From the start of the Cold War, American presidents based U.S. foreign policy on fighting that war with the hope of "winning." But the end of the Cold War was anything but easy from the perspective of U.S. foreign policy. The Cold War provided a framework and clear guidelines for foreign and military policy. In the post–Cold War period, U.S. foreign policy has been guided largely by the need to respond to the most pressing crisis or conflict. President George H. W. Bush spoke of a "new world order," but that lofty ideal has yet to be translated into a foreign policy direction for the United States. The war in the Persian Gulf in 1991, fought by a coalition of countries brought together against one enemy, suggested one approach. However, the inability to address the ethnic conflict in the Balkans and the genocide in Rwanda, for example, suggest that such an approach would not be all-encompassing.

President Clinton came into office wanting to focus on the economy but found quickly that he, too, had to respond to more immediate foreign policy issues and that they could easily deflect time, attention, and political capital from domestic priorities. Clinton authorized a number of military actions (e.g., in Somalia, Haiti, and Bosnia) that were justified on humanitarian and human rights grounds. Clinton presented these to the American public by defining "national interest" rather broadly. But these cases also indicated a significant change in the use of military force in the post–Cold War environment to support more idealistic goals, specifically the U.S. military as a "force for good."[44] This hinted at the start of a new pattern in the direction of U.S. foreign policy, or a return to a policy advocated unsuccessfully by Jimmy Carter and by Woodrow Wilson decades earlier.

When George W. Bush came into office, his primary foreign policy goal was for the United States to return to a more unilateralist policy guided by pragmatic priorities, rather than the more idealistic goals of humanitarian aid, nation building, or preventing genocide. Once again, events beyond a president's control intervened, and with that the course of U.S. foreign policy changed. George H. W. Bush, Bill Clinton, and George W. Bush each started to frame a new direction for U.S. foreign policy in the post–Cold War world, only to be confronted with events demanding a different response. The events of September 11 severely disrupted the foreign policy course that George W. Bush had laid out. More important, September 11 carried a warning that the future of U.S. foreign policy will require anticipating the actions of and threats from nonstate actors as well as traditional nation-states. Since all aspects of foreign policy are premised on the nation-state, this creates another set of challenges for America. Just as the Cold War required new thinking about foreign policy, the notion of the threat, the military force structure and types of weapons needed to meet the threat, and the domestic governmental structure, so the post–September 11 world means rethinking all of these factors once again.

Applying Foreign Policy Concepts:
The Use of U.S. Troops for Humanitarian Purposes

One of the dilemmas that any president faces comes in trying to decide when to deploy U.S. troops and how that deployment is in the national interest of the United States. This has been especially true since Vietnam, when members of Congress and the American public felt that the president had abused his power to send troops to fight and die in a war that was not in the national interest. Since Woodrow Wilson reframed U.S. foreign policy to inject the role of values, presidents have had to balance when, and whether, to take this country to war in support of ideals such as democracy and freedom. Especially since the end of the Cold War and the apparent rise of ethnic and civil conflicts, the United States has tried to determine whether it would be appropriate to intervene in the affairs of another country. In making this determination, the dilemma facing presidents has been balancing issues of the sovereignty of the state, which would preclude external interference, with the moral right to intervene in cases of human rights abuses. If, in fact, one of the roles of the military is to be used as a "force for good" to support basic values and human rights, then is it not part of the national interest of the United States to intervene when those rights are abridged?

Both Presidents George H. W. Bush and Clinton faced this issue during their presidency. Clinton, even more than Bush, chose to intervene early on in his administration and then paid a heavy political price later on. In retrospect, however, did he make the right decision and draw the wrong lesson in choosing *not* to intervene in Yugoslavia?

The Case

When Bill Clinton became president in January 1993, U.S. troops were already deployed in Somalia. They had been sent by his predecessor specifically to address what was seen as a humanitarian crisis, resulting from civil war in that country. Among the conditions for that deployment were supposed to be that the troops would be there for a limited amount of time and would be out by the time Clinton took office, which proved not to be the case. Clinton made the decision to authorize the military to try to capture the warlord, Mohammed Farah Aidid, which resulted in a major battle on the streets of Mogadishu. Ultimately, the U.S. withdrew, leading to congressional and public criticism about the wisdom of the decisions made both to intervene and then to withdraw. As Clinton was dealing with the situation in Somalia, he also had to deal with a crisis unfolding in Haiti and, once again, Clinton made the decision to send in U.S. troops. This, too, resulted in another foreign policy and military fiasco for Clinton.

One result of these two early lessons on the dangers of deploying troops in support of humanitarian missions was Clinton's decision to restrict "U.S. involvement in future peacekeeping missions and by refusing to intervene in other failed states."[45] A consequence of this decision was that "When a much bloodier conflict broke out in nearby Rwanda and Burundi, leaving 1 million dead, the United States, fearing a repeat of the Somalia disaster, let the carnage run its course. With no other major powers willing to step in, the UN, too, stood by as the genocide unfolded."[46]

Not only did the U.S. choose not to intervene in Rwanda, but it also stood by as Bosnia erupted into civil war, ultimately resulting in the deaths of at least two hundred thousand Bosnian Muslims in an act of "ethnic cleansing," with more than two million refugees who were displaced during the war. Despite his campaign rhetoric that "the United States should take the lead in seeking United Nations Security Council authorization for air strikes against those who are attacking the relief effort," and that "the United States should be prepared to lend appropriate military support to that operations,"[47] when he became president, Clinton proved to be unwilling to use force. Rather, not only did Clinton refer to the war in Bosnia as a "frustrating and complex foreign policy issue," but he also was unsure as to what to do. While he saw his main priority as the domestic economic situation, he also realized that he had inherited this situation, as he had the case of Somalia, and he stated that "if the United States does not act in situations like this nothing will happen." He also said that "a failure to do so [to act] would be to give up American leadership."[48] As one political scientist notes, "Presidents inherit the leftover problems that their predecessors fail to resolve, or the tasks that simply require more time or resources to be completed."[49] This was the situation that Clinton faced.

Thus, Clinton had a dilemma. On the one hand, he knew that unless the United States took action, the fighting and genocide in Bosnia would continue. On the other hand, he had already suffered a number of military defeats in Somalia and Haiti, the Congress was skeptical because he had initiated these attacks without congressional approval,[50] and he was not sure how to tie any U.S. involvement in Bosnia to U.S. national interest.

What Would You Do If . . .

The time is 1994. This is an election year, something that President Clinton is acutely aware of. He and his advisors are also aware of the fact that they had inherited a situation in Somalia, but it was his administration that was blamed for the failure. It was Clinton's decision to move forces into Haiti, but that proved to be disastrous for the United States, both politically and in terms of public perceptions. The war in Bosnia is escalating, and the Europeans have proven themselves unable to contain the situation. Only the force of the United States would possibly make a difference.

What would you do if you were an advisor to President Clinton? You see a human rights catastrophe unfolding in Bosnia, but the United States has suffered when it chose to intervene in other cases. On the other hand, to do nothing would fly in the face of many of the values that the United States holds dear. Given what you know now, what policies would you recommend the president engage in, and why? In formulating a policy decision, you need to take into account how this will be presented to the American public, the Congress, and the U.S. allies and how any decision ties directly to U.S. national interest.

6

September 11 and After

A S WE SAW IN EARLIER CHAPTERS, THE POLICIES that the United States followed from its founding to the Second World War were guided by national interest defined by economic growth and also imperialist expansion, both placed primarily under the broad umbrella of unilateralism. Principles, values, and ideals were paramount in justifying U.S. involvement in different places and parts of the world. After 1945 U.S. leaders, driven by realist thinking, made policy based on the perceived need to be ahead of the USSR. This changed in 1991 with the demise of the USSR and the end of the Cold War. Between 1991 and 2001, the framework of international relations in general and U.S. foreign policy in particular seemed to be based on the need to respond to various crises as they emerged, although without any single set of guiding principles. In other words, U.S. foreign policy was characterized largely by *reaction to* world events.

After ten years of apparent drift, the direction of U.S. foreign policy became clearer following the attacks of September 11, 2001. While the Bush administration initially came into office with a call for a neo-unilateralist, almost isolationist foreign policy, 9/11 changed that direction quickly. Suddenly, the United States was actively involved internationally, pursuing wars in Afghanistan and Iraq and following an "either you are with us or against us" brand of foreign policy. The election of 2008 seemed to repudiate that approach. This left incoming president Obama to address both an economic crisis and the need to restore U.S. credibility and leadership internationally, the latter having been damaged by George W. Bush's go-it-alone attitude.

George W. Bush:
Foreign Policy Before and After September 11

The foreign policy of George W. Bush can be divided into two parts: before and after September 11, 2001. The implications of the shift in foreign policy were far-reaching, as the United States, in seeking to establish itself as a global leader, ended up pursuing policies that alienated many of its traditional allies. Rather than making the United States and its people more secure, many felt more threatened and believed that the world was less predictable and scarier than it had ever been, even during the height of the Cold War.

Before September 11

During the presidential campaign of 2000, then-candidate George W. Bush made it clear that the United States would chart its own course in foreign policy. Bush indicated that under his administration, the United States would return to a more unilateralist policy characterized by U.S. action consistent with what the president perceived to be in the national interest. He stressed his desire to strengthen ties south of the border (especially to Mexico), rather than look primarily to the traditional allies in Europe. And he made it clear that the United States should not be in the business of "nation building," stating his intention to pull U.S. troops out of places like the Balkans. In short, candidate Bush outlined a marked shift in the direction of U.S. foreign policy, especially compared with that of his predecessor, Bill Clinton.

In the January/February 2000 volume of *Foreign Affairs*, Condoleezza Rice, a Stanford University professor who had become part of the Bush inner circle and who would become Bush's national security advisor and then secretary of state, laid out what she saw as the priorities of the United States in a Republican (George W. Bush) administration. She began by stating that "the United States has found it exceedingly difficult to define its 'national interest' in the absence of Soviet power." But she also notes that such times "of transition" are important because "one can affect the shape of the world to come."[1] While many of the subsequent Bush administration policies were affected by the events of September 11, the article is instructive for the priorities and policies it outlined.

Rice foreshadowed Bush administration policy when she stated, "The president must remember that the military is a special instrument. It is lethal, and it is meant to be . . . it is certainly not designed to build a civilian society." Rather, in her estimation, "Military force is best used *to support clear political goals*, whether limited, such as expelling Saddam from Kuwait, or comprehensive, such as demanding the unconditional surrender of Japan and Germany during World War II" (emphasis added).[2] At the time of the publication of this article, Rice, and presumably the entire Bush defense and foreign policy team, appeared to be focused on defining national interest in the absence of the Soviet threat.[3]

The events of 9/11 significantly altered the priorities of the Bush administration, creating the "global war on terror" and making this the highest foreign policy priority. From that time forward, all aspects of Bush administration foreign and security policy stemmed from, and were justified by, the need to support the war on terror. It is therefore instructive to go back to the Rice article and note the attention that she paid to U.S. national interest, which she defined "by a desire to foster the spread of freedom, prosperity and peace."[4] It was the desire to spread freedom and democracy that ultimately was used to justify the United States decision for war in Iraq, eclipsing the initial rationale for the attack, which was "regime change" and the desire to eliminate the spread of weapons of mass destruction allegedly found in Iraq. And despite his willingness to use military force, a realist characteristic, Bush's emphasis on spreading freedom and democracy is inherently idealist in perspective.[5]

Contested Election and Implications for U.S. Foreign Policy

In order to put the Bush administration's decisions into broader perspective, it is necessary to go back to the election of 2000, which was fraught with controversy from the beginning. Marked by questions about election fraud in Ohio, a critical swing state, and the "hanging chads" and butterfly ballots in Florida, the election process was characterized by accusations of irregularities in voting procedures as well as the ways in which ballots were counted. The Florida issue was especially contentious, and ultimately the issue of a recount went to the U.S. Supreme Court for a decision. On December 12, 2000, by a vote of 5 to 4, the members of the Court agreed to halt any recount, thereby overruling the verdict of the Florida Supreme Court and effectively ensuring the election of George W. Bush as president.

Despite—or because of—his disputed victory in the presidential election, Bush moved quickly to fulfill the campaign promises he made. In June 2001, over the objections of the European allies as well as many environmentalists in the United States, Bush declared that the Kyoto Protocol to the UN Framework Convention on Climate Change, negotiated and agreed to in 1997 under the Clinton administration, "was fatally flawed in fundamental ways," and that the United States would not participate in that agreement but would offer an alternative. The United States, Bush said, was committed to "work within the United Nations framework and elsewhere to develop with our friends and allies and nations throughout the world an effective and science-based response to the issue of global warming."⁶ These statements left other countries wondering how the United States was going to live up to this commitment or to others that had been made by previous administrations, as the Bush reaction seemed to be especially negative toward anything done by the Clinton administration.

Bush also withdrew the United States from the 1972 Anti-Ballistic Missile Treaty so that the United States would not be constrained by its terms in developing new weapon systems, especially a ballistic missile defense system. He said that the United States would limit continued engagement in the Middle East peace process, which had been a hallmark of U.S. foreign policy since the Carter years. In effect, Bush halted the Oslo process that had been pursued by Clinton. In another repudiation of his predecessor's policies, Bush also suspended talks with North Korea and criticized the agreement signed in 1994 by the United States and North Korea under the Clinton administration.⁷ He said that the United States would not send additional troops to the Balkans as part of the peacekeeping force and implied that he would withdraw those which were there. And he made it clear that the United States should not be in the business of "nation building," a direct slap at previous administrations' foreign policy decisions, including his father's.

These early policy decisions led to a raft of criticism domestically and internationally about the future direction of U.S. foreign policy. The European allies charged that this policy of unilateralism was undermining the basis of U.S. (and European) national security. They also raised concerns not only about the apparent destruction of the existing foreign policy framework, but about what (if anything) Bush was putting in its place. To many opponents both within and outside the United States, the perception was that the Bush administration's policies were tied to the desire to please special interests and were made for domestic political reasons rather than in the greater national interest. These criticisms stopped abruptly on September 11, 2001.

September 11 and the Responses

Using the military actively as an instrument of foreign policy was the hallmark of Bush administration foreign policy after September 11. On that day hijackers captured four aircraft, crashing two into the World Trade Center in New York and one into the Pentagon in Washington. The fourth, which by all accounts was also headed to Washington, crashed in Pennsylvania after passengers wrestled control of the aircraft from the hijackers and diverted it from its target. The responses to these events are instructive as they pertain to U.S. foreign policy.

One of the most immediate effects of September 11 was that NATO invoked Article 5 for the first time in its history. The North Atlantic Council issued a press release on September 12, 2001, affirming that Article 5 "stipulates that in the event of attacks falling within its purview, each Ally will assist the Party that has been attacked by taking such action as it deems necessary. Accordingly, the United States' Allies stand ready to provide the assistance that may be required as a consequence of these acts of barbarism."[8] By early October, under the framework of Article 5, NATO had started to deploy Airborne Early Warning Aircraft (AWACS) to the United States. However, it should be noted that this was the *only* act that NATO took in support of the United States at that time, not because NATO did not want to do more, but because the United States, under the Bush administration, preferred to work independently of NATO or any other formal alliance relationship. In fact, in its role as a collective security alliance, NATO was prepared to work with the United States to formulate a response to the attack. However, the Bush administration determined that it was in U.S. interest to work outside the NATO framework in determining next steps.

At the same time, the Bush administration was working to determine how to respond to the attacks.[9] The administration quickly began exploring military options, including "a strike against al Qaeda forces in Afghanistan, where Osama bin Laden had been given sanctuary by the country's Taliban government, led by Muslim fundamentalists who had imposed a rigid Islamic regime."[10] The decision to attack Afghanistan was to be part of a larger "global war on terror" that would not end "until every terrorist group that had attacked Americans in the past, up to and including the 9/11 assaults, or might launch attacks in the future, had been destroyed."[11] As political scientist Robert Irons described it, perhaps the more important point about the decisions that Bush made following 9/11 was that "the 9/11 attacks created abrupt, far-reaching changes in the nation's political and military situation—changes that would, in turn, *raise significant constitutional issues*" (emphasis added).[12] These issues pertained to the decision to prosecute the war not only with Afghanistan but also Iraq, and especially in the expansion of the role of the executive branch to make decisions not only about military and foreign policy, but about domestic issues, all justified under the broad umbrella of the war on terror.

War with Afghanistan

After gathering intelligence information that linked the hijackers to the terrorist group Al Qaeda, based in Afghanistan, the Bush administration made the decision to send military forces to attack that country and oust the Taliban government, which supported and harbored terrorists. Consistent with the terms of the War Powers Act,[13] the president consulted with Congress and got its support for this venture. According to the president, this was a clear-cut case of an attack on the United States and a military response to that attack. The draft joint resolution was sent to the leaders of the House and Senate on September 12, 2001. It was passed by the Senate on September 14 by a vote of 98 to 0, and in the House later that same day by a vote of 420 to 1.[14]

According to a Congressional Research Service report, the floor debates surrounding the resolution "make clear that the focus of the military force legislation was on the *extent* of the authorization that Congress would provide to the President for use of U.S. military force against the international terrorists who attacked the U.S. on September 11, 2001 and those who materially assisted them in carrying out their actions" (emphasis in original).[15] The resolution that was passed includes five "whereas clauses," "expressing opinions regarding why the joint resolution is necessary."[16] But the critical part is Section 2, "Authorization for Use of United States Armed Forces," which states that "the President is authorized to use all necessary and appropriate force against those nations, organizations, or persons he determines planned, authorized, committed, or aided the terrorist attacks that occurred on September 11, 2001, or harbored such organizations or persons, in order to prevent any future acts of international terrorism against the United States by such nations, organizations or persons." The document also makes it clear that "Nothing in this resolution supersedes any requirement of the War Powers resolution."[17] (See chapter 4 for a description of the War Powers Resolution.)

In negotiating the wording of the resolution, and then in signing it, Bush asserted that S.J. Res. 23 "recognized the authority of the *President* under the Constitution to take action to deter and prevent acts of terrorism against the United States." He also stated that "in signing this resolution, *I maintain the longstanding position of the executive branch regarding the President's constitutional authority to use force*, including the Armed Forces of the United States" (emphasis added).[18] Although the president made it clear that he was complying with the terms of the War Powers Resolution and that the military action requested was necessary to protect the American people and homeland, he clearly was also asserting what he saw as the authority of the president to make these decisions. This is another example of the way in which the Bush administration expanded the power of the executive branch in general, and the president in particular.

However, some in Congress were already concerned about the broad scope of the war on terror envisioned by Bush. In fact, both Senate majority leader Tom Daschle and Senator Robert Byrd, the senior member of the Senate, urged the president to "choose his words carefully" in a proposed speech to the Congress and the nation. "Disturbed by the sweeping language [of the resolution initially proposed], congressional negotiators finally persuaded the president to accept a resolution that limited him to retaliating only against those nations, organizations, or persons responsible for the 9/11 attacks."[19] After some compromise, Bush signed the resolution into law on September 18, 2001, and less than three weeks later, the United States launched ground and air strikes against Afghanistan.

Despite the reservations expressed by some in Congress, such as then-Senate majority leader Tom Daschle and elder statesman Robert Byrd, both Democrats, few would argue with the president's decision to respond to the attacks of September 11 by attacking Afghanistan in October 2001.[20] In fact, Bush's public approval rating hit a high of 90 percent following September 11, the highest popularity rating ever recorded.[21] The swift military victory over the Taliban in Afghanistan proved that the Bush administration was willing to take a decisive stand militarily when it mattered, reinforcing the confidence of both the allies and the American public in the president and his policies. What Bush did not take into account at that time was the fact that removing the Taliban was not going to end the war in Afghanistan. Nor did the president appear to consider the impact of the ongoing war in Afghanistan on perceptions that other countries had of the United States, nor of its impact on its allies and also on the American public.

The initial decision to attack Afghanistan, one of the known homes for Al Qaeda bases, was seen as justified and, on the whole, was received positively. Then-British prime minister Tony Blair stated that "even if no British citizens had died [in the attacks of September 11], it would be right to act. This atrocity was an attack on us all."[22] Within a few months the war expanded and ultimately became a NATO mission. The International Security Assistance Force (ISAF) was created as a UN-mandated international force in December 2001 after the United States had ousted the Taliban regime. It was created initially to assist the Afghan Transitional Authority to reconstruct the country. Although other countries joined in this NATO mission, the United States had, and continues to have, the largest number of troops deployed.

Despite the lofty goals of ousting the Taliban, confronting Al Qaeda, mounting a serious NATO mission, and rebuilding the country, the war in Afghanistan did not go as planned. In fact, between 2001, when the war with Afghanistan started, and January 2009, when the Obama administration came into office, attention given to Afghanistan by the United States became secondary to what became the major foreign policy issue of the Bush years: the war with Iraq.[23]

The Bush Doctrine and the War with Iraq

By early 2002, Bush made it clear that the United States would not stop with the attack on Afghanistan but would expand the "war on terror." In his State of the Union speech in January 2002, Bush identified Iraq, Iran, and North Korea as an "axis of evil," and he stated that "some governments will be timid in the face of terror. . . . If they do not act, America will."[24] He followed that up in a speech on March 11, 2002, the six-month anniversary of September 11. At that time, he said: "Our coalition must act deliberately, but *inaction is not an option*" (emphasis added).[25] In other words, President Bush was sending notice to the American public and the world that the war on terror was going to expand beyond Afghanistan.

The Bush Doctrine, as it became known, became the basis for the decision to go to war against Iraq in March 2003 and to do so without the formal backing of the international community. Formally titled the "National Security Strategy of the United States," this document, which was issued in September 2002 and then summarized by the president in October, puts forward a new direction for American foreign policy: "While the United States will constantly strive to enlist the support of the international community, *we will not hesitate to act alone, if necessary, to exercise our right of self-defense by acting pre-emptively*" (emphasis added).[26]

This doctrine states clearly and unequivocally that the United States is justified in going to war preemptively against any group that potentially threatens the country or its allies, and that it will do so alone if necessary. This is a departure from the policies that the United States followed since the end of World War II, when much of its foreign policy was tied to formal alliances and the belief that security is best achieved if countries work together against a common enemy, rather than trying to defeat the enemy alone. Furthermore, it is a marked departure from the stated idealistic goals for the Bush administration that now made clear it would be relying on U.S. hard power to do whatever it thought was necessary. For the first time since the Cold War, the United States was again relying on its military might to pursue its foreign policy goals. And, once again, foreign and security policy became inextricably linked.

When Bush authorized the attack on Iraq in March 2003 without United Nations approval, he charted another new course for U.S. foreign policy. Unlike his father, who was able to build a strong international coalition before mounting the 1991 Persian Gulf War, George W. Bush had the support of only a few major nations when he took the United States to war against Iraq in 2003. And, perhaps more important, that action was directly opposed by many of the United States' traditionally strongest allies, such as France and Germany.[27] This resulted in a significant schism between the United States and its allies, which proved to be especially damaging at a time when the United States was building support for, and needed to sustain allied commitment to, the war in Afghanistan.

The Path to War with Iraq

It was the war against Iraq that became the defining moment for the Bush administration. There is ample evidence that for at least a year prior to the attack in March 2003, the Bush administration was building support at home, among the public and members of Congress, to justify this expansion of the war on terror. The American public, which had heard a great deal about the need to expand the global war on terror, proved relatively easy to convince, especially when the administration started making the case about the need to stop Saddam Hussein because of his alleged development of weapons of mass destruction. Despite the fact that there was no evidence to prove it, any number of high-level officials supported the claim, which, in turn, justified the need to go to war. This was something that especially the neoconservatives ("neocons") in the administration had been pushing. In public speeches as well as congressional testimony, members of the administration kept reiterating the point and stressed the need for the United States to do something to stop Saddam. The clear implication was that Saddam posed a threat to the United States in some way, either directly or indirectly, unless he was stopped *now*.

Then-vice president Dick Cheney's speech to the Veterans of Foreign Wars in August 2002, seven months before the actual attack on Iraq, is instructive for the way in which the administration was setting the stage:

> The case of Saddam Hussein, *a sworn enemy of our country*, requires a candid appraisal of the facts. After his defeat in the Gulf War in 1991, Saddam agreed under U.N. Security Council Resolution 687 to cease all development of weapons of mass destruction. He agreed to end his nuclear weapons program. He agreed to destroy his chemical and biological weapons. He further agreed to admit U.N. inspection teams into his country to ensure that he was in fact complying with these terms.
>
> In the past decade, Saddam has systematically broken each of these agreements. . . . Simply stated, *there is no doubt that Saddam Hussein now has weapons of mass destruction.* There is no doubt he is amassing them to use against our friends, against our allies, and *against us.* (emphasis added)

Thus, in this part of the speech, Cheney was suggesting that Saddam was developing these weapons, no doubt to be used against the United States and its allies, although without providing any proof of this allegation. In fact, the UN weapons inspectors found no clear evidence that Iraq was developing, producing, or storing such weapons.[28] However, the administration was consistent in its statements to the public and in testimony to the Congress that such weapons, in fact, were hidden in Iraq.

With the assertion that Saddam was developing these weapons, which clearly would be a threat to the United States, Cheney continued the speech, reaching the logical conclusion about the need for war:

> America in the year 2002 must ask careful questions, not merely about our past, but also about our future. The elected leaders of this country have a responsibility to consider all of the available options. And we are doing so. . . . As President Bush has said, time is not on our side. Deliverable weapons of mass destruction in the hands of a terror network, or a murderous dictator, or the two working together, constitutes as grave a threat as can be imagined. *The risks of inaction are far greater than the risk of action* (emphasis added).[29]

Aware of the 2002 election campaign and the need to build support for its position both domestically and internationally, the administration continued to use this same story line about weapons of mass destruction through the fall. On October 2, 2002, Bush submitted to the Congress a resolution authorizing the use of force against Iraq. The resolution itself includes a litany of all of Saddam Hussein's wrongdoings for more than a decade, going back to the first Persian Gulf War and even earlier. It describes an Iraq that was building weapons of mass destruction and demonstrated willingness to use such weapons in the past; the clear implication is that it will do so again, this time against the United States. And it *suggests* that Iraq was somehow involved in the attacks of 9/11—"Whereas the attacks on the United States of September 11, 2001, underscored the gravity of the threat posed by the acquisition of weapons of mass destruction by international terrorist organizations"— although it does not mention Iraq by name in that particular clause.[30]

The resolution then concludes with the important clauses: "Whereas the President and Congress are determined to continue to take all appropriate actions against terrorists and terrorist organizations, including those nations, organizations, or persons who planned, authorized, committed, or aided the terrorist attacks that occurred on September 11, 2001, or harbored such persons or organizations"; and then, "Whereas, the President has authority under the Constitution to take action in order to deter and prevent acts of international terrorism against the United States" the president "*is authorized to use the Armed Forces of the United States as he determines to be necessary and appropriate*" (emphasis added).[31]

On October 11, 2002, the resolution was passed by both houses, in the Senate by a vote of 77 to 23, and in the House by a vote of 296 to 133, and it was signed into law by President Bush on October 16, 2002. All the dissenters were Democrats with the exception of Republican Senator Lincoln Chaffee of Rhode Island, who subsequently was voted out of office.

The U.S. attack against Iraq began on March 19, 2003.

The War with Iraq and Its Aftermath

Where the first Persian Gulf War in 1991 was covered widely in the media (the "CNN effect"), this invasion was characterized by reporters "embedded" with troops, thereby enabling the U.S. public to watch the progress of the war in virtually real time and with first-person commentary. The course of the first phase of the war—"shock and awe"—was swift and apparently successful. The initial military attack was sufficient to bring about the end of the regime of Saddam Hussein. In a show of victory aboard the USS *Abraham Lincoln* on May 2, 2003, Bush spoke under a banner that declared, "Mission Accomplished." However, that declaration of victory proved to be premature. What Bush did not count on was the difficulty of both ending the war and building the peace.[32]

Much has been written about the issues and problems associated with the war in Iraq,[33] and we are not going to review or critique the decision here. Suffice it to say, the decision to invade Iraq without UN or allied support had a devastating impact on perceptions of the United States internationally. It also divided the country domestically.[34] Further, the longer the war continued, the more skeptical the American public and especially the allies became. But this did not stop George W. Bush from winning a second term in the election of 2004. When it comes right down to it, the American public does not like to change leaders during a war. And, as Bush kept reminding the American public, he was a wartime president.

Freedom and Democracy for All

As George W. Bush started his second term in office in January 2005, public opinion polls showed an increasing number of Americans were skeptical about the mission in Iraq and whether the goal of establishing a truly democratic Iraq would succeed. At that time, polls found an overall approval rating for Bush of 50 percent, versus a disapproval rating of 43 percent. A poll taken in May 2004, about six months prior to the election and just about a year after the war in Iraq started, indicated that overall, 50 percent thought that the war was going well, while 46 percent thought it was not. What this suggests is a country that was deeply divided.[35]

Despite candidate Bush's claim that the United States should not engage in nation building, a direct criticism of the Democrats, as President Bush began his second term, not only was the United States engaged in doing so in Iraq, but Bush's inaugural address suggested that the United States would continue its involvement globally, pursuing the Wilsonian ideals of freedom and democracy for all. The war on terror in general and the war in Iraq in particular were part of President Bush's broader policy agenda to spread freedom and democracy. He articulated this concept in his second inaugural address when he said: "There is only one force of history that can break the reign of hatred and resentment, and expose the pretensions of tyrants, and reward the hopes of the decent and tolerant, and that is the force of human freedom." And in language reminiscent of an earlier era, he continued: "So it is the policy of the United States to seek and support the growth of democratic movements and institutions in every nation and culture, with the ultimate goal of ending tyranny in our world."[36]

In his foreign policy decisions following September 11, and especially going into his second term, Bush appeared to be drawing on Wilsonian idealism using America's military might to accomplish this goal.[37] The term coined by the administration to describe this foreign policy direction was "practical idealism," which refers to "the policy's underlying premise that in a post-Sept. 11 world, America's national security is tied directly to the spread of free and open societies everywhere, including the Middle East."[38]

In his book *Winning the Right War*, foreign policy analyst Philip Gordon notes that the Bush administration, early in its second term, started to recognize the reality that an America "that is popular, respected, reliable, and admired has a far better chance of winning needed cooperation than an America that is not." He also contends that the administration was aware of the high price it paid "for gratuitously alienating allies and that diplomatic efforts to repair relations were worthwhile."[39] This awareness resulted in an effort by then-secretary of state Rice to attempt to mend relations with the allies by traveling to Europe. President Bush made similar trips, including one to European capitals in June 2008, dubbed his "farewell tour." According to one account of that visit, "The question of his legacy hangs over his eight-day visit to Europe." But this account also notes the fact that the war in Iraq "did more to strain relations with Europe—not to mention with the Muslim world—than any issue since Ronald Reagan deployed intermediate missiles in Europe in 1984 at the height of the cold war. As a result, he [Bush] remains deeply unpopular in Europe, as he does at home."[40]

What is clear is that during most of its tenure, the Bush administration was trying to define a new direction for U.S. foreign policy in the post–Cold War world and that despite the administration's protestations to the contrary, this policy was formulated in response to external events. In many ways, these events and the Bush administration's reactions to them defined the direction of U.S. foreign policy for the early part of the twenty-first century. They are also further proof that regardless of how much a president might try to initiate a particular course of action, ultimately he (or she) will be forced to react to the most immediate and pressing issues that arise.

While it is still too soon to determine the long-term impact of the Bush administration decisions, some factors can already be identified. What is clear is that shortly before he left office, December 2008 polls show that his approval rating had dropped to 24 percent and his disapproval rating had gone up to 68 percent. The only group that overwhelmingly remained supportive was conservative Republicans.[41]

It is important to note that it was not just his decisions about Iraq that undermined Bush's popularity at home. Domestic events, such as his handling of Hurricane Katrina and the failure to enact some of his signature policies such as Social Security and immigration reform, combined with skepticism about what was going on in the prison at Guantanamo in the wake of Abu Ghraib and the deteriorating situation in Iraq and Afghanistan contributed to rising doubts among the American people about Bush's leadership.

President Bush and Wilsonian Idealism

Even though the Bush administration initially justified the war with Iraq based on the need to find weapons of mass destruction, it quickly morphed into the need for "regime change" to get rid of a nasty dictator who used such weapons against his own people and who posed a threat to the United States and its allies. There was talk of the ways in which the United States would be greeted as "liberators" who freed the Iraqi people from their dictator, and the assumption was that tribal differences within the country would be swept aside as the people of Iraq worked together to rebuild their country as a democracy. Using religious terms, Bush often spoke of America's mission to "'rid the world of evil' and to promote 'God-given values' around the world. The ability of the United States to 'shape events' added to that mission a license to depose 'evil' leaders such as Saddam Hussein."[42]

Bush is often equated with Wilson in the zeal with which he pursued the ideals of promoting democracy and pursuing a foreign policy based on values. However, Bush did not learn all the lessons of history, specifically, that values such as "democracy" and "freedom" cannot be imposed. For example, after becoming president in 1913, Wilson boasted "that he could transform Latin America, if not the rest of the world, into constitutional democracies in America's image." He was vocal in his opposition to Mexican dictator Victoriano Huerta, but, as he discovered, "attempts to instill American-style constitutional democracy and capitalism through force were destined to fail.

. . . In Mexico, Wilson came to understand in practice what he had written in his theories of government—that 'self-government is not a thing that can be "*given*" to any people'" (emphasis added).[43]

In the Bush administration, the forces of the neoconservatives, who had been pushing for war with Iraq and the overthrow of Saddam Hussein since the end of the first Persian Gulf War, adopted Wilson's values but "insisted upon employing McKinley's and Theodore Roosevelt's means to achieve it. They believed in transforming the world in America's image, but sought to do so through the unimpeded use of American power rather than through international cooperation and organization."[44] As author Judis notes, "If the administration's experience in Iraq increasingly resembles past American imperial ventures, Bush's experience was remarkably similar to McKinley's in the Philippines more than a century before."[45]

Wilson had changed the underlying framework of American foreign policy to inject values, such as democracy, which he saw as a universal given. However, Bush tempered that set of values with his own beliefs of the United States as an imperial power with a preordained role to play in the world. These values guided his decisions to go to war with Iraq. But as one political scientist notes, "As the Iraq war turned into a protracted and costly struggle, both the rationale for the American presence in Iraq and the aim of the war shifted substantially. The Iraq war was less about relinquishing Iraq of its weapons of mass destruction than about bringing freedom and democracy to the Middle East."[46]

Clearly, Bush's foreign policy embodies some of the idealism of Wilson with the imperialism of McKinley and Theodore Roosevelt. In understanding the impact of this blend of foreign policy orientations, Judis summarizes it well when he states that "America's true power has always rested not only in its economic and military strength, but in its determination to use that strength *in cooperation with others* on behalf of the equality of individuals and nations" (emphasis added).[47]

Iraq and Its Aftermath

In November 2008, while the Bush administration was still in office, the governments of the United States and Iraq signed a Status of Forces Agreement (SOFA) that would govern the withdrawal of American troops from Iraq. Under the terms of this agreement, all U.S. forces "shall withdraw from all Iraqi territory no later than December 31, 2011." The agreement also specifies clearly that "All United States *combat* forces shall withdraw from all Iraqi cities, villages and localities no later than the time at which Iraqi Security Forces assume full responsibility for security in an Iraqi province, *provided that such withdrawal is completed no later than June 30, 2009"* (emphasis added).[48] In other words, according to the terms of the agreement, while the government of Iraq acknowledges the need to look to the United States to "support" Iraq "in its efforts to maintain security and stability in Iraq," the primary responsibility would fall to the government of Iraq.

As the time got closer for the withdrawal of U.S. forces from Iraq, concerns mounted in both countries. An article in the *New York Times* on June 26, 2009, summarized the ambivalence surrounding this withdrawal. On the one hand, to Iraqi prime minister Nuri al-Maliki, the event was seen as a "great victory" and one that "he compares to the rebellion against British troops in 1920." The Americans, for their part, have been willing "to suspend virtually all American operations—even in support roles—for the first few days in July to reinforce the perception that Mr. Maliki desires: that Iraq's security forces are now fully in control of Iraq's cities." However, according to this news report, "the deadline has provoked uncertainty and even dread among average Iraqis, underscoring the potential problems that Mr. Maliki could face if bloodshed intensifies."[49] The concern, clearly, is a return to the sectarian violence that characterized much of the war prior to the increase in the number of American troops, known as "the surge," early in 2007.

Under the terms of the Status of Forces Agreement, there would not be a total withdrawal of U.S. troops; thousands will remain in Iraq but with their role shifted from combat to support, primarily training and advising. They would also conduct operations "that the Iraqis would not yet do on their own, like emergency medical evacuation."[50] A paramount goal for both Iraq and the United States was to stress the importance of Iraq as a sovereign nation headed by a democratically elected leader (Mr. Maliki), and to ensure that, eventually, a sense of "normalcy" returns to that country. The SOFA allows for continued U.S. assistance "to strengthen the political and military capabilities of the Republic of Iraq to deter threats against its sovereignty, political independence, territorial integrity, and its constitutional deferral democratic system."[51] Despite the withdrawal of its combat forces and the timeline for the withdrawal of all U.S. troops, the role of the United States in Iraq is far from over.

The Obama Administration: The First Year

It appeared that the major issue of the presidential election campaign of 2008 would be the United States' place in the world in general, and the war in Iraq in particular. Writing in *Foreign Affairs* in 2007, then-candidate Obama confronted what he saw as the failures of American leadership and issued a call for the United States to "rebuild the alliances, partnerships, and institutions necessary to confront common threats and enhance common security."[52] Obama echoed many of those same themes in a speech in Berlin in July 2008, when he said that "we know that sometimes, on both sides of the Atlantic, we have drifted apart, and forgotten our shared destiny." He then continued, "Just as American bases built in the last century still help to defend the security of this continent, so does our country still sacrifice greatly for freedom around the globe."[53] Once again, the emphasis appeared to be on the ideals of freedom and sacrifice that had been themes in U.S. foreign policy since Wilson. But, unlike Bush, if elected president, Obama was going to do this in a way that was consultative, with an emphasis on building and/or rebuilding the partnerships and alliances that were a mainstay of U.S. foreign policy in the past.

As a candidate, Obama's areas of emphasis regarding U.S. foreign policy were on the need to rebuild the alliances that he felt had been undermined during the years of the Bush administration and to allow the United States to regain its place as a global leader. He was criticized during the primaries by his Democratic rivals and then by John McCain, his Republican opponent, for his naiveté in stating that he wanted to reach out to, and negotiate with, hostile countries such as Iran. But Obama remained adamant that the most effective foreign policy would not be based solely on reliance on military might, but that it must be balanced with cooperation, negotiation, and diplomacy.

Going into the elections, the image that had been painted of then-candidate Obama was of someone who was weak on foreign policy, at least compared with his far more experienced opponent, John McCain. Obama's selection of his running mate, Joe Biden, a senior senator known for his experience in foreign policy, helped deflect that charge somewhat. But it was assumed that in any McCain-Obama debate on foreign policy, it would be Obama who would be seen as too young and inexperienced to be president in this dangerous time.

However, just a few months prior to the election, the global economic crisis hit and eclipsed all other issues in the campaign. Here the Obama campaign quickly proved to be more adept and was quick to address the situation. Rightly or not, the United States was being blamed for the economic downturn that affected not only it, but most of the rest of the world. A 2008 Pew poll found that "the U.S. image is suffering almost everywhere," due, at least in part, to the fact that "in the most economically developed countries, people blame America for the financial crisis."[54] Thus, the emphasis of the campaign quickly shifted, although Obama also made it clear that, if elected president, among his first priorities would be ending the war in Iraq, giving renewed attention to the war in Afghanistan, closing the prison camp at Guantanamo

Bay, and, in general, working to restore the United States' position in the world. But to the American electorate, foreign policy was a secondary concern compared with the economy, a pattern that seems to be a given. This helped sway the public to elect Obama in an election that also brought a significant Democratic majority to the House and Senate.

Obama and Iraq and Afghanistan

After eight years in which U.S. influence internationally waned and its power—especially soft power—was undermined, many around the world as well as at home were waiting to hear what the new president would say and were eager to learn in what direction he would take the United States. As he made clear in his inaugural address, Barack Obama came into office facing critical challenges to United States foreign and security policy. In that address on January 20, 2009, Obama identified what his U.S. foreign policy priorities would be as president. To all who were watching and listening, both at home and abroad, he sent these words: "Know that America is a friend of each nation and every man, woman, and child who seeks a future of peace and dignity, and that *we are ready to lead once more*" (emphasis added).[55]

Philip Gordon notes simply that "having a new face in the White House will itself do more to restore many allies' disinclination to work closely with the United States."[56] While that might be true at least for a start, the burden will be on the Obama administration to show that it can follow through on its campaign promises and that the United States can lead once again. But this will not be an easy task. As the report of the Pew Global Attitudes Project noted, "When Barack Obama is sworn in as America's new president in January, he will inherit two wars in distant lands, one highly unpopular and the other going badly, along with a worldwide financial crisis that is being measured against the Great Depression. He will confront the prospect of destructive global climate change and the spread of nuclear weapons to rogue states." From a foreign policy perspective, the report also states that "opposition to key elements of American foreign policy is widespread in Western Europe, and positive views of the U.S. have declined steeply among many of America's longtime European allies."[57] In short, President Obama began his presidency facing a number of challenges, both domestic and international, and many will be watching his first year in office to get a sense of the new president and the direction of U.S. foreign policy.

One of candidate Obama's priorities was to end the war in Iraq. In some ways, the course for this was set for him in the SOFA and the commitment that U.S. combat forces withdraw by June 30, 2009. Nonetheless, as noted above, this withdrawal by no means suggests the end of U.S. involvement in that country. Certainly, U.S. forces will remain to aid the Iraqi government and its security forces. But technically, their role is only to support the Iraqi forces.

Clearly, this was not a war of Obama's making, and his administration has consistently made it clear that it is not a war that he would have chosen to fight. But since that decision was made by his predecessor, leaving the United States committed, a larger question remains, and that is what *should* the United States do if sectarian violence increases in the wake of U.S. withdrawal? The answer to that question will be up to this president and is unknown at the time this book went to press.

From the time he was a candidate, Obama made it clear that his focus would be on the war in Afghanistan, which he felt suffered under the Bush administration's attention to Iraq. In remarks that he made as early as August 2007, then-candidate Obama was critical of the war in Iraq, which he termed "a dumb war, a rash war," but he also stressed the need to pay more attention to Afghanistan. In one of many speeches that he gave on the subject, he claimed that by focusing on Iraq, "We did not finish the job against al Qaeda in Afghanistan. We did not develop new capabilities to defeat a new enemy, or launch a comprehensive strategy to dry up the terrorists' base of support. We did not reaffirm our basic values, or secure our homeland." And he outlined the direction that an Obama administration would take: "We will wage the war that has to be won, with a comprehensive strategy with five elements: getting out of Iraq and on to the right battlefield in Afghanistan and Pakistan; developing the capabilities and partnerships we need to take out the terrorists and the world's most deadly weapons; engaging the world to dry up support for terror and extremism; restoring our values; and securing a more resilient homeland." He then continued to emphasize his main points: "The first step must be getting off the *wrong battlefield* in Iraq, and taking the fight to the terrorists in Afghanistan and Pakistan" (emphasis added).[58]

Less than two years later, as a relatively new president, Obama started to bring to fruition those policies he had outlined as a candidate. As noted above, the issue of withdrawing troops from Iraq had been set by the SOFA agreement, and that moved forward. As promised, he turned his attention to Afghanistan, and shortly after taking office, he ordered the deployment of additional combat troops to that country, with more deployments to follow contingent on the results of a policy review that he ordered. And, in another indicator of how serious he was about shifting priorities, he appointed Richard Holbrooke, former U.S. ambassador to the United Nations and architect of the Dayton Agreement that ended the war in Bosnia, as his special representative to Afghanistan and Pakistan, thereby raising the profile of these two countries still further.

Obama reinforced this message about shifting priorities in remarks he made on March 27, following the results of the comprehensive policy review. Obama couched his remarks in terms that made it clear that there would be a new direction in U.S. foreign policy: "So I want the American people to understand that we have a clear and focused goal: to disrupt, dismantle and defeat al Qaeda in Pakistan and Afghanistan, and to prevent their return to either country in the future." He framed the changes in policy that he would announce by noting that "our troops [in Afghanistan] have fought bravely against a ruthless enemy. Our allies have borne a heavy burden. Afghans have suffered and sacrificed for their future. But for six years, Afghanistan has been denied the resources that it demands because of the war in Iraq. Now, we must make a commitment that can accomplish our goals." And in words that harkened back to the idealism of the past, he continued, "*That is a cause that could not be more just*" (emphasis added).[59]

In a shift in policy from the Bush administration and consistent with Obama's emphasis on diplomacy and negotiation (soft power) rather than solely depending on military might, the president also announced at that time that there will be a "standing, trilateral dialogue among the United States, Afghanistan and Pakistan. Our nations will meet regularly with Secretaries Clinton [Secretary of State] and Gates [Secretary of Defense][60] leading our effort." And he announced the deployment of additional U.S. troops to Afghanistan to engage in direct combat with the Taliban and to help secure the borders, but also to train the Afghan forces specifically for the purpose of building an Afghan army. Clearly the goal here is to build the Afghan army "as our plans to turn over security responsibility to the Afghans go forward."[61] Contrary to the decision to go to war with Iraq, which continued with no exit strategy or plan to end U.S. involvement until the SOFA was signed, under the Obama administration, the United States would be involved with Afghanistan for a limited amount of time and with specific goals in mind. How successful this plan actually is remains to be seen.

Ties to the Islamic World

Obama understood quickly that diminished relations with the Islamic world was one of the major results of the Bush administration policies. Although he is a Christian, because he had spent some of his childhood in Indonesia, the world's most populous Islamic country, Obama knew that he was in a unique position to heal the rift that had emerged between the United States and the Islamic world. But he also understood that the world was watching and that he had to move relatively quickly. For the Obama administration, the outreach to the Islamic world was important not only to mend fences, but because if the United States were once again to be an active participant in the quest for peace in the Middle East, then the country needed to establish credibility among the Islamic nations. He decided to begin the process by making a speech about U.S. relations with the Islamic world in June 2009, about five months after taking office, and to do so in a Muslim country. Hence, the content of the speech had far-reaching consequences.

There was a great deal of speculation as well as secrecy surrounding the venue for the proposed speech. The decision that the president give the speech at Cairo University in Egypt was, in itself, fraught with symbolism. While some were puzzled by his choice of Egypt, which has been less than democratic in presidential elections as well as having a relatively poor human rights record, the White House stressed the importance of Cairo as the "heart of the Muslim world." Furthermore, if the United States is to play a role in negotiating peace between the Palestinians and Israel, the speech in Cairo would virtually guarantee a Palestinian audience as well as send an important symbolic message by choosing the first country to sign a peace agreement with Israel as the venue.

The speech itself was closely watched and parsed not only for what it did say, but for what it did not. Obama began by recognizing the tensions that have emerged between the United States and the Muslim world in general as well as acknowledging the need for a "new beginning between the United States and Muslims around the world: one based upon mutual interest and mutual respect; and one based upon the truth that America and Islam are not exclusive, and need not be in competition. Instead, they overlap, and share common principles—principles of justice and progress; tolerance and the dignity of all human beings."[62]

And then Obama outlined what he called "specific issues that . . . we must finally confront together," beginning with the need "to confront violent extremism in all of its forms." And in saying this, Obama echoed a point that he had made during a speech in Ankara, Turkey, a few months prior: "America is not—and never will be—at war with Islam.[63] We will, however, relentlessly confront violent extremists who pose a grave threat to our security. Because we reject the same thing that people of all faiths reject: the killing of innocent men, women, and children. And it is my first duty as President to protect the American people."[64]

In saying this, President Obama drew an important distinction between the Islamic people and the terrorists or extremists that attacked and threatened the United States and its allies. Here, too, he distinguished himself and his administration from the previous one, where terrorists were often conflated with Muslims in general, leading to the further isolation of the United States from a large portion of the world. Obama made it clear that he understood the difference between a war of necessity (Afghanistan) and war of choice (Iraq), and that he would engage in the former only when it becomes necessary. In saying this, however, he also stressed that his emphasis will be on the use of diplomacy and soft power: "I believe that events in Iraq have reminded America of the need to use diplomacy and build consensus to resolve our problems whenever possible."[65]

In identifying the issues that countries need to address together, Obama focused on many that were of special interest to his audience in the Middle East and Islamic world, including the countries of Iraq and Israel and the Palestinian people. And in a point directed especially to Iran, he spoke of the need to stop the spread of nuclear weapons. Among the other issues that he addressed was democracy, a point that had been stressed by the Bush administration and that was one of the justifications for the war in Iraq. But here Obama specifically stated that "no system of government can or should be imposed upon one nation by another." And he reiterated his commitment "to governments that reflect the will of the people," but continued that this principle must be "grounded in the traditions of its own people." And, again reflecting the Wilsonian principles that have been heard in the past, Obama spoke of his "unyielding belief that all people yearn for certain things: the ability to speak your mind and have a say in how you are governed; confidence in the rule of law and the equal administration of justice; government that is transparent and doesn't steal from the people; the freedom to live as you choose. These are not just American ideas, they are human rights, and that is why we will support them everywhere."[66]

In a clear criticism of Egyptian president Mubarak as well as other autocratic leaders, Obama also spoke of those who "once in power . . . are ruthless in suppressing the rights of others" and of how "you must maintain your power through consent, not coercion. . . . Without those ingredients, elections alone do not make a true democracy."[67] But implied in his words were not the rhetoric of "regime change" or "axis of evil" states, but rather, the recognition that ultimately it must be up to the people of the state to make decisions about their form of government. Clearly, the United States would be a partner and would help promote the ideals that are important by providing economic aid and assistance, expanding access to education, technological development, and so on. But to be effective, it would have to be a partnership, and the goals that he outlined could be achieved only if countries work together.

In going to Cairo and also in a separate meeting with Israeli prime minister Netanyahu, Obama made it clear that the United States would again be an active participant in peace talks between Israel and the Palestinians. Working toward Middle East peace had been a priority of the United States in the past but was something that had languished under the Bush administration. The

Bush administration had hosted a summit in Annapolis, Maryland, in 2007 to "facilitate" a peace process, but little came of it beyond the outline of a "road map." In contrast, the Obama administration signaled early on that the United States would be actively engaged once again. The decision to appoint George Mitchell as special envoy to the Middle East was another sign of the seriousness with which this administration took the Middle East negotiations. Mitchell, the former Senate majority leader, had been appointed by President Clinton to help negotiate a settlement in Northern Ireland, which resulted in the signing of the Good Friday Agreement in 1998. Appointing Mitchell was proof positive of this administration's commitment to the peace process.

Obama also made it clear that the position of the United States is that Israel would have to freeze all settlement activities, a point that was reiterated by Secretary of State Clinton. After both Mrs. Clinton's meetings and President Obama's with both Netanyahu and Palestinian president Mahmoud Abbas, George Mitchell began negotiating with Israel and its neighbors. While it is too soon to tell what, if anything, will come out of those meetings, the Obama administration has given every sign not only of wanting to be involved, but of wanting to reach an agreement.

Relations with Europe and Other Challenges

Relations between the United States and its European allies were strained severely because of the decision to go to war with Iraq. If transatlantic relations are really to improve, then the United States must go beyond reaching out to Europe as a whole through NATO and the European Union (EU) and also work directly with individual countries to assuage their particular concerns. The United States has been looking to Europe to provide additional troops to help fight the escalating war in Afghanistan, something that the Europeans are hesitant to do. The enmity that many in Europe feel toward the United States was heightened by the onset of the economic crisis, which, correctly or not, many blame on the United States.

Obama has met with many of the European leaders either individually or as part of summits, and he remains wildly popular in Europe. But the European leaders themselves are facing domestic challenges, both economic and political, that suggest that they will remain distant from the United States. For example, British prime minister Gordon Brown's Labor government will no doubt be replaced by a Conservative one (if it has not been already). Angela Merkel in Germany is under attack at home because of her close ties to the Bush administration and her decision to lend German support to the war in Afghanistan. While Germany has been criticized by some for not pulling its weight in the conflict, Merkel cannot risk further domestic anger by increasing German support for the U.S. mission there. By all accounts, President Obama and French president Sarkozy appear to be getting along well, and the fact that Sarkozy agreed to bring France back into the NATO unified military structure can be construed as a sign of support for the United States. However, what the past few years have made clear is that Europe is no longer an unquestioning ally, willing to go along with whatever the United States wants or wherever the United States leads. While it is clear that there are, and will continue to be, close ties between the United States and the countries of Europe, the Obama administration will have to prove that it will not simply dictate policy but will consult with this group of economic, as well as political and military, allies.

There will be a number of areas in which the United States and Europe disagree, as they have at various times in the past. One of those pertains to Turkey and its accession to the EU. In his speech in Ankara, President Obama stressed the relationship between the United States and Turkey and was unambiguous when he said that "the United States strongly supports Turkey's bid to become a member of the EU. We speak not as members of the EU, but as close friends of both Turkey and Europe." He sent an important signal to both Turkey and the EU when he said that "Turkey has pursued difficult political reforms not simply because it's good for EU membership, but because it's right for Turkey." And in framing the speech, he harkened back to the Truman Doctrine, which "committed our nation to the defense of Turkey's freedom and sovereignty, and Turkey committed itself to the NATO Alliance."[68] Like Bush, Obama was stressing the importance of democracy and democratic reforms, but additionally, what Obama did was praise Turkey for moving forward with these for reasons beyond conditions for EU membership. As in the past, democracy seems to be a theme of the Obama administration, but democracy pursued from within rather than imposed from without.

The Obama administration is facing a number of other international security and foreign policy challenges beyond those mentioned above. The questionable presidential election in Iran in June 2009 that resulted in the reelection of President Ahmadinejad was another indicator of how difficult it will be for the United States to deal with that state. However, rather than trying to isolate it, as was the policy of the Bush administration, the Obama administration has given signs that it plans to pursue the dual tracks of negotiation and diplomacy, as well as threats when necessary.

Similarly, it appears that North Korea is testing the mettle of the new president at a time when the leadership of North Korea appears to be unsettled. Here, too, rather than simply trying to isolate that regime, the Obama administration has indicated plans to pursue negotiations as well as threats. Since threats have not been successful in bringing about the desired outcome (the end of their nuclear weapons programs) in the case of either North Korea or Iran, Obama seems to be looking toward a more cooperative strategy, albeit one backed up by threats if or as necessary.

Bush versus Obama

How different will Obama's foreign policy be from that of his predecessor? Those who were opposed to President Bush's policies hope to see a radical change in policy from one that was premised on the use of hard power and military force as the means for asserting U.S. principles to one that acknowledges the role of negotiation and diplomacy; from one that was based on a go-it-alone-if-necessary attitude to one that is firmly committed to cooperation; from one that used Wilsonian ideals as the justification for military intervention to one that supports ideals and principles but does not seek to impose them on any country. On the other hand, those who supported Bush are concerned about whether Obama's talk about diplomacy and cooperation will undermine the perception of U.S. strength at a time when the United States needs to appear strong. But is it really that simple? Are the contrasts as stark as they might appear to be?

As noted above, the early indicators are that the Obama administration's foreign policy will be quite different from the policies pursued under Bush. But that, too, can lead to mistakes and errors. In fact, among the traps that the Bush administration fell into was that it did not want to replicate the Clinton administration policies and what were seen as the flaws in Clinton's foreign policy. In seeking to be different, to show that the United States was not afraid to use force and was not dependent on soft power, the Bush administration went to the extreme, resulting in the decision to engage in a "war of choice" that resulted in isolation for the United States. While there is little doubt that the Bush administration pursued the policies that it believed to be in the best interest of the United States, with hindsight, it is clear that such policies made the world a more dangerous place and the United States more, rather than less, vulnerable.

If foreign policy is a continuous process, as we indicated in chapter 1, then can an Obama administration really turn aside or reverse the course of Bush administration policy? Or would it be more prudent to build on some of the more popular policies, such as staying true to U.S. values of democracy and freedom while moving away from those policies that were unpopular, including the unfettered use of force that has so isolated the United States? These are tough questions that do not yet have any answers, and certainly not easy ones.

In the next and final chapter, based on some of the general conclusions about American foreign policy, we will reiterate some of the basic themes and see whether some conclusions can be drawn about the future of U.S. foreign policy.

Applying Foreign Policy Concepts: Response to September 11

In this chapter, we looked at the decisions made by the Bush administration based on its understanding of the events of September 11. We now have a more complete understanding of what happened and why, as well as who was behind the awful events. However, at the time, the Bush administration felt that it had to respond, which it did based on what was then known, the advice of those within the administration, and also the underlying ideological perspective that was guiding the administration at that time. If you were an advisor to President Bush, and you knew then what you know now, what would you have recommended, and why?

In order to determine this, you need to identify the critical players at the time (e.g., the terrorist groups involved and the role of Congress, the military, the public, the allies, etc.), what position or positions each of them took on this issue, and what you think was in the national interest at the time. This all must be put into the framework of U.S. foreign policy direction (unilateralist versus expansionist) as well as your own understanding of resources available to the United States, specifically, the use of hard versus soft power. Put another way, would you have resorted to the use of military power against either Afghanistan and/or Iraq or pursued a different option, and why?

The Case

On September 11, 2001, nineteen men hijacked four aircraft. They crashed two into the World Trade Center in New York and one into the Pentagon, and the fourth crashed in Pennsylvania, short of its target in Washington, D.C., when passengers fought back. Approximately three thousand people lost their lives in those attacks. One of the highest priorities of the Bush administration was to find out what happened and then formulate a response to the event.

The United States' allies rallied behind the country and invoked Article 5 of the NATO treaty for the first time in the history of the alliance. But outside of allowing AWACS aircraft to help patrol the skies over the United States in case of further attack, the United States chose not to seek an allied response.

Investigations into the attacks found that the hijackers were all part of the Al Qaeda terrorist network founded and led by Osama bin Laden. The men, all of whom were from the Middle East, were believed to have been part of a group trained in the radical *madrasas* in Pakistan and Afghanistan and to have received their terrorist training at camps in those countries. Through its investigations the United States also learned that bin Laden probably was in Afghanistan, but the Taliban government refused to turn him over to U.S. authorities.

The period immediately following September 11 was a time of confusion and uncertainty for much of the United States. For the president, however, the attacks "confirmed what Bush already believed: The world was a danger-ous place. Terrorists bent on doing harm were not stopped by a smile and an open hand, but by grim determination and a closed fist. International agree-ments and institutions could not protect the American people; only the might of the American military could." And for President Bush, "foreign policy, or more precisely, the war on terrorism, became the defining mission of his presidency."[69]

President Bush was determined that the United States had to respond force-fully to those attacks. But the question was where and how to respond. Any response would have to send a signal to future groups or even countries that the United States was a major force to be reckoned with. Clearly, the terror-ists came from a number of different places and relied on different countries for support. Further, Al Qaeda, a nonstate organization, was the "bad guy" rather than any single country. The American public looked to the president for direction, and the polls showed that he had the support of the public. The Congress understood that this was a direct attack on the country and looked to the executive for a response, albeit with congressional approval. It would be up to the president to determine what to do next and to be sure that the Congress and the public supported him.

What Would You Do If . . .

The time is October 2001. George W. Bush has been president for nine months, and he came into office after a disputed election. His priority was to begin to withdraw the United States from some of its commitments abroad and refocus the country's priorities. Rather than looking toward the traditional European allies, Bush felt that the United States should be strengthening its ties to Central and Latin America. Initially Bush was accused of pursuing an isolationist foreign policy, as he refused to endorse the Kyoto Protocol, and he withdrew the United States from the 1972 ABM Treaty as an example of how the United States would chart its own foreign policy course. September 11 changed the direction of U.S. policy, and the responses to that event would define U.S. foreign policy for the Bush administration and beyond.

What would you do if you were a close advisor to President Bush and he looked to you for recommendations about how to respond to the attacks of September 11? By late September and early October, you have some essential information about the attacks, but there is still a lot that is not yet known. You know that you would have the support of the American people and the Congress as well as allies for a military response, but against which country should the attack be directed? What should be the short- and long-term goals, and how will you achieve them? Given what you know now, including the consequences (both intended and unintended), what would you recommend that President Bush do, and why? And finally, although we can never know this for certain, speculate as to whether you think the outcome would have been different if Al Gore, Bill Clinton's vice president, had won the contested presidential election of 2000 rather than George W. Bush.

7

The Future of U.S. Foreign Policy

<hr />

CHAPTER 1 POSED SEVERAL QUESTIONS ABOUT U.S. FOREIGN POLICY, starting with why it is important to learn about the subject. The goal of this chapter is to tie together the themes and ideas raised throughout the book so that you can begin to answer some of those questions for yourself. Remember that in many cases there are no clear-cut answers, nor are there objective "right" or "wrong" answers. Rather, the main point is that you need to know how to gather and analyze information so that you have the tools to better understand U.S. foreign policy.

It is beyond the scope of this book to try to speculate or predict what the shape of U.S. foreign policy will be in the future. However, by looking at the past and understanding the ideas that have governed the creation of U.S. foreign policy, you will be in a better position to understand what *might* happen in the future and why, as well as to evaluate what *did* happen in the past.

The Cold War as a Framework for U.S. Foreign Policy

The Cold War provided a clear framework for guiding U.S. foreign policy.[1] According to the realist theorists, power is the ability of one country to influence another to do what it wants or to influence the outcome of events. During the Cold War, "power" was thought of primarily as hard power (i.e., tied to military might), and foreign policy was based on the belief that it was necessary to maintain a balance of power between the United States and the Soviet Union. This did not mean that both sides needed to have exactly the same number of weapons; rather, it meant that there had to be a sense that if one side attacked, the other side had the capability to respond, at least enough so that it would not be worth it for either side to attack first (i.e., deterrence).

While it is not often placed in the same category as military might, economic power is another important factor that was used to leverage the outcome of events. The decision to "reward" a country by giving it financial aid or other assistance was one economic approach used during and after the Cold War to sway countries to a particular side. Conversely, imposing economic sanctions or tariffs to "punish" countries is an approach that is still used. Hence, economic tools can be used to influence a country's position. In a world that has become increasingly interdependent, economic power is an important commodity.

The Changing Notion of Power

One of the things that has changed most dramatically since the Cold War ended has been the very notion of what "power" is or means. It still is important to have economic power as well as enough military power to deter, defend, and protect as necessary, and both are considered examples of "hard power." But the concept of power can be broadened to include what has been called "soft power." According to Nye, "Hard power rests on inducements (carrots) or threats (sticks)," whereas "soft power rests on the ability to set a political agenda in a way that shapes the preferences of others."[2] While soft power has always been a component of U.S. foreign policy, it has become more prominent since the end of the Cold War.

However, soft power carries with it dangers, some of which have become apparent in the wake of September 11, 2001. Where "soft power arises in large part from our values" and from the desire for other countries or for people in other countries to want to emulate the United States,[3] it also carries with it the risks that those values are, or are perceived to be, antithetical to the core values of another country or culture. The imposition of one country's values on another is known as "cultural imperialism," something that the United States has been accused of.

As noted above, Nye divides power into two broad categories, hard and soft. Another author, Walter Russell Mead, makes a further distinction when he divides American power in particular into four types: sharp (military), sticky (economic), sweet (culture and ideals), and hegemonic. Sharp, sticky, and sweet "contribute to hegemonic power," as they come together and create a whole that is greater than the sum of the parts.[4] His point is that power can be looked at in any number of ways; American power is hegemonic because when the various types of power are applied together, as they have been since the end of World War II, they allow the United States to grow in strength and importance in the international arena. In his estimation, the United States has been so effective because of the use of the *full range* of the power that it has and has used.

Nye, Mead, and others who try to categorize power would affirm that there is a time and situation within which applying one or the other type in pursuit of national interest would be most appropriate. A major foreign policy challenge facing the United States in the twenty-first century is how to use its hegemonic power—the application of its military, economic and "soft" power of culture, ideals, and values—and to what ends. Or, put another way, how and when should the United States assume that soft power is the best option versus resorting to the use of hard power which is, by its nature, a less cooperative and more conflictual option? That is the challenge now facing the Obama administration. After years of resorting to primarily hard (military) power with little success, should the country rethink its approach to power and, as Obama has suggested thus far, be more willing to pursue policies that are more cooperative and based on soft power?

U.S. Power and National Interest

As we look to U.S. foreign policy in the twenty-first century, it is essential to go back to first principles and ask what policies are in the national interest. How should the United States use its power and its superpower status? Is the goal of U.S. power, as President Bush outlined in his second inaugural address, "to seek and support the growth of democratic movements and institutions in every nation and culture, with the ultimate goal of ending tyranny in our world"?[5] Is the goal, as Mead suggests, that the United States act as "the chief agent in a global revolutionary process through which liberal capitalism and liberal democracy are sweeping the world"?[6] Or is our goal "to join with citizens and governments; community organizations, religious leaders, and businesses . . . around the world to help our people pursue a better life," as President Obama stated in his address in Cairo?[7] All of these represent an idealist interpretation of the role of the United States, one tied to values and cooperation for mutual good. If those are the priorities, then U.S. foreign policy should be directed toward achieving those goals using the appropriate type and amount of power to achieve them.

In a world in which there is no single country that can match the power of the United States, it is easy to overlook the realist perspective that framed U.S. foreign policy through the Cold War. From that perspective, Mearsheimer suggests that "the central aim of American foreign policy . . . is to be the hegemon in the Western Hemisphere and have no rival hegemon in Europe or Northeast Asia. The United States does not want a peer competitor. In the wake of the Cold War, U.S. policymakers remain firmly committed to that goal."[8] If U.S. decision-makers decide that this more realist perspective better defines the goals for the country, then U.S. foreign policy decisions should support that perspective. Ultimately, however, the major task is to define the national interest and determine the most effective means to achieve it.

Since September 11, 2001, many people have discussed and debated why the United States is perceived as it is. Being a superpower carries with it both responsibilities and dangers. Other countries look to the United States to take the lead on important international issues, such as global warming, the fight against HIV/AIDS, or eradicating global poverty. If not leading, the role of the United States should not be to interfere with the place of these issues on the global agenda.[9] When the United States does not live up to other countries' expectations of what the United States should do, then America is seen as failing in some way. Yet, when it does take action, the desire of the United States to aid other countries can all too easily be interpreted as imposing its will on others, leading to charges of cultural imperialism. The lesson here is that the United States must be as careful with its use of soft power as it is with its use of hard power.

By 1991, the Cold War was over. Since that time the United States has yet to develop a cohesive foreign policy framework that can guide the country through the many challenges it faces in the twenty-first century. Much as George H. W. Bush advocated for a new world order, or Bill Clinton tried to focus on the economy, or George W. Bush stressed the imposition of freedom and democracy, the reality is that U.S. foreign policy in the twenty-first century will be as much a product of reactions to various events as it will be the result of proactive decisions. "Each generation of Americans must reinvent its country and its foreign policy to meet the demands of a world that, thanks in large part to our own success, is perpetually more complex and more explosive."[10]

In a globalized world, as American companies such as Starbucks or McDonald's open stores in more countries, they bring with them the perception of American dominance. McDonald's is ubiquitous, and Starbucks has been able to make inroads in China and Japan, both tea-drinking countries.[11] On the one hand, this means that people in those countries are accepting the image that Starbucks is selling, which is tied closely to American culture. On the other hand, that success also represents an assertion of American cultural values that not everyone in those countries likes or accepts. It is also an indirect and very visible assertion of American power and influence, that is, soft power.

The Changing Notion of Threat

A "threat" is anything that endangers or potentially could endanger a country or its people. Since the end of the Cold War, U.S. foreign policy has had to confront the changing perception of threat. Traditionally, threat has been tied to military might, as threats were generally perceived as the dangers from one country's attacking another. But in the late twentieth and early twenty-first centuries, a threat could emerge from situations other than military attack or an attack from one country against another. It is not necessary to belabor the impact of September 11, 2001. Suffice it to say that the attacks of that day were one example of a direct threat coming from a nonstate actor, in this case an Islamic fundamentalist group. But other threats need to be considered as well, for they, too, pose a threat to the security of the people of the United States and will—or should—influence American foreign policy decisions.

One of the characteristics of a globalized world has been a breakdown in national borders, as people, products, and ideas are transmitted easily from one country to another—communication between and among countries is virtually seamless. One can travel around the world in less than a day. Ideas and knowledge are shared easily, as scientists collaborate with colleagues in other countries using e-mail and computer technology. However, a globalized world also means that contraband materials, such as weapons and drugs, can be shipped from one place to another virtually undetected. Illegal immigrants can move from one country to another, some seeking economic opportunity, others intent on terrorism. Infectious diseases, such as SARS or "swine flu" (the H1N1 virus), can spread quickly as one person who is unknowingly carrying the disease gets on a plane and spreads it among fellow passengers, who then disperse and spread it still further.[12] Each of these examples represents a security threat that can be addressed by a foreign policy response. The decision to close the border or make it more difficult to enter a country, imposing stricter controls at entry areas (such as ports), and screening passengers for health problems are possible responses to the challenges noted above. However, while such policies might be designed to protect the population, they are also subject to cries of human rights abuses, depending on the application of the policies. Thus, all of these challenges and potential responses have foreign policy implications.

The existing approaches to American foreign policy decision-making are not necessarily ready or able to deal with these new and emerging threats; U.S.

foreign policy is still premised on a threat coming from another country and taking a particular form. However, as the examples above show, the nature of the threat has changed. Although the Bush administration created the Department of Homeland Security to try to address the terrorist threat (a threat by a nonstate actor), no administration to date has arrived at a way to create U.S. foreign policy that can anticipate and respond to the changing nature of the threats or the range of potential dangers that this country now faces. The inability to confront these threats and the difficulty in even identifying the sources of such threats are among the foreign policy challenges that the United States and other countries face in the twenty-first century.

Identifying the threats from nonstate actors does not mean that other nation-states do not also pose a threat to the United States. In his State of the Union address in January 2002, then-president Bush identified three countries that he called the "axis of evil," Iraq, Iran, and North Korea.[13] Since the time he made that speech, the government in Iraq has changed, although the situation is far from stable. Iran and North Korea both remain threats, if not to the United States directly, then certainly to U.S. allies and potentially the world, if each continues to pursue the development of nuclear weapons. While the Bush administration tried unsuccessfully to deal with each by using the threat of military action, economic sanctions, and political isolation, the Obama administration has promised a new approach that will be tied to diplomacy and negotiation to try to persuade each of these two countries to become more integrated into the international system.

Pakistan, a country that had been a strong ally of the United States in its war on terror, has become increasingly unstable as Taliban and other militant factions have become active around the border between Pakistan and Afghanistan. In Afghanistan, as noted in the previous chapter, the war continues. Under the leadership of Vladimir Putin, Russia became more militant and aggressive in its foreign policy, resulting in growing tensions between the United States and Russia once again. Although President Obama and President Medvedev of Russia agreed on the framework of a treaty to reduce their strategic nuclear arsenals, there are significant differences between the two countries regarding implementation of this treaty, as well as other foreign policy priorities.

China is another country currently vying for major power status, a perspective that will certainly affect U.S. foreign policy. China "is unlikely to surpass [the United States] on any dimension—military, political, or economic—for decades, let alone have dominance in all areas."[14] Nonetheless, "on issue after issue, it has become the second-most-important country in the world, adding a wholly new element to the international system." China has the world's fastest-growing economy and largest population, and it is one of the major military spenders.[15] Furthermore, China "tends to view both Japan and the United States as potential enemies," the former for its perceived militaristic tendencies and the latter, the United States, because of the country's relationship to Taiwan as well as concerns that the United States will stand in the way of China becoming the dominant power in Northeast Asia.[16] Whether those perceptions are correct or not, they will certainly color the way in which China acts toward the United States. And the United States must anticipate and prepare its own policies toward that country accordingly.

Africa on the whole has been an area that has largely been outside the U.S. sphere of influence and has not been an area of major foreign policy focus. Egypt, which is in North Africa, has generally been considered a Middle Eastern country rather than an African one, and U.S. policy regarding that country has been tied to policy regarding the Middle East as a whole. Similarly, Libya under Muammar Qaddafi has been a foreign policy challenge to the United States. Under the Reagan administration, the United States broke all ties with that country because of its links to international terrorism. In 2003, Libya announced that it would give up its nuclear weapons program and, subsequently, that it was working with Britain to help curtail terrorism. These events led the United States to remove Libya from its list of countries that sponsor terrorism ("state-sponsored terrorism") and to begin the process of normalizing diplomatic relations. In May 2006, the United States announced that it was reversing its previous policy and reestablishing diplomatic ties.

The countries of sub-Saharan Africa had generally been removed from areas of focus of U.S. foreign policy. Even during periods of civil war and genocide in countries such as Rwanda and Sudan, the United States remained removed from any active policies beyond verbally condemning the acts. Successive presidents, including Clinton and Bush, could not justify U.S. military intervention in those cases. And the attempt to intervene in Somalia was a foreign policy disaster. However, early indicators are that some of this will change under an Obama administration. As the first African American president, and with a Kenyan father, Obama has stronger ties to Africa than any previous president. His decision to visit Ghana following the G8 summit in July 2009 is further evidence that U.S. policy toward Africa might become more proactive in an Obama administration.

What this all suggests is that the United States is confronting more and different types of threats and challenges from other nation-states as well as nonstate actors than it did in the past, and the Obama administration needs to develop a foreign policy better suited for the challenges that the United States is facing. This might mean injecting more diplomacy, thereby balancing soft with hard power. Or it may mean more reliance on allies once again. The critical factor should be to ensure that the foreign policy is appropriate to the situation and existing political and economic realities.

The Actors and the Domestic Balance of Power

In the first chapter, we talked about the actors who make foreign policy and the constitutional framework that was to guide this process. However, what has become clear, especially in the wake of 9/11, is the emergence of a very strong executive (the "imperial presidency") at the expense of the Congress. There can be little doubt that the Congress was willing to abrogate some of its oversight responsibilities under the administration of George W. Bush and to allow the administration to pursue policies that, in retrospect, were questionable. Among these policies were the circumvention of the Foreign Intelligence Surveillance Act (FISA) and authorization of wiretaps on American citizens; the use of torture, such as waterboarding, on terrorism suspects; and the use of extraordinary rendition to send suspects to countries for extreme forms of interrogation. These policies were all enacted in the name of national security and were justified as essential to safeguarding the security of the United States. What have emerged subsequently have been charges and countercharges about what information Congress was given and how much members of Congress actually knew. But, as of the time this book went to press, former vice president Dick Cheney continued to speak out in support of the policies enacted by the Bush administration and, more important, their right to make many of those decisions, while Congress continues to complain that it was unaware of many of that administration's policies.

What history has shown is a pendulum swinging between the assertion of presidential authority and congressional prerogatives given in the Constitution if not to oversee that authority, at least to balance presidential power. The last time the perception arose that the pendulum had swung too far and that the president was abusing his power was during the administration of Richard Nixon. This resulted in passage of the War Powers Resolution and a belief in the need to check the power of the president. What followed was a series of fairly weak presidents (Ford and Carter), until Reagan once again started asserting executive power. But what we saw under Bush was an unapologetic assertion of executive power justified by events of the time.

It will be up to Obama as well as the Congress to determine how to redress the apparent imbalance. Obama has the advantage of coming into office as a popular president and with a strong Democratic majority in Congress. Like Johnson before him, he also has a robust domestic agenda that he wishes to accomplish, including addressing the economic downturn and the crisis in health care. Having learned the lessons of the past, Obama has been actively working with the Congress to help bring these policies to fruition. Both Congress and Obama seem to understand that they will accomplish more if they work together in consultation and cooperation.

This is not to suggest that the Congress will allow Obama to do whatever he wants; in fact, after what many saw as the abuses of the Bush administration, Congress seems to be more willing to engage in oversight of the executive branch once again. The fact that the two branches appear to be consulting with, rather than working against, each other bodes well for future policy decisions. After all, Obama is aware of the fact that he will not get funding for the war in Afghanistan without congressional approval. And the members of Congress, in turn, are aware of the fact that they will benefit from the perception that they are working with, rather than in opposition to, a popular president.

Challenges to U.S. Foreign Policy in the Future

As we have seen, the United States is facing a number of challenges. The decisions that are made regarding how to respond to those challenges and the direction that the United States chooses to take have far-reaching implications for the future of U.S. foreign policy. It is clear that major events, such as 9/11, can dramatically alter the direction of U.S. foreign policy. But it is also clear that when policies are formulated in reaction to events before enough time has elapsed to gain perspective, those policies can result in damage to a country's national interest.

When Barack Obama became president in January 2009, he also became the person who would reframe American foreign policy and set it on a new course. Certainly he has made clear his intention to do so. What is unknown, however, is what events might intervene that will deflect the direction of U.S. foreign policy and set it off in a new direction once again.

The world of the twenty-first century is a difficult and complicated place, and it will be up to present as well as future decision-makers to determine how to frame foreign policy that will meet those challenges and also serve U.S. national interest.

Notes

Preface to the Second Edition

1. Patricia Cohen, "Great Ceasar's Ghost! Are Traditional History Courses Vanishing?" *New York Times*, June 11, 2009.

2. John B. Judis, *The Folly of Empire: What George W. Bush Could Learn from Theodore Roosevelt and Woodrow Wilson* (New York: Scribner, 2004), 46.

Chapter 1: Setting the Stage for Understanding U.S. Foreign Policy

1. For a more complete description of these approaches to American foreign policy, see Walter Russell Mead, *Special Providence: American Foreign Policy and How It Changed the World* (New York: Alfred A. Knopf, 2002).

2. See, for example, Don Oberdorfer, "Cuban Missile Crisis More Volatile than Thought," *Washington Post*, January 14, 1992; and Martin Tolchin, "U.S. Underestimated Soviet Force in Cuba during '62 Missile Crisis," *New York Times*, January 15, 1992. Both these articles describe what became known as the result of a conference held in 1992, thirty years after the Cuban Missile Crisis. For a more comprehensive and recent book that includes new information about this event, see Michael Dobbs, *One Minute to Midnight: Kennedy, Khrushchev, and Castro on the Brink of Nuclear War* (New York: Alfred A. Knopf, 2008).

3. Mead, in *Special Providence*, notes that "foreign policy and domestic politics were inextricably mixed throughout American history" (26). That said, throughout the book he also condemns Americans, even those in positions of leadership and responsibility, for their "lack of interest in the history of American foreign policy" (7).

4. While many political science texts refer to the early period of U.S. foreign policy as "isolationist," diplomatic historians, such as Walter McDougall, make the point that the period is better described as "unilateralist." According to McDougall, "the essence of Unilateralism was to be *at Liberty* to make foreign policy independent of the 'toils of European ambition.' Unilateralism never meant that the United States should, or for that matter could, sequester itself or pursue an ostrich-like policy toward all foreign countries. It simply meant . . . that the self-evident course for the United States was to avoid permanent entangling alliances and to remain neutral in Europe's wars." Walter A. McDougall, *Promised Land, Crusader State* (New York: Houghton Mifflin, 1997), 40. The concept of *unilateralism* describes a foreign policy through which the United States is engaged with the world although steering clear of formal alliances or political obligations.

5. "The National Security Strategy of the United States of America," http://www.mtholyoke.edu/acad/intrel/bush/doctrine.htm.

6. As we will see in chapter 6, the Bush administration justified the decision to go to war in Iraq based on alleged evidence that Saddam Hussein had weapons of mass destruction, an allegation that was subsequently disproved.

7. John B. Judis makes the case that "the End of the Cold War created the conditions for finally realizing the promise of Wilson's foreign policy" (7). John B. Judis, *The Folly of Empire: What George W. Bush Could Learn from Theodore Roosevelt and Woodrow Wilson* (New York: Scribner, 2004). In many ways, it also set the stage for the policies of George W. Bush, specifically the idealistic desire to spread democracy worldwide, which in many ways harkens back to the idealism of Wilson.

8. For a detailed description of the ways in which an American corporation affects other countries, see the three articles on "the Wal-Mart effect" in the *Los Angeles Times*: Abigal Goldman and Nancy Cleeland, "An Empire Built on Bargains Remakes the Working World," November 23, 2003; Nancy Cleeland, Evelyn Iritani, and Tyler Marshall, "Scouring the Globe to Give Shoppers an $8.63 Polo Shirt," November 24, 2003; Nancy Cleeland and Abigal Goldman, "Grocery Unions Battle to Stop Invasion of the Giant Stores," November 25, 2003. The series won a Pulitzer Prize in 2004.

9. Joseph Nye, *The Paradox of American Power: Why the World's Only Superpower Can't Go It Alone* (Oxford: Oxford University Press, 2000), 9.

10. Hans J. Morgenthau, *Politics among Nations: The Struggle for Power and Peace* (Boston: McGraw-Hill, 1993), 5.

11. According to Barry Hughes, core interests "flow from the desire [of the state] to preserve its essence: territorial boundaries, population, government, and sovereignty." Barry Hughes, *Continuity and Change in World Politics: The Clash of Perspectives*, 2nd ed. (Englewood Cliffs, N.J.: Prentice Hall, 1994), 79.

12. Cynthia Enloe makes a persuasive argument about the need to take women's experiences in foreign policy and international relations seriously. For example, she writes about why and how "Carmen Miranda's movies helped make Latin America safe for American banana companies at a time when U.S. imperialism was coming under wider regional criticism." This is but one example of the ways in which women's images have been used to shape international business and economics as well as

foreign policy. Cynthia Enloe, *Bananas, Beaches, and Bases* (Berkeley: University of California Press, 2000), 124.

13. See J. Ann Tickner, *Gendering World Politics* (Cambridge: Cambridge University Press, 2001).

14. John Shattuck, "Human Rights and Humanitarian Crises: Policy-Making and the Media," in *From Massacres to Genocide: The Media, Public Policy, and Humanitarian Crises*, ed. Robert I. Rotberg and Thomas G. Weiss (Washington, D.C.: Brookings Institution, 1996), 174.

15. A series of polls released in June 2005 showed that public support for the conflict in Iraq was dropping. One poll found that 37 percent of those polled approved of the president's handling of the situation in Iraq, down from 45 percent in February (Robin Toner and Marjorie Connelly, "Bush's Support on Major Issues Tumbles in Poll," *New York Times*, June 17, 2005). A *Washington Post*-ABC News poll found that 50 percent of the respondents "now disapprove of the way Bush is handling both the economy and the situation in Iraq." This poll also found that "support for the war is the lowest yet recorded in this poll" (David Broder, "A Growing Public Restlessness," *Washington Post*, June 12, 2005, B9). Also see "Bush's Approval Ratings Stay Low," CBS News poll, http://www.cbsnews.com/stories/2005/06/16/opinion/polls/main702487.shtml.

16. "Less Optimism about Iraq," Pew Research Center for People and the Press, May 1, 2008, http://people-press.org/report/?pageid=1296.

17. As noted above, most political science texts refer to the early period of U.S. foreign policy as a period of "isolationism," meaning that the United States was "isolated" (removed) from the rest of the world, preferring to focus within. In fact, the United States was involved in a limited way, thereby making the word *unilateralist* more appropriate. However, Mearsheimer makes the case that U.S. policy in the period between the two world wars really was isolationist, in that "the United States made no serious move toward a continental commitment when the war [World War II] broke out." In fact, he notes, from the period from 1923 to the summer of 1940, the "United States committed no forces to Europe," suggesting a return to the policy advocated by George Washington. John Mearsheimer, *The Tragedy of Great Power Politics* (New York: W. W. Norton, 2001), 254. For purposes of this text, both terms will be used to describe policies that are slightly different, as appropriate at various periods in U.S. history.

18. Eugene R. Wittkopf, Charles W. Kegley Jr., and James M. Scott, *American Foreign Policy*, 6th ed. (Belmont, Calif.: Wadsworth/Thomson Learning, 2003), 27.

19. George Washington's Farewell Address, September 17, 1796, http://usinfo.state.gov/usa/infousa/facts/democrac/49.htm.

20. Mead, *Special Providence*, 14.

21. Mead, *Special Providence*, 17.

22. Mearsheimer writes that "the United States achieved great-power status in about 1898" and that "the United States was no ordinary great power by 1900. It had the most powerful economy in the world and it had clearly gained hegemony in the Western Hemisphere." Mearsheimer, *The Tragedy of Great Power Politics*, 234–35.

23. A joint U.S.-Soviet commission was established as part of the 1972 summit, when the two countries also initialed the SALT I agreement. The purpose of this commission was to begin the process for granting most favored nation trade status to the Soviet Union by the United States. The trade patterns between the two countries ebbed and flowed throughout the Cold War.

24. The U.S.-North Korean Agreed Framework of 1994 allowed for the export of U.S. oil to North Korea as well as assistance in dismantling its graphite-moderated nuclear reactors to replace them with water-moderated reactors, which is a safer method of nuclear power production. See U.S.-DPRK Agreed Framework between the United States of America and the Democratic People's Republic of Korea, October 21, 1994, http://www.kedo.org/pdfs/AgreedFramework.pdf.

25. For a more detailed explanation of the various actors and their relationship to one another and to the "rings" of power, see Roger Hilsman (with Laura Gaughran and Patricia A. Weitsman), *The Politics of Policy Making in Defense and Foreign Affairs: Conceptual Models and Bureaucratic Politics*, 3rd ed. (Englewood Cliffs, N.J.: Prentice Hall, 1993).

26. For more detail as to the relationships among the various branches of government specifically regarding war powers, see Donald L. Westerfield, *War Powers: The President, the Congress, and the Question of War* (Westport, Conn.: Praeger, 1996). Westerfield goes through a number of cases and reviews issues of constitutionality as well as how "the sense of the Congress" plays a role in limiting the power of the president.

27. Article II, Section 2, Clause 2, Constitution of the United States, http://www .house.gov/Constitution/Constitution.html.

28. Article II, Section 2, Clause 1, Constitution of the United States, http://www .house.gov/Constitution/Constitution.html.

29. Article I, Section 8, Clause 11, Constitution of the United States, http://www .house.gov/Constitution/Constitution.html.

30. "Truman's Korean War Statement," June 27, 1950, http://encarta.msn.com/ sidebar-761594739/Truman's_Korean_War_Statement.html.

31. The Tonkin Gulf Resolution is described and explored in more detail in chapter 4, "The Cold War."

32. The Constitution made Congress the branch of government that is closest to the people. This is especially true of the House of Representatives, where all members must stand for election every two years. This means that they are most sensitive to public opinion.

33. The term *military-industrial complex* was coined by President Eisenhower in his farewell address, delivered on January 17, 1961, in which he said: "We must guard against the acquisition of unwarranted influence, whether sought or unsought, by the military industrial complex. The potential for the disastrous rise of misplaced power exists and will persist." http://nas.ucdavis.edu/Forbes/Efarewell.htm.

34. Article 5 states that "an armed attack against one or more of them [the parties to the treaty] in Europe or North America shall be considered an attack against them all." The full text of the North Atlantic Treaty can be found at the NATO website, http://www.nato.int/docu/basictxt/treaty.htm.

35. Avery Johnson, "Sticker Shock at the Lumberyard," *Wall Street Journal*, August 11, 2004, D1.

Chapter 2: Unilateralism to Engagement: The Founding to the End of World War I

1. Quoted in "Bush Pushes Middle East Democracy," November 6, 2003, http://www.cnn.com/2003/ALLPOLITICS/11/06/bush.democracy/.

2. Jean E. Smith, *The Constitution and American Foreign Policy* (St. Paul, Minn.: West Publishing, 1989), 14.

3. Article II, Section 2, Clause 2 of the Constitution states: "He [the president] shall have Power, by and with the Advice and Consent of the Senate, to make Treaties, provided two thirds of the Senators present concur." Available at http://www.house.gov/Constitution/Constitution.html.

4. Quoted in Smith, *The Constitution and American Foreign Policy*, 16–17.

5. Charles Tilly makes the point that the evolution of the European state system was tied, in large measure, to war (i.e., the means of coercion), especially at a time when the United States was being created and established. "As European states moved into the phase of nationalization (especially between 1700 and 1850 . . .) dynasties lost much of their ability to make war on their own behalf, and something we call vaguely 'national interest' came to dominate states' involvement or non-involvement in wars. National interest synthesized the interests of the dominant classes, but compounded them with a much stronger drive to control contiguous territories and populations within Europe, as well as a fiercer competition for land outside Europe." It appears that Washington and some of the other founders of the country saw what was going on in Europe and, understanding that drive for competition leading to war, wanted to keep the United States removed from it as much as possible. Charles Tilly, *Coercion, Capital, and European States: AD 990–1990* (Cambridge, Mass.: Basil Blackwell, 1990), 185.

6. Alexander Hamilton, *The Federalist Papers*, No. 24 (New York: Mentor, 1961), 160–61. Also available at http://www.foundingfathers.info/federalistpaper/hamilton.htm.

7. Walter A. McDougall, *Promised Land, Crusader State* (New York: Houghton Mifflin, 1997), 31–32.

8. The entire Farewell Address is well worth reading for the way in which Washington perceived the country at that time, as well as for the argument that he made about what U.S. foreign policy should be. The address is available at http://avalon.law.yale.edu/18th_century/washington.asp.

9. The entire quotation from John Adams is: "This principle was that we should make no treaties or alliance with any European power; that we should consent to none but treaties of commerce; that we should separate ourselves, as far as possible and as long as possible from all European politics and wars." Quoted in Alan Taylor, "Adams and American Leadership: Aristocracy and Empire," available at http://web.princeton.edu/sites/jmadison/calendar/conferences/Adams%20Alan%20Taylor.pdf.

10. Eugene R. Wittkopf, Charles W. Kegley, Jr., and James M. Scott, *American Foreign Policy*, 6th ed. (Belmont, Calif.: Wadsworth/Thomson Learning, 2003), 28.

11. Mearsheimer makes the point that "the phrase 'Manifest Destiny' was not actually coined until 1845." By that time, the United States was well into its westward expansion and had already acquired the Louisiana Purchase and the Texas territories. John Mearsheimer, *The Tragedy of Great Power Politics* (New York: W. W. Norton, 2001), 487, fn. 11.

12. "The Monroe Doctrine," http://avalon.law.edu/19th_century/monroe.asp.

13. Quoted in McDougall, *Promised Land, Crusader State*, 92.

14. T. Harry Williams, *The History of American Wars: From Colonial Times to World War I* (New York: Alfred A. Knopf, 1981), 144–45.

15. Robert Ryal Miller, "The War between the United States and Mexico," http://www.pbs.org/kera/usmexicanwar/dialogues.

16. Mearsheimer, *The Tragedy of Great Power Politics*, 244.

17. Walter Russell Mead, *Special Providence: American Foreign Policy and How It Changed the World* (New York: Alfred A. Knopf, 2002), 14. In the first chapter of his book, Mead makes the case that U.S. economic interests were directly tied to other parts of the world through interlinked financial markets. This meant not only that "foreign money dug the canals, built the railroads and settled much of the West" but also that "domestic prosperity was threatened or ruined by financial storms that originated overseas" (15–16).

18. Mead, *Special Providence*, 26.

19. Paul Kennedy, *The Rise and Fall of the Great Powers* (New York: Vintage, 1987), 180.

20. The Treaty of Chemulpo between the United States and Korea begins by stating that "there shall be perpetual peace and friendship between the President of the United States and the King of Chosen [Korea] and the citizens and subjects of their respective Governments." "Treaty of Peace, Amity, Commerce and Navigation Between Korea (Chosen) and the United States of America," http://www.koreasociety.org/index2.php?option=com_docman&task=doc_view&gid=479&Itemid=35. This treaty also provided for trade on a most-favored-nation basis, established diplomatic relations between the two countries, allowed for the immigration of Koreans to the United States, and established mutual defense in case of foreign invasion. According to George Herring, although this agreement was part of the United States' search for markets, trade between the two countries was "negligible." George C. Herring, *From Colony to Superpower: U.S. Foreign Relations Since 1776* (Oxford: Oxford University Press, 2008), 287.

21. The DeLome letter can be found at http://www.historicaldocuments.com/DeLomeLetter.htm.

22. Note that there are parallels to the Gulf of Tonkin incident, which led to the resolution passed in 1964 that gave Lyndon Johnson the excuse to escalate the war in Vietnam. In that case, the U.S. destroyers *Maddox* and *Turner Joy* allegedly came under attack while patrolling the Gulf of Tonkin. This was seen as an act of war and gave President Johnson the rationale to go to Congress to secure passage of a resolution authorizing him to take "all necessary measures to repel any armed attacks against the

forces of the United States and to prevent further aggression." The commander of the *Maddox* indicated that "freak weather effects" and "overeager" sonar operators might have been to blame, rather than an actual attack. But it was clear that Johnson, who had the resolution already prepared, and Secretary of Defense Robert McNamara were ready to escalate the conflict, and this incident provided the opportunity for them to do so. See George C. Herring, *America's Longest War: The United States and Vietnam, 1950–1975* (New York: McGraw-Hill, 1996), 133–37.

23. The first Open Door note was sent on September 6, 1899, to Germany, Russia, and England. The second Open Door note, which was similar, was sent later to Japan, Italy, and France. Russia and Japan did not comply but went to war in 1904–1905 over control of Manchuria and Korea (the Russo-Japanese War).

24. "The Roosevelt Corollary to the Monroe Doctrine," Theodore Roosevelt's Annual Message to Congress, December 6, 1904, available at http://www.historical documents.com/TheodoreRooseveltCorollarytotheMonroeDoctrine.htm.

25. Work on the Panama Canal started in 1907, and it was completed and opened in 1914. Its completion meant that the United States could move warships quickly between the Atlantic Ocean and the Pacific, which "transformed naval strategy" and, in fact, "changed hemisphere policy." But it also meant that "a deep distrust had been sown . . . in the minds of Latin Americans, about the ambitions and lack of scruple of American foreign policy." J. M. Roberts, *Twentieth Century: A History of the World, 1901–2000* (New York: Viking, 1999), 105.

26. Robert B. Marks, *The Origins of the Modern World: A Global and Ecological Narrative*, 2nd ed. (Lanham, Md.: Rowman & Littlefield, 2002), 135.

27. "Wilson's First Inaugural Address," March 4, 1913, available at http://www .yale/edu/lawweb/avalon/president/inaug/wilson1.htm.

28. The First *Lusitania* Note, May 13, 1915, available at http://www.lib.byu .edu/~rdh/wwi/1915/lusitania1.html.

29. Daniel J. Boorstein and Brooks Mather Kelley, *A History of the United States* (Lexington, Mass.: Ginn, 1981), 448.

30. "Peace without Victory," address of President Wilson to the U.S. Senate, January 22, 1917, available at http://www.firstworldwar.com/source/peacewithoutvictory .htm.

31. "Wilson's Speech for Declaration of War against Germany," address delivered at joint session of Congress, April 2, 1917, available at http://www.firstworldwar.com/ source/usawardeclaration.htm.

32. "The Fourteen Points," Wilson's address to Congress, January 8, 1918, available at http://www.yale.edu/lawweb/avalon/wilson14.htm.

33. According to John B. Judis, "Wilson understood that the war itself [World War I] was rooted not just in Prussian militarism but in a flawed international system that had encouraged and would continue to encourage war." Judis continues: "Wilson also understood that the United States would have to abandon both its isolationist and imperialist approaches to foreign policy. . . . For Wilson, America's mission was not to create an empire, but a global democracy of equal and independent nations." To do so, the United States would have to be prepared "to abandon forever Washington and Jefferson's injunctions against 'entangling alliances.'" John B. Judis, *The Folly of*

Empire: What George W. Bush Could Learn from Theodore Roosevelt and Woodrow Wilson (New York: Scribner, 2004), 96–97.

34. This principle of "collective defense" is the cornerstone of Article 5 of the North Atlantic Treaty that created NATO (the North Atlantic Treaty Organization) in 1949, after World War II. Article 5 states: "The parties agree that an armed attack against one or more of them in Europe or North America shall be considered an attack against them all and consequently they agree that, if such an armed attack occurs, each of them, in exercise of the right of individual or collective self-defense . . . will assist the Party or Parties attacked."

35. Mead, *Special Providence*, 8–9.

36. For example, see Nancy F. Cott, *Public Vows: A History of Marriage and the Nation* (Cambridge, Mass.: Harvard University Press, 2000); Linda K. Kerber, *No Constitutional Right to Be Ladies* (New York: Hill & Wang, 1998); and Joyce P. Kaufman and Kristen P. Williams, "United States and Derivative Citizenship," in *Women, the State, and War: A Comparative Perspective on Citizenship and Nationalism* (Lanham, Md.: Lexington Books, 2007), 41–77.

37. Judis, *The Folly of Empire*, 37.

38. Judis, *The Folly of Empire*, 39.

39. Judis, *The Folly of Empire*, 46.

40. Herring, *From Colony to Superpower*, 367.

Chapter 3: The Interwar Years through World War II

1. Although the early period might be called unilateralist, I concur with Mearsheimer, who makes it clear that "isolationism was the word commonly used to describe American policy during the years between the world wars" (254). In this case, the distinction between unilateralism and isolationism is that during the period from about 1920 to 1940, the United States really did try to stay removed from the political and military events—especially conflicts—outside its borders. Although the United States did have some gunboats patrolling Asia at this time, their role was limited. A further indicator of the policy of isolationism during this period was that the United States chose not to respond militarily in the 1930s when Japan conquered Manchuria, nor when Japan and the Soviet Union clashed later in that decade (258). John Mearsheimer, *The Tragedy of Great Power Politics* (New York: W. W. Norton, 2001).

2. According to Paul Kennedy, by 1917 the United States "produced half of the world's food exports, which could now be sent to France and Italy as well as to its traditional British market." Thus, the United States played an important role in sustaining the Allies' war effort far beyond just military support. Paul Kennedy, *The Rise and Fall of the Great Powers* (New York: Vintage, 1987), 271.

3. Quoted in John B. Judis, *The Folly of Empire: What George W. Bush Could Learn from Theodore Roosevelt and Woodrow Wilson* (New York: Scribner, 2004), 120.

4. J. M. Roberts, *Twentieth Century: The History of the World, 1901 to 2000* (New York: Viking, 1999), 333–34.

5. The Immigration Act was a direct reaction to the influx of immigrants that had risen to approximately one million per year prior to World War I. Unlike the welcoming notion of America as a "melting pot" that characterized an earlier immigration pattern, the new law tied immigration to country of origin and, according to Ferrell, limited immigration to "3 percent of the number of foreign-born of each nationality residing in the United States in 1910. This reduced European immigrants to a maximum of 355,000 a year. . . . Congress passed it [the act] in the belief that millions of Europeans . . . were about to descend on the United States. By this time, the notion of a melting pot was in disrepute, and there was talk about 'alien indigestion.'" Although the law restricted the number of people who could enter the country from Europe and parts of Asia, it did not place restrictions on immigration from the Western Hemisphere or the Philippines. As a result, there was an influx of immigrants from Mexico and the Philippines. Robert H. Ferrell, *The Presidency of Calvin Coolidge* (Lawrence: University Press of Kansas, 1998), 113–14.

6. Ponting notes that the act stopped the "very low level of black immigration" by prohibiting "aliens ineligible for citizenship." Since 1790, only whites could become naturalized citizens, thereby precluding nonwhite immigrants from entering the country. Clive Ponting, *The Twentieth Century: A World History* (New York: Henry Holt, 1999), 475.

7. The Washington Conference resulted in a number of treaties. Under the Four Power Treaty, signed in December 1921, the United States, Britain, France, and Japan agreed to respect one another's possessions in the Pacific. The Five Power Treaty of February 1922 committed Great Britain, France, Italy, Japan, and the United States to limit the number of their ships with over 10,000 tons displacement. And the countries agreed not to build any more military forts or naval bases on their possessions in the Pacific. "Although the agreement gave Britain and the United States overall superiority, it allowed Japan local dominance in the Pacific." Ponting, *The Twentieth Century,* 256.

A Nine Power Treaty was signed in February 1922, protecting Western interests by binding all countries to respect the Open Door in China as well as China's integrity and not to seek land or special privileges there. The result of these treaties was to head off a naval arms race and to stabilize the situation in the Pacific in the short term, although, as Kennedy notes, while Britain and the United States "economized during the 1920s and early 1930s, Japan built right up to the treaty limits—and secretly went far beyond them." Kennedy, *The Rise and Fall of the Great Powers,* 300.

8. In this phrase, the pact draws on the work of Carl von Clausewitz, who defined war as "a mere continuation of policy by other means." But Clausewitz concludes his treatise *On War* this way: "War is an instrument of policy; it must necessarily bear its character, it must measure its scale: the conduct of War, in its great features, is therefore policy itself, which takes up the sword in place of the pen, but does not on that account cease to think according to its own laws." Carl von Clausewitz, *On War*, ed. Anatol Rapaport (Baltimore: Penguin, 1968), 410.

9. *The Kellogg Peace Pact*, August 27, 1928, available at http://www.yale.edu/lawweb/avalon/imt/kbpact.htm.

10. It should be noted that technically the pact remains in force today.

11. F. D. Roosevelt's first inaugural address, March 4, 1933, available at http://www.bartleby.com/124/pres49.htm.

12. Roberts, *Twentieth Century*, 367.

13. Roberts, *Twentieth Century*, 367.

14. Roosevelt's first inaugural address.

15. Roosevelt's first inaugural address.

16. See the full text of Roosevelt's first inaugural address.

17. In 1938, Mexico nationalized all foreign oil companies, about 60 percent of which were British and 40 percent American. Needless to say, this directly affected American interests. But by that point, U.S. concerns were elsewhere. Roberts, *Twentieth Century*, 375.

18. Roberts, *Twentieth Century*, 421.

19. Roosevelt's address at Charlottesville, Virginia, June 10, 1940, available at http://www.ibiblio.org/pha/7-2-188/188-toc.html.

20. Roberts, *Twentieth Century*, 421.

21. Roosevelt's "Four Freedoms" speech, January 6, 1941, available at http://www.wwnorton.com/college/history/ralph/workbook/ralprs36b.htm.

22. See the Atlantic Charter, August 14, 1941, available at http://avalon.law.yale.edu/wwii/atlantic.asp.

23. President Roosevelt's message asking for war against Japan, December 8, 1941, available at http://www.law.ou.edu/hist/infamy.htm.

24. See Kennedy, *The Rise and Fall of the Great Powers*, 202.

25. Under political pressure, Roosevelt issued Executive Order 8802 affirming the policy of the United States that there shall be "no discrimination of workers in defense industries or government because of race, creed, color or national origin." Available at http://www.eeoc.gov/abouteeoc/35th/theLaw/eo-8802.html. However, members of the military resisted the call for integration of the armed forces out of concern that this change in policy would affect military readiness. President Harry Truman formally ended segregation in the military in 1948 by Executive Order 9981, *On Equality of Treatment and Opportunity in the Armed Forces*, available at http://www.trumanlibrary.org/9981a.htm.

26. Executive Order 9066, signed February 19, 1942, states that "the successful prosecution of the war requires every possible protection against espionage and against sabotage to national-defense material, national-defense premises and national defense utilities." As such, it authorizes the secretary of war and the military commanders to designate areas from which "persons" may be excluded and, similarly, areas to which those people can be relocated. It is important to note that this order does not specifically name Japanese, but it was applied against that group of people, as well as some of German and Italian descent. Executive Order 9066, http://www.pbs.childofcamp/history/eo9066.html.

27. Roosevelt's annual message to the Congress, titled "An Economic Bill of Rights," January 11, 1944, available at http://www.fdrlibrary.marist.edu/011144.html.

28. It is important to note that Japanese cities were constructed largely of wood, so firebombing literally incinerated them. The city of Kyoto, the original capital of Japan (Heian), was spared specifically because of its historical importance.

29. See, for example, work done at the Ohio University Contemporary History Institute, a summary of which was published as "The Great Atomic Bomb Debate," by Bryan McNulty, in *Perspectives* (Spring–Summer 1997). According to McNulty, "President Harry S. Truman's decision to use the atomic bomb on two Japanese cities remains one of the most passionately debated historical events of the twentieth century. . . . Some respected historians say the bombing was avoidable at best, and analogous to Nazi war crimes at worst." McNulty also notes: "While the Institute's historians agree on the bomb's necessity [because of the conduct of the war to that point], some question the necessity of dropping the Nagasaki bomb only three days after Hiroshima." Hence, not only is the decision to drop one bomb debated, but the question of whether the second one was needed is cause for additional discussion and debate.

30. White House press release, August 6, in Robert H. Ferrell, ed., *Harry S. Truman and the Bomb: A Documentary History* (Worland, Wyo.: High Plains Publishing, 1996), 48; for the full text of the release, see 47–52. The text can be found online at http://trumanlibrary.org/whistlestop/study_collections/bomb/small/mb10.htm.

31. White House press release, August 6, in Ferrell, *Harry S. Truman and the Bomb*, 48.

32. Paul Kennedy notes that a "mix of motives" pushed the United States "toward the decision to drop the bomb—the wish to save allied casualties, the desire to send a warning to Stalin, the need to justify the vast expenses of the atomic project," all of which are still debated. What is not debated is that dropping the atomic bombs "marked the beginning of a new order in world affairs." Kennedy, *The Rise and Fall of the Great Powers*, 356–57. And Bill Gordon, scholar of Japanese history and culture, writes: "The concerns of top American leaders about the Soviet Union's future actions had the most significant influence on President Truman's deliberations on whether or not to drop the atomic bomb on Japan. If America did not drop the bomb in order to demonstrate its military superiority, American leaders had concerns that the Soviet Union would occupy Manchuria and would share the occupation of Japan with the U.S. . . . In addition, American leaders believed that dropping of the bomb would strengthen their position in future dealings with the Soviet Union concerning their sphere of influence in Eastern Europe." Bill Gordon, "Reflections on Hiroshima," available at http://wgordon.web.wesleyan.edu/papers/hiroshima.htm.

33. Townsend Hoopes and Douglas Brinkley, *FDR and the Creation of the U.N.* (New Haven, Conn.: Yale University Press, 1997), 9.

34. Hoopes and Brinkley, *FDR and the Creation of the U.N.*, 9.

35. The Atlantic Charter reaffirms that "all nations of the world, for realistic as well as spiritual reasons must come to the abandonment of the use of force. Since no future peace can be maintained if land, sea or air armaments continue to be employed by nations which threaten, or may threaten, aggression outside of their frontiers, they believe, *pending an establishment of a wider system of general security, that the disarmament of such nations is essential*" (emphasis added). Atlantic Charter, August 14, 1941, http://www.avalon.law.yale.edu/wwii/atlantic.asp.

36. Quoted in Hoopes and Brinkley, *FDR and the Creation of the U.N.*, 40.

37. Chiang Kai-shek was the leader of China at the time. Prior to World War II, Chiang had been fighting a civil war against Mao Tse-tung (Mao Zedong), the

leader of the communist forces. The civil war resumed after World War II ended and resulted in Mao's victory over the nationalist forces led by Chiang. In 1949, Chiang Kai-shek and his troops fled mainland China for the island of Taiwan, and on October 1, Mao and the communists declared the creation of the People's Republic of China.

38. Hoopes and Brinkley, *FDR and the Creation of the U.N.*, 108.

39. Atlantic Charter, August 14, 1941, http://www.avalon.law.yale.edu/wwii/atlantic.asp.

40. *Declaration of United Nations*, January 1, 1942, http://www.avalon.law.yale.edu/20th_century/decade03.asp.

41. "Classic Senate Speeches: Arthur H. Vandenberg," http://www.senate.gov/artandhistory/history/common/generic/Speeches_Vandenberg.htm.

42. Arthur H. Vandenberg, Jr., quoted in Herring, *From Colony to Superpower*, 538–39.

43. "Classic Senate Speeches: Arthur H. Vandenberg," http://www.senate.gov/artandhistory/history/common/generic/Speeches_Vandenberg.htm.

44. "Classic Senate Speeches," Arthur H. Vendenverg, January 10, 1945, U.S. Senate: Art & History Home, http://www.senate.gov/artandhistory/history/common/generic/Speeches_Vendenberg.htm.

Chapter 4: The Cold War

1. According to Mearsheimer, "When the Third Reich finally collapsed in April 1945, the Soviet Union was left standing as the most powerful state in Europe. Imperial Japan collapsed four months later (August 1945) leaving the Soviet Union also as the most powerful state in Northeast Asia. . . . The United States was the only state powerful enough to contain Soviet expansion." John Mearsheimer, *The Tragedy of Great Power Politics* (New York: W. W. Norton, 2001), 322.

2. On the role of economics as part of the U.S. policy of containment, Mead notes: "The progress toward free trade and the development of an international legal and political system that supported successive waves of expansion and integration across the entire world economy is one of the great (and unheralded) triumphs of American foreign policy in the second half of the twentieth century." He considers this policy "very much an element of the overall grand strategy of containing communism in part through creating a prosperous and integrated noncommunist world." Walter Russell Mead, *Power, Terror, Peace, and War: America's Grand Strategy in a World at Risk* (New York: Alfred A. Knopf, 2004), 33–34.

3. See Roosevelt's "Four Freedoms" speech, January 6, 1941, available at http://www.wwnorton.com/college/history/ralph/wprkbook/ralprs36b.htm.

4. Truman's "Statement on Fundamentals of American Foreign Policy," October 27, 1945, available at http://millercenter.org/scripps/archive/speeches/detail/3342.

5. Quoted in Eugene R. Wittkopf, Charles W. Kegley, Jr., and James M. Scott, *American Foreign Policy*, 6th ed. (Belmont, Calif.: Wadsworth/Thomson Learning, 2003), 47. Stalin gave this speech in February 1946 about the war and the future of the

economy. He gave a similar speech in October 1946 on the twenty-ninth anniversary of the Great October Socialist Revolution.

6. Referring to Kennan, Gaddis writes: "Rarely in the course of diplomacy does an individual manage to express within a single document, ideas of such force and persuasiveness that they immediately change a nation's foreign policy. That was the effect, though, of the 8,000-word telegram dispatched from Moscow by Kennan on February 22, 1946." John Lewis Gaddis, *Strategies of Containment: A Critical Appraisal of American National Security Policy during the Cold War* (New York: Oxford University Press, 2005), 18–19.

7. Kennan included in the list of potentially vulnerable countries Germany, Argentina, and parts of the Middle East. He also identified Iran as one of the countries of "strategic necessity" to the United States. See George Kennan, "The Long Telegram," February 22, 1946, at www.gwu.edu/~nsarchiv/coldwar/documents/episode-1/kennan.htm.

8. Kennan, "The Long Telegram."

9. On September 27, 1946, Soviet ambassador Nikolai Novikov sent a cable back to Moscow in which he described U.S. foreign policy as expansionistic and part of a drive for world hegemony. Although parts of Novikov's analysis were questioned and Novikov apparently also was dissatisfied with the result of the document, as one observer notes: "The general picture of the world they [Novikov and Kennan] painted was essentially the same: a dichotomous cleavage—on one side the powers of good, on the other, evil." Viktor L. Mal'kov, "Commentary," in *Origins of the Cold War: The Novikov, Kennan, and Roberts "Long Telegrams" of 1946*, ed. Kenneth M. Jensen (Washington, D.C.: United States Institute of Peace Press, 1993), 75. It is well worth reading the three telegrams, by Kennan, Novikov, and Frank Roberts (British chargé d'affaires in Moscow) for the picture each paints of the emerging Cold War.

10. George Kennan, "The Sources of Soviet Conduct," originally in *Foreign Affairs*, July 1947, found in its entirety at http://www.foreignaffairs,com/articles/23331/x/the-sources-of-soviet-conduct.

11. Kennan, "The Sources of Soviet Conduct."

12. Harry S. Truman, "Special Message to the Congress on Greece and Turkey: The Truman Doctrine," March 12, 1947, available at www.pbs.org/wgbh/amex/truman/psources/ps_doctrine.html.

13. The structure of the new Department of Homeland Security was outlined by President Bush in June 2002. The legislation formally creating the agency was passed by the U.S. Congress and signed by the president in November 2002. For the structure and presidential remarks regarding the creation of the Department of Homeland Security, see http://www.c-span.org/executive/presidential/homelandsecurityplan.pdf.

14. The full text of the *National Security Act of 1947* (Public Law 80-253) with some supporting documentation can be found at http://www.state.gov/www/about_state/history/intel/201_214.html.

15. The National Security Act of 1947 gave each of the three military branches (army, navy, and newly created air force) its own civilian service secretary. In 1949, the National Security Act was amended "to give the Secretary of Defense more power over the individual services and their secretaries." U.S. Department of State, *National Security Act of 1947*, http://www.state.gov/r/pa/ho/time/cwr/17603.htm.

16. The text of the "Marshall Plan" speech, given on June 4, 1947, at Harvard University, is available at http://www.marshallfoundation.org/marshall_plan_speech_ harvard.html.

17. The full text of the North Atlantic Treaty can be found at the NATO website, http://www.nato.int. When the treaty was drafted, the stipulation of collective security/defense outlined in Article 5 was assumed to be directed at a Soviet attack from the east on Western Europe, probably an attack on Germany through the Fulda Gap. However, the only time in its history that NATO invoked Article 5 was on September 12, 2001, in response to the September 11 attacks on the United States.

18. As noted in chapter 2, Article 10 of the League charter was the focus of much of the concern by congressional opponents of the League. Their fear was that if the United States signed the charter, Article 10 could have the effect of drawing the United States into wars that did not directly involve the country and, therefore, were not in U.S. national interest.

19. Article 2, the North Atlantic Treaty.

20. This is also one of the reasons that the former communist countries of Eastern Europe, such as Poland, Hungary, the Czech Republic, and others, were so eager to join NATO when it enlarged initially in the 1990s, and why the countries of Eastern Europe and the former Soviet Union have wanted to join as NATO continued to enlarge. To them, this served as a way of formally recognizing that they, too, are members of that democratic capitalist group of countries tied to the West. It was also recognition that the old days of Soviet domination had ended.

21. Soviet communism was based on the idea of a planned economy that had at its hub centralized state planning with large urban bureaucracies/ministries to manage it. The central state made the decisions and choices about the allocation of resources. In contrast, in China, Mao's model relied on the mass mobilization of rural labor as central to his idea of communism. His model was based on the voluntary collectivization of agriculture and the full employment of peasant labor found in a more rural country. Each of the two versions of communism was designed for the needs of the particular country as envisioned by its leaders. Ultimately, the two versions were seen by each country as being at odds with each other.

22. John B. Judis, *The Folly of Empire: What George W. Bush Could Learn from Theodore Roosevelt and Woodrow Wilson* (New York: Scribner, 2004), 142.

23. The entire document of NSC 68, while quite lengthy, lays out in detail U.S. perceptions of the Soviet Union and its intentions, the goals of the United States, and why the two were in conflict. It also describes Soviet military capabilities as then known and a range of options available to the United States to successfully deter and counter the Soviet Union. While it recognizes the "heavy responsibility" placed on the United States, the document also makes clear the need to "organize and enlist the energies and resources of the free world" in support of this effort. NSC 68 also notes the importance of keeping "the U.S. public fully informed and cognizant of the threats to our national security so that it will be prepared to support the measures which we must accordingly adopt." National Security Council, NSC 68: "United States Objectives and Programs for National Security," April 14, 1950, available at http://www.fas .org/irp/offdocs/nsc-hst/nsc-68.htm.

24. This is an important point because the United States was aware that if the vote had come when the Soviet ambassador was present, he probably would have exercised the veto, thereby killing the motion. It is also important to note that the Security Council seat held by "China" was actually held by the government of Taiwan, not the PRC, which was allied with North Korea. It was not until October 1971 that the UN General Assembly voted to seat the PRC in place of Taiwan, which resulted in removing Taiwan from the UN.

25. "Truman's Statement on the Korean War," June 27, 1950, available at http://www.mtholyoke.edu/acad/intrel/pentagon/doc8.htm. According to political scientist Peter Irons, President Truman specifically circumvented the Congress in authorizing U.S. troops into Korea without asking for approval or a formal declaration of war. Irons also makes the case that Truman violated the provisions of the UN charter by taking unilateral action prior to a UN Security Council call for assistance. Thus, Irons concludes, "Truman had no legal or constitutional authority for his actions at the outset of the Korean War. He ordered U.S. forces to undertake acts of war in Korea, despite his claim at a June 29 press conference, that 'we are not at war.'" Peter Irons, *War Powers: How the Imperial Presidency Hijacked the Constitution* (New York: Metropolitan Books, 2005), 171.

26. On April 11, 1951, President Truman called a press conference to announce that General MacArthur had been removed from the command of the forces in Korea. Truman believed that MacArthur had overstepped his bounds when he launched an attack into North Korea that pushed the enemy back toward the Yalu River, bordering China. MacArthur requested support to blockade the Chinese coast and bomb the mainland, which was denied by Washington. MacArthur was then warned to restrict the fighting to the area south of the thirty-eighth parallel, so as not to incite China. When MacArthur spoke out against what he saw as this strategy of "limited war," Truman saw this as a direct challenge to him as president and commander in chief, and he responded by firing MacArthur.

27. Quoted in Paul Kennedy, *The Rise and Fall of the Great Powers* (New York: Vintage, 1987), 382.

28. According to Roberts, "This was to turn out to be one of the most influential acts by a statesman of any nationality since 1945. It shook the monolithic front communism had hitherto presented." J. M. Roberts, *Twentieth Century: A History of the World, 1901–2000* (New York: Viking, 1999), 649. Excerpts of Khrushchev's speech can be found at http://www.marxists.org/glossary/events/p/e.htm.

29. In his memoirs, Khrushchev reflected: "For some time the United States lagged behind us. We were exploring space with our Sputniks. People all over the world recognized our success. Most admired us; the Americans were jealous." Nikita Khrushchev, *Khrushchev Remembers: The Last Testament,* trans. Strobe Talbott (Boston: Little, Brown, 1974), 54.

30. Under President Eisenhower's leadership, spy and intelligence technology made great advances in the 1950s. Specifically designed to monitor the Soviet Union and protect the United States from surprise nuclear attack, the U.S. intelligence apparatus came to depend increasingly on reconnaissance aircraft and spy satellites. For the background story of many of these developments, see Philip Taubman, *Secret*

Empire: Eisenhower, the CIA, and the Hidden Story of America's Space Espionage (New York: Simon & Schuster, 2003).

31. For a fascinating and detailed account of the U-2 incident, see Michael R. Beschloss, *Mayday: Eisenhower, Khrushchev, and the U-2 Affair* (New York: Harper & Row, 1986).

32. Quoted in James MacGregor Burns, *The Crosswinds of Freedom* (New York: Alfred A. Knopf, 1989), 262.

33. Quoted in Burns, *The Crosswinds of Freedom*, 332. The news conference of Friday, April 21, 1961, can be found at http://www.jfklibrary.org/jfk_press_conference_610421.html.

34. Resentment and tensions had been building between the Soviet Union and China since Stalin. Since the 1950s, China had implemented policies to reduce its dependence on the USSR. The tensions between the two countries grew until the Soviet Union withdrew its economic and technical aid and advisors in 1960. Concurrent with that, the two countries engaged in countercharges about border violations, with shots fired across the border as early as 1963. In 1964, China exploded its first nuclear weapon, becoming the fifth country to acquire this technology (following the United States, Soviet Union, Britain, and France). Subsequently, the two countries pursued very different policies, undermining the notion of monolithic communism.

35. See, for example, Graham T. Allison, *Essence of Decision: Explaining the Cuban Missile Crisis* (Boston: Little, Brown, 1971). This is perhaps the classic book on the missile crisis. Also see Raymond L. Garthoff, *Reflections on the Cuban Missile Crisis* (Washington, D.C.: Brookings Institution, 1989) and Robert F. Kennedy, *Thirteen Days: A Memoir of the Cuban Missile Crisis* (New York: W. W. Norton, 1969) for a fascinating first-person account of the event by someone intimately involved. For a work that draws on previously secret documents from Russian and U.S. archives to offer further insights into the crisis, see Aleksandr Fursenko and Timothy Naftali, *"One Hell of a Gamble": Khrushchev, Castro, and Kennedy, 1958–1964* (New York: W. W. Norton, 1997). Also see Michael Dobbs, *One Minute to Midnight: Kennedy, Khrushchev, and Castro on the Brink of Nuclear War* (New York: Alfred A. Knopf, 2008) for a detailed account of the crisis that draws on exhaustive and relatively new research.

36. Don Oberdorfer, "Cuban Missile Crisis More Volatile than Thought," *Washington Post*, January 14, 1992, A1.

37. Quoted in Martin Tolchin, "U.S. Underestimated Soviet Force in Cuba during '62 Missile Crisis," *New York Times*, January 15, 1992.

38. Michael Dobbs, in his 2008 book about the Cuban Missile Crisis, notes that there were many "unintended consequences" of the event, many of which are just being realized. For example, he quotes Clark Clifford, who served as secretary of defense after Robert McNamara, as saying that "the architects of the Vietnam War were 'deeply influenced by the lessons of the Cuban missile crisis.' They thought that concepts like 'flexible response' and 'controlled escalation' had helped Kennedy prevail over Khrushchev—and would work equally as well in Vietnam.'" Dobbs also asserts that "A somewhat different—but equally mistaken—lesson from the Cuban missile crisis was drawn by modern-day neoconservatives. In planning for the war in

Iraq, they shared the conceit that the political will of the president of the United States trumps all other considerations." Dobbs, *One Minute to Midnight*, 347.

39. Quoted in George C. Herring, *America's Longest War: The United States and Vietnam, 1950–1975* (New York: McGraw-Hill, 1996), 38.

40. Quoted in Herring, *America's Longest War*, 78.

41. Statement by President Kennedy on the importance of Laos, at a news conference March 23, 1961, available at http://www.mtholyoke.edu/acad/intrel/pentagon2/ps5.htm.

42. For more detail about Laos and its relationship to Vietnam, see Norman B. Hannah, *The Key to Failure: Laos and the Vietnam War* (Lanham, Md.: Madison Books, 1987). Hannah makes the argument that not only were the situations in Laos and Vietnam related, which seems apparent, but in chapter 2, "The Bay of Pigs and Indochina," he makes the case that "the pattern of our failure in Indochina was set at the Bay of Pigs" (9).

43. Roberts, *Twentieth Century*, 673.

44. According to Doris Kearns Goodwin, "Johnson did worry about the loss of his domestic programs. As a boy of five, he had heard his Populist grandfather describe the devastating impact of the Spanish-American War on social reform. He had lived through the periods of reaction following World War I and World War II, seen a virtual paralysis of domestic action in the aftermath of Korea. And one cannot doubt the intensity of this concern." Doris Kearns, *Lyndon Johnson and the American Dream* (New York: Harper & Row, 1976), 259.

45. Kearns, *Lyndon Johnson and the American Dream*, 251–52.

46. The Southeast Asia Collective Defense Treaty that established the Southeast Asia Treaty Organization (SEATO) was signed in 1954 and entered into force in 1955. It joined the United States and the countries of Australia, France, New Zealand, Pakistan, Philippines, Thailand, and United Kingdom. Article 4 of this treaty is the collective defense provision similar to the one in Article 5 of the NATO treaty. The goal of the treaty and of SEATO was to oppose communist gains in Southeast Asia after the withdrawal of the French. The organization was divided by the U.S. role in Vietnam and was officially disbanded in 1977.

47. "President Johnson's Message to Congress," *Joint Resolution of Congress*, H.J. RES 1145, available at http://www.yale.edu/lawweb/avalon/tonkin-g.htm.

48. "Johnson's Message to Congress."

49. Donald L. Westerfield, *War Powers: The President, the Congress, and the Question of War* (Westport, CT: Praeger Press, 1996), 53. Article I, Section 8, of the Constitution explicitly grants to the Congress the power to declare war.

50. Herring, *America's Longest War*, 136.

51. Quoted in Westerfield, *War Powers*, 84.

52. Herring, *America's Longest War*, 167.

53. Herring, *America's Longest War*, 173.

54. Herring, *America's Longest War*, 173.

55. Walter Cronkite, "We Are Mired in Stalemate," broadcast, February 27, 1968, https://facultystaff.richmond.edu/~ebolt/history398/Cronkite_1968.html. Supposedly,

when Lyndon Johnson heard Cronkite's commentary on the news, he was reported to have said, "If I've lost Cronkite, I've lost Middle America."

56. Burns, *The Crosswinds of Freedom*, 412.

57. Burns, *The Crosswinds of Freedom*, 413.

58. The full text of Lyndon Johnson's announcement of March 31, 1968, can be found at http://www.pbs.org/ladybird/shattereddreams/shattereddreams_doc_re_elect.html.

59. Quoted in Kearns, *Lyndon Johnson and the American Dream*, 343.

60. Roberts, *Twentieth Century*, 675.

61. *War Powers Resolution*, Public Law 93-148, 93rd Congress, H.J. RES. 542, November 7, 1973, Joint Resolution Concerning the War Powers of Congress and the President, http://www.yale.edu/lawweb/avalon/warpower.htm.

62. Despite the caveats built into the War Powers Resolution, in October 2002 Congress gave President George W. Bush virtually the same authority regarding the conduct of the war with Iraq. Congress gave the president authorization "to use the Armed Forces of the United States as he determined to be necessary and appropriate in order to (1) defend the national security of the United States against the continuing threat posed by Iraq; and (2) enforce all relevant United Nations Security Council Resolutions regarding Iraq." Like the Tonkin Gulf Resolution, this resolution was premised upon a case that has since been disproved. *Joint Resolution to Authorize the Use of United States Armed Forces against Iraq*, available at http://www.whitehouse.gov/news/releases/2002/10/20021002-2.html.

63. For a more detailed discussion of the constitutionality of the resolution and these parts in particular, see Westerfield, *War Powers*, 90–92, and many of the sources that he cites. Irons raises an interesting point when he notes that "rather than limiting the president's war-making powers, as it sponsors intended, the War Powers Resolution of 1973 actually expanded them by failing to include any enforcement provisions." This leads him to state that, therefore, "presidents could—and most often did—ignore the resolution's consulting and reporting provisions, or comply in the most perfunctory manner." Irons, *War Powers*, 219. However, as desired, the act has forced presidents to report to the Congress. Whether, when, and how Congress responds is a different question.

64. In addition to the United States and Soviet Union, the United Kingdom became nuclear in 1956, France in 1960, and China in 1964. India conducted its first nuclear test in 1974, and by the 1980s it was clear that Pakistan had nuclear weapons as well. In addition, Argentina, Brazil, and South Africa all had a nuclear capability but chose not to build nuclear weapons. It is an open secret that Israel has nuclear weapons, and North Korea and Iran both made it clear that each would be resuming its own nuclear weapons program.

65. Quoted in Wittkopf, Kegley, and Scott, *American Foreign Policy*, 51.

66. Wittkopf, Kegley, and Scott, *American Foreign Policy*, 51.

67. For a fascinating and brief description of Nixon's position on China, including short excerpts of some of his writings on the topic, see "Finding China," in Burns, *The Crosswinds of Freedom*, 468–75.

68. *Joint Communiqué of the United States and the People's Republic of China*, February 28, 1972, available at http://www.taiwandocuments.org/communique01.html.

69. For a detailed first-person account of the events leading up to the Iranian hostage crisis, the U.S. attempts at diplomatic solution, the failed rescue attempt, and the implications of the crisis, see Gary Sick, *All Fall Down: America's Tragic Encounter with Iran* (New York: Random House, 1985).

70. Henry Kissinger, "Lessons of Vietnam," unpublished memo, available at http://www.thebattleofkontum.com/extras/Kissinger.html.

71. "President Johnson's Message to Congress," *Joint Resolution of Congress*, H.J. Res. 1145, available at http://www.yale.edu/laweb/avalon/tonkin-g.htm.

Chapter 5: The Cold War and Beyond: Reagan through Clinton

1. What Kennedy meant was that he, too, is a citizen of Berlin. Although most people knew what he was trying to say, the colloquial translation of this statement is, "I am a jelly-filled donut," since a "Berliner" is a popular type of pastry. This is one example of how language, especially in translation, can confound international relations. This example is cited in Raymond Cohen, *Negotiating across Cultures* (Washington, D.C.: United States Institute of Peace Press, 1992).

2. President Reagan delivered the speech on June 12, 1987, at the Brandenburg Gate in West Berlin. It is important to note that the speech could be heard on the eastern side of the Berlin Wall and sent an important message. About halfway through the speech, Reagan directed his comments not only to the people of Berlin but to Mikhail Gorbachev in the Soviet Union when he said, "General Secretary Gorbachev, if you seek peace, if you seek prosperity for the Soviet Union and Eastern Europe, if you seek liberalization: Come here to this gate! Mr. Gorbachev, open this gate! Mr. Gorbachev, tear down this wall!" http://www.reagan.utexas.edu/archives/speeches/1987/061287d.htm.

3. The beginning of the end of the Cold War started in 1989 when "the Soviet Union suddenly reversed course . . . and abandoned its empire in Eastern Europe." John Mearsheimer, *The Tragedy of Great Power Politics* (New York: W. W. Norton, 2001), 201–2. In the most tangible example of the changes taking place, in November 1989 the Berlin Wall came down. Two years later, in 1991, the Soviet Union broke apart and became fifteen separate states. With that, the Cold War ended.

4. Roberts, *Twentieth Century: A History of the World, 1901–2000* (New York: Viking, 1999), 742.

5. For a detailed discussion of "soft" and "hard" power and the role that each has played in American foreign policy, see Joseph S. Nye, Jr., *The Paradox of American Power: Why the World's Only Superpower Can't Go It Alone* (New York: Oxford University Press, 2002).

6. President Reagan delivered the first "evil empire" speech, as it came to be known, to the British House of Commons on June 8, 1982. Although Reagan did not label the Soviet Union the "evil empire" per se, in speaking to the British people about

the contest of democracy versus communism and West versus East, he did say: "Given strong leadership, time, and a little bit of hope, the forces of good ultimately rally and triumph over evil." Available at http://www.fordham.edu/halsall/mod/1982reagan1. html. Reagan reprised many of these themes in a speech he gave on March 8, 1983, to the National Association of Evangelicals in Florida. However, he was even more blunt this time, given his audience: "So, in your discussions of the nuclear freeze proposals, I urge you to beware the temptation of pride—the temptation of blithely declaring yourselves above it all and label both sides equally at fault, to ignore the facts of history and the aggressive impulses of an *evil empire*, to simply call the arms race a giant misunderstanding and thereby remove yourself from the struggle between right and wrong and good and evil" (emphasis added). Available at http://www.president reagan.info/speeches/empire.cfm.

7. Roberts, *Twentieth Century*, 747.

8. The arms control process did continue under Reagan, but unsuccessfully, at least initially. For more detail about the progress of some of the negotiations, see Strobe Talbott, *Deadly Gambits* (New York: Alfred A. Knopf, 1984). Especially instructive is chapter 6, "A Walk in the Woods" (117–51), describing the informal talks that took place between U.S. negotiator Paul Nitze and Soviet negotiator Yuli Kvitsinsky, and why those negotiations were doomed to fail.

9. Jack F. Matlock, Jr., *Reagan and Gorbachev: How the Cold War Ended* (New York: Random House, 2004), 302. This is an example of how a powerful individual actor can play an important role in international relations and the direction of a particular nation-state.

10. Mikhail Gorbachev, *Perestroika: New Thinking for Our Country and the World* (New York: Harper & Row, 1987).

11. See Matlock, *Reagan and Gorbachev*. One of the more interesting insights that can be seen in this book is the role of both Raisa Gorbachev and Nancy Reagan. In a number of places, Matlock describes the important behind-the-scenes roles that the two wives had in influencing their husbands at this critical point. If one is looking at foreign policy through "gender-sensitive lenses," although the two women had the traditional role of wife, in both cases they were extremely important in influencing the outcome of events.

12. See Howard Zinn, *The Twentieth Century* (New York: HarperCollins, 2003), 355–57. The "Boland Amendment" was the name given to three congressional amendments sponsored by Congressman Edward Boland (D-MA) between 1982 and 1984, all of which dealt with limiting U.S. assistance to the Contras. The first one, passed in 1982, was an amendment to the Defense Appropriations Act. The second one was an amendment to the Intelligence Authorization Act for Fiscal Year 1983 and was passed on November 3, 1983. It was initially introduced as a House resolution "to prohibit United States support for military or paramilitary operations in Nicaragua." It also amended the Intelligence Authorization Act "to prohibit the Central Intelligence Agency or any other agency involving intelligence operations from using FY 1983 or FY 1984 appropriations to support military or paramilitary operations in Nicaragua" (http://www.milnet.com/boland.htm). The third was passed as part of a defense appropriations bill in 1984 for fiscal year 1985, again limiting funding for Nicaragua.

13. *The Tower Commission Report: The Full Text of the President's Special Review Board* (New York: Random House, 1997), 6.

14. *The Tower Commission Report*, 87.

15. "Toward a New World Order," President George H. W. Bush's address to a joint session of Congress and the nation, September 11, 1990. Available at http://www.sweetliberty.org/issues/war/bushr/htm.

16. The text of Resolution 678 can be found at http://www.fas.org/news/un/iraq/sres/sres0678.htm. Twelve of the fifteen members of the Security Council voted in favor of the resolution. Two countries, Cuba and Yemen, voted against it; China, one of the permanent members and therefore with veto power, chose to abstain. It is interesting to note that the resolution referred to "member states" at a time when one of the major changes in the international system was the emergence and predominance of nonstate actors. This, too, created a dilemma for U.S. foreign policy, since policy had always been premised on nation-to-nation interaction. This issue of how to deal with nonstate actors became especially acute after September 11, 2001, and the attack that was mounted by Al Qaeda, a terrorist organization.

17. In his memoirs, George H. W. Bush notes that while preparing to go to Congress, he studied the way in which Johnson "had handled Congress at the time of the Gulf of Tonkin Resolution in 1964." Bush acknowledges that "the Vietnam War was different, but his effort made a big impression on me, and I began to think about seeking a similar congressional vote of support." George Bush and Brent Scowcroft, *A World Transformed* (New York: Alfred A. Knopf, 1998), 371.

18. Bush and Scowcroft, *A World Transformed*, 446.

19. In 1995, Andrew Kohut and Robert Toth of the Pew Center for People and the Press issued a report that stated: "Until a generation ago, elites were probably the only Americans interested in foreign news. . . . Today, much broader and less sophisticated U.S. audiences are exposed to the world, but because most Americans lack much knowledge about international affairs, they can be easily stirred to demand action by dramatic stories that they read and that they see." What they are describing is what we have come to know as "the CNN effect." Andrew Kohut and Robert C. Toth, "A Content Analysis: International News Coverage Fits Public's Ameri-Centric Mood," http://www.people-press.org/reports/pdf/19951031.pdf.

20. Roberts, *Twentieth Century*, 775.

21. For an excellent history of Yugoslavia leading up to the breakup, see John R. Lampe, *Yugoslavia as History: Twice There Was a Country*, 2nd ed. (Cambridge: Cambridge University Press, 2000). Also see Susan L. Woodward, *Balkan Tragedy: Chaos and Destruction after the Cold War* (Washington, D.C.: Brookings Institution, 1995).

22. The country of Yugoslavia was a federation of six republics: Serbia, Croatia, Bosnia-Herzegovina, Montenegro, Macedonia, and Slovenia. With the exception of Bosnia, the other five were fairly homogeneous, that is, Serbia was primarily Serb, Croatia was primarily Croat, and so on. In general, all the groups are ethnically similar. The main difference is religion. Serbs tend to be Eastern Orthodox, Croats are generally Catholic, and Bosnians are generally Muslim. Prior to the war, intermarriage among the groups, especially in Bosnia, was not unusual. (In Bosnia, prior to the war, as many as 30 percent of marriages were between different groups.) The emergence

of leaders such as Milosevic in Serbia and Tudjman in Croatia fueled the nationalist fervor within each group and led directly to ethnic conflict. The most destructive and longest war was in Bosnia, and it involved fighting among the Serbs, Croats, and Bosnian Muslims.

23. Eugene R. Wittkopf, Charles W. Kegley, Jr., and James M. Scott, *American Foreign Policy*, 6th ed. (Belmont, Calif.: Wadsworth/Thomson Learning, 2003), 263.

24. Wittkopf, Kegley, and Scott, *American Foreign Policy*, 452–53.

25. Elizabeth Drew, *On the Edge: The Clinton Presidency* (New York: Simon & Schuster, 1994), 323.

26. For a harrowing description of the battle in Mogadishu, Somalia, and the issues surrounding it, see Mark Bowden, *Black Hawk Down* (London: Corgi Books, 1999).

27. Drew, *On the Edge*, 318.

28. Quoted in Fraser Cameron, *American Foreign Policy after the Cold War: Global Hegemon or Reluctant Sheriff?* (New York: Routledge, 2002), 22.

29. The fact that the United States chose not to intervene in genocide in various places has been condemned by a number of authors who felt that an important role that the United States could and should play in the post–Cold War world was as a moral leader. For example, one journalist who covered the wars in the Balkans told me that, in her opinion, the lack of action by the Bush administration meant that the United States exercised no "moral authority" regarding policies in Bosnia, and that this lack of action set a precedent that would hamper the Clinton administration's ability to take action. (Interview with the author in December 2000.) For more detail about specific cases, see Samantha Power, *"A Problem from Hell": America and the Age of Genocide* (New York: HarperCollins, 2002).

30. *Regarding United States Policy toward Haiti*, SJ Res 229, October 7, 1997, available at http://thomas/loc.gov/cgi-bin/query/.

31. According to one author, "This enabled American troops to land unopposed in order to restore order and to carry out peacekeeping duties, pending the return of Aristide." Cameron, *American Foreign Policy after the Cold War*, 20.

32. Quoted in Woodward, *Balkan Tragedy*, 6.

33. According to a Pew poll, Clinton's approval rating in September 1994 was 41 percent, and disapproval was at 52 percent. "Americans Unmoved by Prospect of Clinton, Lewinsky Testimony," Pew Research Center for People and the Press, August 4, 1998, http://www.people-press.org.

34. A number of books deal with the war in Bosnia and the negotiations surrounding the Dayton peace agreement. See, for example, Ivo H. Daalder, *Getting to Dayton: The Making of America's Bosnia Policy* (Washington, D.C.: Brookings Institution, 2000); Saadia Touval, *Mediation in the Yugoslav War: The Critical Years, 1990–1995* (London: Palgrave, 2002); and Joyce P. Kaufman, *NATO and the Former Yugoslavia: Crisis, Conflict, and the Atlantic Alliance* (Lanham, Md.: Rowman & Littlefield, 2002).

35. "National Security Strategy for a New Century" (1997), available at http://clinton3.nara.gov/WH/EOP/NSC/Strategy.

36. In an interview in Washington, D.C., in August 2000, one high-level official in the Clinton administration told me that the United States should not have publicly

taken the position that it did about its unwillingness to use ground forces. He claimed that doing so clearly sent the wrong signal to Milosevic, limited negotiating options, and further damaged relations within NATO and between the United States and its NATO allies.

37. Wittkopf, Kegley, and Scott, *American Foreign Policy*, 263.

38. Wittkopf, Kegley, and Scott, *American Foreign Policy*, 265.

39. When George W. Bush became president in 2001, he defied convention because the first foreign leader he met with was President Vicente Fox of Mexico, rather than one of the leaders of Canada or Europe, which had been the tradition.

40. It is important to remember that terrorist attacks against the United States or Americans abroad were not limited to the Clinton administration. The suicide bombing of the U.S. Marine barracks in Beirut, Lebanon, in October 1983, under Reagan resulted in the deaths of 241 marines and other U.S. personnel. In fact, a State Department survey of international terrorist attacks for the period 1981 through 2000 showed a decline in the overall number of attacks, down from a high of 666 in 1987. However, what has changed has been an increase in the intensity of attacks directed specifically at U.S. citizens or interests. While the overall number of attacks might have declined, the loss of life from attacks such as those in Beirut, the USS *Cole* in Yemen (2000), the American embassies in Kenya and Tanzania (1998), the first World Trade Center bombing (1993), and, of course, September 11 all have resulted in a significant increase in the number of American lives lost. Statistics are drawn from Wittkopf, Kegley, and Scott, *American Foreign Policy*, 193.

41. In an op-ed piece in the *New York Times* following the terrorist bombs detonated in London on July 7, 2005, Robert A. Pape makes the point that since 1990, most of the suicide terrorists "came from America's closest allies in the Muslim world—Turkey, Egypt, Pakistan, Indonesia and Morocco—rather than from those the State Department considers 'state sponsors of terrorism,' like Iran, Libya, Sudan and Iraq." Robert A. Pape, "Al Qaeda's Smart Bombs," *New York Times*, July 9, 2005, A29.

42. A Gallup poll released on August 22, 1998, just after the raid, indicated that "the American public continued to give Bill Clinton high marks for the job he is doing as president." At that point, his job approval rating was 66 percent. Frank Newport, "Clinton Maintains High Job Approval Ratings throughout Tumultuous Week," Gallup Organization, August 22, 1998, http://www.gallup.com/poll.

43. "Remarks of President Clinton to the UN General Assembly," September 21, 1998, available at http://daccessdds.un.org/doc/UNDOC/GEN/N98/858/28/PDF/N9885828.pdf?OpenElement.

44. Despite Clinton's willingness to deploy U.S. forces in support of humanitarian missions, Samantha Power claims that the United States waited too long to act in many of these cases, which resulted in further genocide. She is one of the most outspoken critics of U.S. foreign policy for its apparent hesitancy to use military force in order to address—and halt—genocide. See Power, *"A Problem from Hell."*

45. Steven W. Hook, *U.S. Foreign Policy: The Paradox of World Power*, 2nd ed. (Washington, D.C.: CQ Press, 2008), 57.

46. Hook, *U.S. Foreign Policy*, 56.

47. Quoted in David Owen, *Balkan Odyssey* (New York: Harcourt Brace, 1995), 14.

48. Ivo H. Daalder, *Getting to Dayton: The Making of America's Bosnia Policy* (Washington, D.C.: Brookings Institution Press, 2000), 150.

49. Irons, *War Powers*, 212.

50. See chapter 11, "We Were Going to War," in Irons, *War Powers*, 204–20. Irons argues that in the cases of Somalia, Haiti, and eventually Bosnia, "Clinton failed to comply with the War Powers Resolution; he claimed that he was acting according to his powers as commander in chief, not as a result of Congressional approval. His assertions, in fact, provoked a response in the Senate" (211).

Chapter 6: September 11 and After

1. Condoleezza Rice, "Promoting the National Interest," *Foreign Affairs*, January/February 2000, 45.

2. Rice, "Promoting the National Interest," 53.

3. In her article, Rice also states that "a Republican administration should refocus the United States on the national interest and the pursuit of key priorities" (46). She then outlines what these should be. But even more instructive now, she foreshadowed what became a Bush administration priority of spreading and promoting democracy: "America is blessed with extraordinary opportunity. It has had no territorial ambitions for nearly a century. Its national interest has been defined instead by a desire to foster the spread of freedom, prosperity, and peace. Both the will of the people and the demands of modern economies accord with that vision of the future" (62). See Condoleezza Rice, "Promoting the National Interest," *Foreign Affairs*, January/February 2000, 45–62.

That same issue included a companion piece, "A Republican Foreign Policy," by Robert Zoellick, deputy secretary of state in Bush's second term and then director of the World Bank. He was quite blunt that "a primary task for the next president of the United States is to build public support for a strategy that will shape the world so as to protect and promote American interests and values for the next 50 years" (63). Zoellick was very critical of Clinton and his foreign policy, particularly the fact that he "failed to define a new internationalism for the United States" (64). He outlined a "modern Republican foreign policy" built on five principles. The last of these is recognition of the fact that "there is still evil in the world—people who hate America and the ideas for which it stands" (70). One of his proposed solutions included the need to "deter and even replace" their brutal regimes, and it assumed that the United States will have a strong military—and use it when necessary. Although Zoellick warned that "It is a mistake for the United States simply to react to events," the reality is that the events of September 11, 2001, overshadowed all other aspects of U.S. foreign policy and redefined the policy direction. Robert B. Zoellick, "A Republican Foreign Policy," *Foreign Affairs*, January/February 2000, 63–78.

4. Rice, "Promoting the National Interest," 62.

5. There is a great deal of documentation suggesting that there were some in the Bush administration, generally grouped under the heading of the "neocons," as well as

Bush himself, who were looking for ways to invade Iraq even before the 9/11 attacks. For example, Godfrey Hodgson notes that "from the very first days of his administration, well before 9/11, George Bush showed an interest in attacking Iraq" (169). He continues that "Bush had been preoccupied with the danger from Iraq long before 9/11" (170). Hodgson builds a case that for some in the administration, especially Paul Wolfowitz, concern about Iraq goes back to the Cold War, especially concern about control of Iraq's oil fields. Godfrey Hodgson, *The Myth of American Exceptionalism* (New Haven, Conn.: Yale University Press, 2009). Judis also notes that "the nationalists and neoconservatives had begun to call for Saddam Hussein's ouster in the late 1990s after the UN inspectors left Iraq. In 1998, Rumsfeld joined Wolfowitz and other conservatives in signing the Project for the New American Century's open letter to [President] Clinton calling for Saddam's ouster." John B. Judis, *The Folly of Empire: What George W. Bush Could Learn from Theodore Roosevelt and Woodrow Wilson* (New York: Scribner, 2004), 175. Philip Gordon is another author who also identifies both the individuals and the policies, going back to the 1990s, who made the case of war against Iraq way before 9/11. Philip H. Gordon, *Winning the Right War* (New York: Times Books, 2007).

6. "President Bush Discusses Global Climate Change," press release, June 11, 2001, http://georgewbush-whitehouse.archives.gov/news/releases/2001/06/20010611-2.html.

7. According to the terms of the 1994 U.S.-North Korea Framework Agreement, North Korea was required to freeze and eventually dismantle its nuclear facilities that could be used to manufacture fuel for nuclear weapons. In exchange, North Korea was promised light-water reactors (that could not be used for nuclear weapons) and the U.S. promise to send tons of heavy fuel to the country. As a result of these talks, North Korea was encouraged to engage in negotiations with Asian countries as well. One effect has been increased trade between North Korea and South Korea, China, and Japan. http://www.armscontrol.org/documents/af.asp.

8. "Statement by the North Atlantic Council," September 12, 2001, http://www.nato/int/docu/pr/2001/p01-124e.htm.

9. As stated in note 5 (above), the Bush administration had been looking for an excuse to invade Iraq and to get rid of Saddam Hussein. Although there was never any proof that Iraq had anything to do with 9/11, that attack became the justification for the invasion and subsequent "regime change."

10. Peter Irons, *War Powers: How the Imperial Presidency Hickjacked the Constitution* (New York: Metropolitan Books, 2005), 217–18.

11. Irons, *War Powers*, 218.

12. Irons, *War Powers*, 218.

13. *War Powers Resolution*, Public Law 93-148, November 7, 1973, http://www.yale.edu/lawweb/avalon/warpower.htm.

14. The lone "no" vote in the House was cast by Barbara Lee, Democrat of California. For the complete roll call in the House and Senate as well as the full text of S.J. Res. 23, see http://www.govtrack.us/congress/bill.xpd?=sj107-23.

15. Richard F. Grimmett, "Authorization for Use of Military Force in Response to the 9/11 Attacks (P.L. 107-40): Legislative History," CRS Report for Congress, Order Code RS22357, Updated January 16, 2007, CRS-3.

16. Grimmett, "Authorization for Use of Military Force," CRS-4.

17. S.J. Res. 23, passed September 14, 2001, http://www.law.cornell.edu/background/warpowers/sj23.pdf.

18. "President Signs Authorization for Use of Military Force Bill," Statement by the President, September 18, 2001, http://avalon.law.yale.edu/sept11/president_022.asp.

19. Irons, *War Powers*, 219.

20. On September 18, 2001, the Congress passed Public Law 107-40, granting President Bush authorization to attack Afghanistan. The air strikes started on October 7. Available at http://www.yale.edu/lawweb/avalon/sept_11/sjres23_eb.htm.

21. Eugene R. Wittkopf, Charles W. Kegley, Jr., and James M. Scott, *American Foreign Policy*, 6th ed. (Belmont, Calif.: Wadsworth/Thomson Learning, 2003), 261.

22. Alan Cowell, "A Nation Challenged: Britain; Blair Declares the Airstrikes Are an Act of Self-Defense," *New York Times*, October 8, 2001, http://query.nytimes.com/gst/fullpage.html?res=9F00E2DF103CF93BA35753C1A9679C8B63&sec=.

23. As of January 2009, when Obama took office, there were 33,000 U.S. troops in Afghanistan, 15,000 troops with the NATO ISAF mission, and 18,000 fighting insurgents and training the Afghan army and police. By contrast, there were 142,000 U.S. troops in Iraq. *Canadian American Strategic Review*, January 2009, http://www.casr.ca/ft-new-afghan-strategy-obama-1.htm.

24. George W. Bush, "State of the Union Address," January 29, 2002, http://www.presidency.ucsb.edu/ws.index/php?pid=29644.

25. George W. Bush, "Remarks on the Six Month Anniversary of the September 11 Attacks," http://www.whitehouse.gov/news/releases/2002/03/20020311-1.html.

26. "The National Security Strategy of the United States of America," http://www.mtholyoke.edu/acad/intrel/bush/doctrine.htm.

27. While some NATO allies, primarily Great Britain, Poland, and Spain, did support the United States and send troops to fight in Iraq, others, most notably Germany and France, were vocal in their opposition. After a major bombing in Madrid in March 2004, elections brought a socialist government to power in Spain. One of the first acts of newly elected prime minister Zapatero was to authorize the withdrawal of Spanish troops from Iraq.

28. UN weapons inspectors left Iraq on March 17, 2003, after President Bush "issued a final ultimatum for Saddam Hussein to step down or face war." "Weapons Inspectors Leave Iraq," http://www.cbsnews.com/stories/2003/03/17/iraq/main544280.shtml. During their four months in Iraq looking for banned weapons of mass destruction, they did not find any.

29. It is instructive to read the speech in its entirety to see the way in which Vice President Cheney, and by implication the Bush administration, was framing the issue and preparing the American public for the war that would follow. "Full Text of Dick Cheney's Speech," delivered to the Veterans of Foreign Wars national convention, Nashville, Tennessee, August 27, 2002, http://www.guardian.co.uk/world/2002/aug/27/usa.iraq/print.

30. Public Law 107-243, October 16, 2002, *Authorization for Use of Military Force Against Iraq Resolution of 2002*, http://www.c-span.org/content/pdf/hjres114.pdf.

31. Public Law 107-243, October 16, 2002, *Authorization for Use of Military Force Against Iraq Resolution of 2002*, http://www.c-span.org/content/pdf/hjres114.pdf.

32. Leslie Gelb, a former reporter for the *New York Times* as well as former president of the Council of Foreign Relations, wrote a very insightful piece in the *Wall Street Journal* in which he proposed some solutions. He concluded: "Even the wisest of strategies will confront the odds in making Iraq a better place. . . . A good strategy fashioned with Iraqis, fitted to Iraq's political realities plus a U.S. withdrawal plan, can tap that volcano." Leslie H. Gelb, "Tap the Volcano," *Wall Street Journal*, August 2, 2005.

33. See, for example, Thomas Ricks, *Fiasco: The American Military Adventure in Iraq* (New York: Penguin Press, 2006); Andrew Bacevich, *The Limits of Power: The End of American Exceptionalism* (New York: Metropolitan Books, 2008); and Philip H. Gordon, *Winning the Right War: The Path to Security for America and the World* (New York: Times Books, 2007).

34. See "Global Public Opinion in the Bush Years (2001–2008)," The Pew Global Attitudes Project, December 18, 2008, http://global.org/reports/pdf/263.pdf. The results of these polls, which were administered in fifty-four countries, show unambiguously that "The U.S. image abroad is suffering almost everywhere. Opposition to key elements of American foreign policy is widespread in Western Europe, and positive views of the U.S. have declined steeply among many of America's longtime European allies. In Muslim nations, the wars in Afghanistan and particularly Iraq have driven negative ratings off the charts" (1).

35. "Reviewing the Bush Years and the Public's Final Verdict: Bush and Public Opinion," The Pew Research Center for the People & the Press, December 18, 2008, http://www.people-press.org.

36. George W. Bush, second inaugural address, January 20, 2005, http://www.bartleby.com/124/press67.html.

37. See chapters 9 and 10 in Judis, *The Folly of Empire*, 165–212.

38. Tyler Marshall, "Bush's Shifting Foreign Policy," *Los Angeles Times*, June 5, 2005, A1.

39. Philip H. Gordon, *Winning the Right War: The Path to Security for America and the World* (New York: Times Books, 2007), 96.

40. Steven Lee Myers, "Question of Bush's Legacy Lingers over His Farewell Visits to European Capitals," *New York Times*, June 14, 2008.

41. "Reviewing the Bush Years and the Public's Final Verdict: Bush and Public Opinion," The Pew Research Center for the People & the Press, December 18, 2008, http://www.people-press.org.

42. Irons, *War Powers*, 231.

43. Judis, *The Folly of Empire*, 5.

44. Judis, *The Folly of Empire*, 171.

45. Judis, *The Folly of Empire*, 200.

46. G. John Ikenberry, Thomas J. Knock, Anne-Marie Slaughter, and Tony Smith, *The Crisis of American Foreign Policy: Wilsonianism in the Twenty-first Century* (Princeton: Princeton University Press, 2009), 9.

47. Judis, *The Folly of Empire*, 212.

48. "Agreement between the United States of America and the Republic of Iraq on the Withdrawal of United States Forces from Iraq and the Organization of Their Activities during Their Temporary Presence in Iraq," http://www.mnf-iraq.com/images/CGs_Messages/security_agreement.pdf, 20.

49. Steven Lee Myers and Marc Santora, "Premier Casting U.S. Withdrawal as Iraq Victory," *New York Times*, June 26, 2009.

50. Myers and Santora, "Premier Casting U. S. Withdrawal as Iraq Victory."

51. "Agreement between the United States of America and the Republic of Iraq," 22.

52. Barack Obama, "Renewing American Leadership," *Foreign Affairs*, July/August 2007, http://foreignaffairs.org/20070701faessay86401/barack-obama/renewing-american-leadership.html., 5.

53. "Full Script of Obama's Speech," July 24, 2008, Berlin, Germany, http://edition.cnn.com/2008/POLITICS/07/24.obama.words/.

54. Pew Global Attitudes Project, "Global Public Opinion in the Bush Years (2001–2008)," http://global.org/reports/pdf/263.pdf., 1.

55. "Barack Obama's Inaugural Address," prepared text as provided by the Presidential Inaugural Committee, http://www.iht.com/bin/printfirendly.php?id=19532874.

56. Gordon, *Winning the Right War*, 97.

57. Pew Global Attitudes Project, "Global Public Opinion in the Bush Years (2001–2008)," http://global.org/reports/pdf/263.pdf, 1.

58. "Remarks of Senator Obama: The War We Need to Win," delivered at the Woodrow Wilson Center, Washington, D.C., August 1, 2007, http://www.barackobama.com/2007/08/01/the_war_we_need_to_win.php.

59. "Remarks by the President on a New Strategy for Afghanistan and Pakistan," March 27, 2009, http://www.whitehouse.gov/the_press_office/Remarks-by-the-President-on-a-New-Strategy-for-Afghanistan-and-Pakistan.

60. One of then-candidate Obama's campaign promises was to reach out across the aisle and appoint Republicans to his cabinet. One of the key decisions that he made was to keep Robert Gates as his secretary of defense. Gates was appointed in December 2006 to succeed Donald Rumsfeld, who resigned in the wake of the election of 2006, which gave the Democrats a majority in Congress. The outcome of that election was seen by many political scientists as an indicator of public dissatisfaction with the course of the wars in Iraq and Afghanistan; Rumsfeld had been widely criticized by members of the Congress as well as by the press for his glib answers to tough questions about the wars and for his apparent inability or unwillingness to change the course of action. Gates was seen as more reasonable and moderate than Rumsfeld, plus he had over two years' experience in dealing with both wars when Obama asked him to stay on.

61. "Remarks by the President on a New Strategy for Afghanistan and Pakistan," March 27, 2009, http://www.whitehouse.gov/the_press_office/Remarks-by-the-President-on-a-New-Strategy-for-Afghanistan-and-Pakistan.

62. "Remarks by the President on a New Beginning," Cairo University, Cairo, Egypt, June 4, 2009, http://www.whitehouse.gov/the_press_office/Remarks-by-the-President-at-Cairo-University-6-04-09/.

63. In his earlier speech in Ankara, President Obama said, "The United States is not, and never will be, at war with Islam. In fact, our partnership with the Muslim world is critical not just in rolling back the violent ideologues that people of all faiths reject, but also to strengthen opportunity for all its people." "Remarks by President Obama to the Turkish Paraliament," Ankara, Turkey, April 6, 2009, http://www.whitehouse.gov/ the_press_office/Remarks-By-President-Obama-To-The-Turkish-Parliament.

64. "Remarks by the President on a New Beginning," Cairo University, Cairo, Egypt, June 4, 2009, http://www.whitehouse.gov/the_press_office/Remarks-by-the -President-at-Cairo-University-6-04-09/.

65. "Remarks by the President on a New Beginning," Cairo University, Cairo, Egypt, June 4, 2009, http://www.whitehouse.gov/the_press_office/Remarks-by-the -President-at-Cairo-University-6-04-09/.

66. "Remarks by the President on a New Beginning," Cairo University, Cairo, Egypt, June 4, 2009, http://www.whitehouse.gov/the_press_office/Remarks-by-the -President-at-Cairo-University-6-04-09/.

67. "Remarks by the President on a New Beginning," Cairo University, Cairo, Egypt, June 4, 2009, http://www.whitehouse.gov/the_press_office/Remarks-by-the -President-at-Cairo-University-6-04-09/.

68. "Remarks by President Obama to the Turkish Paraliament," Ankara, Turkey, April 6, 2009, http://www.whitehouse.gov/the_press_office/Remarks-By-President -Obama-To-The-Turkish-Parliament.

69. Ivo H. Daalder and James M. Lindsay, *America Unbound: The Bush Revolution in Foreign Policy* (Washington, D.C.: Brookings Institution, 2003), 80.

Chapter 7: The Future of U.S. Foreign Policy

1. For example, see John Lewis Gaddis, "Toward the Post–Cold War World," in *The Future of American Foreign Policy*, ed. Charles W. Kegley, Jr., and Eugene R. Wittkopf (New York: St. Martin's Press, 1992), 16–32; and John J. Mearsheimer, "Why We Will Soon Miss the Cold War," in Kegley and Wittkopf, *The Future of American Foreign Policy*, 48–62. Also see Gaddis, *Strategies of Containment: A Critical Appraisal of American National Security Policy during the Cold War* (New York: Oxford University Press, 2005); and Gaddis, *The Cold War: A New History* (New York: Penguin, 2005).

2. Joseph S. Nye, Jr., *The Paradox of American Power: Why the World's Only Superpower Can't Go It Alone* (New York: Oxford University Press, 2002), 8–9.

3. Nye, *The Paradox of American Power*, 9.

4. Walter Russell Mead, *Power, Terror, Peace, and War: America's Grand Strategy in a World at Risk* (New York: Alfred A. Knopf, 2004), 42.

5. George W. Bush, second inaugural address, January 20, 2005, http://bartleby. com/124/pres67.html.

6. Mead, *Power, Terror, Peace, and War*, 60.

7. "Remarks by the President on a New Beginning," Cairo University, Cairo, Egypt, June 4, 2009, http://www.whitehouse.gov/the_press_office/Remarks-by-the -President-at-Cairo-University-6-04-09/.

8. John Mearsheimer, *The Tragedy of Great Power Politics* (New York: W. W. Norton, 2001), 386.

9. For example, British prime minister Tony Blair put global warming and aid for Africa at the center of the discussions at the G8 summit meeting that he chaired at Gleneagles, Scotland, in July 2005.

10. Mead, *Power, Terror, Peace, and War*, 62.

11. Geoffrey A. Fowler, "Converting the Masses: Starbucks in China," *Far Eastern Economic Review*, July 17, 2003, 34–36; and Jason Singer and Martin Fackler, "Japan's Starbooze," *Far Eastern Economic Review*, July 17, 2003, 36. I was in Guangzhou, China, in 1993 when the first McDonald's was opening in that city. There were major traffic jams and huge lines as everyone wanted to experience this phenomenon.

12. SARS (Severe Acute Respiratory Syndrome) is believed to have originated in the city of Guangzhou, in southern China, in late 2002 or early 2003. From there, it was spread unknowingly by a doctor to Hong Kong, where it spread globally as people who were unaware that they were contaminated started to travel, infecting others. Cases were diagnosed as far away as Canada, and tourism to and within Asia came to a virtual halt. It took months to bring the situation under control, although no new cases of the disease have been diagnosed since. But in order to control the situation, governments quarantined anyone who appeared to have the disease; responses included stopping air flights coming from areas that were known to have outbreaks of SARS and examining passengers who appeared to be ill. While some saw this as an infringement on basic human rights and freedoms, few objected if it meant stopping the spread of the disease. This is one example of how quickly dangerous diseases can spread globally.

13. George W. Bush, "State of the Union Address," January 29, 2002, www .presidency.ucsb.edu/ws.index/php?pid=29644.

14. Fareed Zakaria, *The Post-American World* (New York: W. W. Norton, 2008), 93.

15. Zakaria, *The Post-American World*, 92.

16. Mearsheimer, *The Tragedy of Great Power Politics*, 375.

Suggested Readings

Books

A more detailed list of readings can be found in the notes for each chapter. Among the books that are especially recommended are the following:

Allison, Graham T. *The Essence of Decision: Explaining the Cuban Missile Crisis.* Boston: Little, Brown, 1971. This is the classic book explaining the Cuban Missile Crisis.

Bacevich, Andrew. *The Limits of Power: The End of American Exceptionalism* (New York: Henry Holt and Company, 2008). This is one of two relatively recent books by Andrew Bacevich that offers a critique of current U.S. foreign policy for what he sees as the errors in many of the decisions that have been made.

Gordon, Philip H. *Winning the Right War: The Path to Security for America and the World* (New York: Times Books, 2007). This relatively short book draws some parallels between the war on terror and the Cold War to draw conclusions about the future direction of U.S. foreign policy.

Herring, George C. *America's Longest War: The United States and Vietnam, 1950–1975.* New York: McGraw-Hill, 1996. This classic and concise description of the Vietnam War and U.S. involvement in Vietnam is straightforward and relatively easy to read and understand.

Ikenberry, G. John, Thomas J. Knock, Anne-Marie Slaughter, and Tony Smith. *The Crisis of American Foreign Policy: Wilsonianism in the Twenty-first Century* (Princeton, N.J.: Princeton University Press, 2009). Four scholars look at and compare the foreign policies of George W. Bush and Woodrow Wilson to arrive at some conclusions about Bush's foreign policy decisions.

Judis, John B. *The Folly of Empire: What George W. Bush Could Learn from Theodore Roosevelt and Woodrow Wilson.* New York: Scribner, 2004. Judis puts the policies of George W. Bush into a historical framework by contrasting them with the policies of Theodore Roosevelt in his quest for American empire and with Woodrow Wilson's idealism.

McDougall, Walter A. *Promised Land, Crusader States.* New York: Houghton Mifflin, 1997. McDougall is a diplomatic historian who frames the evolution of U.S. foreign policy in broadly conceptual terms, including what he sees as the role that religion has played in influencing many of the country's leaders.

Mead, Walter Russell. *Special Providence: American Foreign Policy and How It Changed the World.* New York: Alfred A. Knopf, 2002. Mead believes that Americans, and especially American leaders, are ahistorical. He goes back to the start of the country to arrive at some important and general conclusions about the reasons for some U.S. foreign policy decisions.

Mearsheimer, John. *The Tragedy of Great Power Politics.* New York: W. W. Norton, 2001. Mearsheimer puts U.S. foreign policy and the emergence of the United States as a great power into a broad historical context that takes into account the emergence of other major powers. He takes us to the present to assess the major threats/dangers facing the United States today and how the country is likely to meet those threats.

Websites

Be aware that the specifics of a site can change, but you can go to the main page and navigate from there or use a search engine to find a site.

Government sites are particularly important for accessing primary source documents. Among the most helpful to navigate is the State Department site, http://www.state.gov; also see http://usinfo.state.gov. See the U.S. House of Representatives site at http://www.house.gov for the Constitution and other documents.

Copies of presidential speeches (especially recent ones) and related documents can be found at http://www.whitehouse.gov. This site then requires additional navigation to get to the particular places that are most relevant.

The main site for the North Atlantic Treaty Organization (NATO) is http://www.nato.int. From that point, it is possible to navigate through all important NATO documents, including the NATO Treaty. The United Nations site is http://www.un.int.

News organizations are an important source for current information, including recent poll numbers. Some news sites require navigation to get to the desired story or information. Helpful sites are http://www.cnn.com; http://www.pbs.org; http://www.c-span.org; http://www.cbsnews.com; and http://www.nytimes.com. Also see http://www.people-press.org for Pew Center reports and polls and http://www.gallup.com for Gallup organization polls.

One of the most valuable sites is accessible through Yale University's Avalon Project. It contains a host of primary source documents often cited in this text. The general URL is http://www.yale.edu/lawweb/avalon. Another helpful source for historical documents is http://www.historicaldocuments.com. Also see http://www.bartleby .com.

Presidential libraries and universities with presidential papers are an important source for primary documents. All of these require some navigation to get to the parts that are most valuable and germane. Among these sites are http://www.fdrlibrary .marist.edu; http://trumanlibrary.org; http://millercenter.virginia.edu; http://www .marshallfoundation.org; http://www.mtholyoke.edu; and http://www.reagan foundation.org. One of the best sites for Cold War documents, such as the Long Telegram, is http://www.gwu.edu/~nsarchiv/coldwar/documents.

Index

Note: Figures on pages are indicated by *italic* page numbers.

About the Author

Joyce P. Kaufman is professor of political science and director of the Whittier Scholars Program at Whittier College. She is the author of *NATO and the Former Yugoslavia: Crisis, Conflict, and the Atlantic Alliance* (Rowman & Littlefield, 2002) and numerous articles and papers on U.S. foreign and security policy. With Kristen Williams, she is coauthor of *Women, the State, and War: A Comparative Perspective on Citizenship and Nationalism* (Lexington Books, 2007). As a faculty member at an institution that focuses on undergraduate education, she regularly teaches a political science class on American foreign policy. She received her B.A. and M.A. from New York University and her Ph.D. from the University of Maryland.